Urban Intersections

Urban Intersections

Meetings of Life and Literature in United States Cities

SIDNEY H. BREMER

UNIVERSITY OF ILLINOIS PRESS
Urbana and Chicago

© 1992 by the Board of Trustees of the University of Illinois
Manufactured in the United States of America
C 5 4 3 2 1

This book is printed on acid-free paper.

Library of Congress Cataloging-in-Publication Data
Bremer, Sidney H., 1944–
    Urban intersections : meetings of life and literature in United
States cities / Sidney H. Bremer.
       p.   cm.
    Includes bibliographical references and index.
    ISBN 0-252-01886-9 (cl. : alk. paper)
    1. American literature—History and criticism.   2. City and town life in literature.   3. Cities and towns in literature.   I. Title.
PS169.C57B7   1992
810.9′321732—dc20   91-29509
                                                                                    CIP

Dedicated to
the many voices of our diverse cities,
the writers who speak them
even against powerful cultural muffling,
and all those who try to hear
—including Jerry, Estella, Karon, Therese,
Bill, and Mama Dorey.

Contents

Preface ix

Acknowledgments xv

Introduction: Locating Urban Texts and Contexts in United States Literature   1

1 Pre–Civil War City-Towns   19

2 Toward a National Economic City   36

3 The Standard Chicago Novel   60

4 Chicago's Residential Novels and Their Social Roots   81

5 New York's Megalopolitan Nightmares   113

6 The Urban Home of the Harlem Renaissance   132

7 Neighborhood-City Dreams   165

8 Regional Perspectives and Situated Insights   185

Notes   203

Works Cited   223

Index   245

Illustrations

Figure 1. Jerrold C. Rodesch photograph, Long House, Mesa Verde — 6

Figure 2. Thomas Cole, *The Course of Empire: Consummation* — 8

Figure 3. Thomas Cole, *The Architect's Dream* — 10

Figure 4. Unknown artist, *Landscape* — 11

Figure 5. John Marin, *Brooklyn Bridge* — 33

Figure 6. Cecilia Beaux, *After the Meeting* — 50

Figure 7. John Sloan, *The City from Greenwich Village* — 55

Figure 8. Isabel Bishop, *Homeward* — 83

Figure 9. Little Room, *Cap. Fry's Birthday Party* — 106

Figure 10. Joseph Stella, *Brooklyn Bridge* — 117

Figure 11. Ralph Fasanella, *Sunday Afternoon—Stickball Game* — 118

Figure 12. James Van Der Zee, *Parade on Seventh Avenue* — 153

Figure 13. John Biggers, *Shotguns* — 177

Preface

In writing *Urban Intersections,* I have been continually aware of the personal implications in my authorial argument. As contemporary literary theorists and participants in today's "growing ethnic-feminist consciousness" keep reminding us, "writing itself [is] a practice located at the intersection of subject and history," and every writer is a "historical subject" (Minh-ha 1990, 245). Likewise my investigation of urban literature and the urban situations out of which authors write intersects with the current movement in U.S. cultural studies to explore issues of race, gender, class, and region. Of course, this movement, like every academic school of vision or revision, is historically conditioned by matters that extend well beyond ideas. So, too, specific places and social circumstances have intersected with the dialectic of my own learning and living to shape the argument of this particular book. Many of these personal and collective intersections have taken place in specifically urban "grids of Them-and-Us experiences" (Piercy 1981, 209–10).

Undoubtedly this book takes some of its shape from my circumstances as an Anglo-American woman who yelled her first breath in the middle of Manhattan during World War II; who roller-skated and sledded and read her way through early childhood along the residential sidewalks of Portland, Oregon; who awakened to adulthood in California suburbs and learned the virtues of so-called country living from the San Francisco airwaves in the 1960s; and who now looks out on the Great Lakes water and channel markers, woods and interstate highway, fields and TV towers that edge the mid-sized, mid-continental city of Green Bay, Wisconsin.

To use the terminology I develop in this book, my birthplace was the megalopolis—specifically, its East Coast epicenter, New York City. I began my life many stories off the ground—physically and socially uprooted—my parents having left their home state of Washington to seek "the center of things" in New York—like the characters in *Manhattan Transfer*. My family moved west after the disruptions of the war, and I spent my formative elementary school years in Oregon's "City of Roses." From my perch in a cherry tree surveying my homogeneous, stable neighborhood, with its tree-lined boulevard leading toward Reed College's ivied halls, Portland embodied the natural, residential, and cultural characteristics of a regional city-town. When our family moved on to California, Portland became for me what Minneapolis was in *The Great Gatsby,* an image of an urban home lost in the past and covered with nostalgia.

In a white suburban "bedroom community" linked by highways and television to the rest of the San Francisco Bay Area, I bypassed the class conflicts and industrial machinery of what this book calls the economic city, as well as the street life of ethnic neighborhood cities, to plunge into the modern electronic mainstream. I became a teenager in the California of bebop records and movie magazines. A private university there in the 1960s allowed me an early baby boomer's box seat to watch hippies meet Black Panthers. The persistence of middle-class gender roles directed me toward the traditionally feminine field of teaching and encouraged me to internalize rather than act out the era's alienation. Meanwhile, the literary curriculum I studied explicated the city only in political-economic imagery from Howells to Herrick; its focus on great works and its thematic dichotomies of American romance and realism, machines and gardens, native wit and expatriate modernism, all confirmed the alienated "urbanism" that I was experiencing as a pervasive "way of life" (Wirth 1938). I identified myself as a Californian precisely because I did not find myself at home there—or anywhere. I came to Wisconsin as a mobile modern American riding the megalopolitan mainstream, a visitor everywhere.

Natives of Green Bay have impressed me with their powerful sense of being at home, and sometimes homebound, at the harbor end of a 100-mile urban strip of more than 250,000 people. A population of 100,000 makes Green Bay itself as big as New York in 1820, San Francisco after the Civil War, Minneapolis at the turn of the century, and Little Rock during the school desegregation crisis. It is a heavily industrial city that shares meat packing with *The Jungle*'s Chicago. But this and its other major industries, paper and cheese making, also link it to a regional environment of woods and dairyland. Moreover, continuities of multigenerational family ties are strong; ethnic accents, traditions, and religious practices maintain a comfortable sense of flexible familiarity. Though it has significant populations of Oneida and Menominee Indian people and Southeast Asian Americans, Green Bay lacks the large numbers of African Americans that spell urban heterogeneity for white Americans in the North, making nearby Milwaukee seem a more "real" industrial city.

As Green Bay's 100,000 residents have questioned whether they are a city, resisted recognizing their share of "urban problems," and neglected the urban resources their community ties and regional continuities offer, they have made me question whether our recognized urban imagery of skyscraper machinery and alienation is adequate. Coexisting elements of the supposedly lost city-town, the industrial economic city of our best-known urban literature, and modernism's megalopolitan synapses make Green Bay typical of the mid-sized cities in which most urban Americans live today. But it is the experience of only some, who live in a very few big cities, that we recognize as urban. Green Bay has no well-imaged sense of its own cityness. It has had no articulated ground on which to make its past a part of its present, its regional identity a part of its social life, its community a part of its government as a city. And that has left its citizens culturally adrift, defensive and sometimes angry—as at their inability, for instance, to stop the removal of an age-polished German-American neighborhood restaurant to make room for a predictable downtown mall with its attendant acres of parking lot. Supporters of "our local Kaap's"—as a button reads from the still-remembered, failed protest two decades ago—were participating in our nation's recently emergent interest in urban historical preservation but without the sense of city identity that served to support crusades for Boston's Faneuil Hall, Milwaukee's Grand Avenue Mall, or San Francisco's cable car project.

Even my students at the regional University of Wisconsin-Green Bay have had no ready answer to the question of whether or not Green Bay is a city. Nonetheless, they have always been quick to applaud Upton Sinclair's *The Jungle* for showing the city as it really is. When I have assigned *The Awakening*, Kate Chopin's novel set in New Orleans and its Gulf region, they have been just as quick to object that I was trying to turn an urban studies class into a women's studies class. They repeatedly demonstrate the power of the national image of the economic city to shape their assumptions. At the same time, they keep asking me what literature has to do with their lives. As the teacher of these first-generation college students in interdisciplinary studies, I have not been able to satisfy them simply by invoking—in Hans-Georg Gadamer's (1975) terms—established disciplinary "method" to ward off the potentially revolutionary "truth" of their challenges. I have had to find chapter and verse to demonstrate alternative definitions of historical and regional towns as cities, and I have had to provide graphic and experiential confirmations for my literary exhibits.

Undoubtedly, the growth of my ideas about urban literature has been forced in part by my participation in interdisciplinary programs at the University of Wisconsin-Green Bay. Probably reflecting the greater likelihood for women than men to find themselves on the edges of our cultural institutions, my academic career has developed outside the established disciplines. I have been challenged to bring my Stanford doctorate in American literature to bear on urban, women's, and ethnic studies. In these academic borderlands I have confronted urban literature's intersections with a variety of urban environments and biased social situations. Based in the social sciences and in professional studies, urban studies has enabled me to make the case—to my colleagues as to my students—that literature is a form of knowledge and cultural action that informs real cities. The volatile fields of women's and ethnic studies have raised critical questions for me about canonical content, personal and political interests, and civic implications in literature and urban studies alike.

In my approach to Chicago literature, for example, urban studies directed my attention toward the physical structures corresponding to literary images—the skyscraping Loop, the el, and the 1893 world's fair. Consequently, on my first visit to Chicago I ended up taking a cross-town walk through the African-American South Side in order to get from the now extended el to the one building remaining from the fair, the Museum of Science and Industry. When a white police officer stopped me and asked, "Lady, do you know where you are?" I realized how powerfully the literature I'd read had traced its own urban map in my mind. The officer's question also activated another lesson I had learned from literature—that Chicago is a dangerous place to be alone, especially on the "other" side of a racial class division. Ethnic studies confirmed the resulting limitation of my white middle-class perspective. As I dug further into the foundations of Chicago history, planning, sociology, and political economics, women's studies led me to certain other questions. I wondered whether any of the women I encountered as culture builders—Jane Addams of the Hull-House settlement, Mrs. Potter Palmer of the fair, Ida B. Wells-Barnett of its protests, Edith Wyatt of the Consumers' League, Harriet Monroe of *Poetry,* and Susan Glaspell of the Little Theatre—had created literary imagery for their urban experience. Why was it that all the Chicago novels I knew were by men? And why didn't my students think *The Awakening* appropriate for an urban studies class?

Being a woman and an academic in the 1970s, the era that saw the field of women's studies first develop, I was certainly predisposed to appreciate the shaping impact of gender on urban experience. Patterns of continuity and community, similar to those differentiating white women's experiences from white men's, stood out for me when I then focused my attention on the marginalized urban lives and literature of African Americans and Jews. Having never experienced the material underside of class, the press of poverty, I was not totally preoccupied with the economic-city imagery in novels protesting racial injustice. I have been well situated—in my personal urban history of mobility, my social history as a woman, and my intellectual history in interdisciplinary borderlands—to see the connective, creative potential in Harlem Renaissance and Lower East Side images of the city as neighborhood home.

Perhaps the ultimate homeward thrust of *Urban Intersections* toward a multicultural regionalism also has to do with my personal development into middle age. While our parents' generation approaches dying and our children's generation approaches birthing, my friends, colleagues, and I are all discovering a mid-life concern with roots. During the past few years, again and again, I have found us discussing what home means. With a gentle man raised in the South I have learned how deeply we can be moved by the smells and sights of a physical landscape. In the delicious phrasing of William Faulkner (1932, 111), my "memory believes before knowing remembers" that I am home whenever I see the rising city and settling suburbs of the Bay Area's golden hills, despite all the vaunted alienation I learned there. And with a wise sister of women artists and the mythic figures they develop, I have learned that home can also be a community that extends beyond any one place. Powerful reverberations of shared history, imagery, societal bias, and bodily experience bind us in a birthright community with other women—a necessary, unsentimental home often rent with dissention within and besieged from without. And finally, a historian who cares passionately about the conversations of intellectual culture, extending well beyond the givens of his working-class upbringing, has taught me how important the symbolic home of one's ambitions can be. Sometimes attained only in imagination, sometimes in a circumstantial way (like the book-lined "old house home" that Chicagoan Elia Peattie treasured as the objective correlative of her cultural ambitions), such a spiritual home is where a person feels most fully realized.

During the past few years, as I have been finishing this book, I have also been consciously making the city of Green Bay my home—creating resonant connections with my physical surroundings, taking time to care for and be cared for by friends, and pursuing my aspirations. I have learned that a city home can be built on a sense of belonging that does not depend on residential permanence. In this new home life, which I have heard voiced by once marginalized ethnic and women writers, I have become convinced that we need to be at home in the world for our own survival, separately and collectively. Otherwise we treat the earth as disposable plastic that we can always leave behind for some new outer space. Otherwise we treat others as some monolithic "them" whose supposed inhumanity becomes our own, as the "white looming mountain of hate" opposes Bigger Thomas in Richard Wright's *Native Son* ([1940] 1966, 334). Otherwise we become alienated from ourselves—like Nella Larsen's Danish-African-American heroine in *Quicksand* (1928)—and may sink, as she finally does, into dulled, unfeeling existence. We need to be fully at home in the cities as well as the pastures of our world in order to be responsibly human.

Acknowledgments

My writing of *Urban Intersections* has been a long journey home, winding for nearly twenty years through the many intersections of experience and ideas involved in teaching, reading, writing, and thinking aloud with others. I am particularly grateful to the interdisciplinary circles that have challenged me to connect my literary thinking to civic issues, student lives, and communal experience—especially the public forums of the Wisconsin Humanities Committee, my classes at the University of Wisconsin–Green Bay, and the fellowship of the Society for Values in Higher Education. My research has benefited, too, from the financial support of the University of Wisconsin and the University of Wisconsin–Green Bay Research Council, the American Philosophical Association, the National Endowment for the Humanities, and the American Council of Learned Societies. I would like to thank the staffs of the Newberry Library, the James Weldon Johnson Memorial Collection at Yale University, the Countee Cullen Memorial Collection at Atlanta University, the Houghton Library at Harvard, the Mungar Library at Boston University, the Regenstein Library at the University of Chicago, the *Chicago Tribune,* the YIVO Yiddish Institute, the University of California–Santa Barbara Library, the New York Public Library, the Chicago Historical Society, and the State Historical Society of Wisconsin for the use of their manuscript holdings and archives. I especially thank Mark and Noel Peattie for sharing with me the memoirs of their Chicago grandmother, Elia Peattie, and her husband, Robert. I also appreciate the extensive interlibrary loan services at the University of Wisconsin–Green Bay.

I have shaped my research into this book through a process of thinking and rethinking that has involved many other minds. As they midwifed into print the essays that honed my thinking for chapters 3, 4, and 5,

Soundings editors Thomas Ogletree and Donald Sherburne, Susan Squier, Carol Orr (formerly of the University of Tennessee Press), *PMLA* editor John Cronin and special editor Henry Louis Gates, Jr., gave me essential encouragement while also challenging me to focus my arguments. By offering critical analyses of my book as a whole in its earliest versions, Albert Gelpi, Joan Catapano, and several anonymous readers helped me to begin making the first hard decisions about scope and organization. In making the final hard decisions—about presentational style, too—I have been given persistent support and thoughtful suggestions from the University of Illinois Press's director and editor, Richard Wentworth, his several anonymous readers, associates Robert Bray and James Hurt, and copy editor Margaret Welsh.

Out of the best of colleagueship and friendship, I have also received critical readings and continuing support from Estella Lauter, William Walling Bremer, Alan Trachtenberg (many times over), Thomas Bender, Nellie McKay, and Carl Smith—and from Jane Tompkins a timely reminder to "historicize, historicize, historicize." My companion, Jerrold Rodesch, has given me the inspiration of his intrepid intellectual curiosity and the nurture of his love, faith, and fun during the final stages of my writing and revision. To all, my thanks.

I also gratefully acknowledge the permission of the Houghton Library and W. W. Howells to quote from the unpublished papers of William Dean Howells. I am pleased to be able to acknowledge several journals for permission to use materials from my previously published articles:

"American Dreams and American Cities in Three Post-World War I Novels," in *South Atlantic Quarterly* 79 (2): 274–85. Copyright © 1980 by Duke University Press.

"Lost Continuities: Alternative Urban Visions in Chicago Novels, 1890–1915," *Soundings: An Interdisciplinary Journal* 64, no. 1 (Spring 1981): 29–51.

"Willa Cather's Lost Chicago Sisters," in Susan Merrill Squier, ed., *Women Writers and the City: Essays in Feminist Literary Criticism,* 210–29. Copyright © 1984 by the University of Tennessee Press.

"Home in Harlem, New York: Lessons from the Harlem Renaissance Writers," *PMLA* 105 (Jan. 1990): 47–56.

"From Boston via New York/Chicago to L.A.: The Dismissal of Regionalism in American Urban Literature," *Urban Resources* 4, no. 2 (Winter 1987): 41–46.

Urban Intersections

Introduction

Locating Urban Texts and Contexts in United States Literature

The skyscraper has cast a long shadow over twentieth-century literature and thought about cities in the United States. Rising up "with startling suddenness at the end of the nineteenth century," the skyscraper organized cities that "before...had expanded without any...characteristic shape" (Taylor 1979, 247). It also catalyzed urban culture. Of course, cities had existed before and they continue to take other distinctive shapes—in literature as well as in life. But the skyscraper, long since topped by a broadcast antenna, epitomizes what we "assume" of cities, and its shadow obscures whatever does not fit the "characteristic shape."

Our understandings of urban culture have focused on the economic functions, publicity, and technological reach epitomized by the skyscraper. We have concentrated on the problems of class conflict and psychological alienation at its base and looked to domination and singular success as means to rise above them. In our formulations of urban phenomena, we have emphasized the areas and eras that bring skyscrapers into high relief—especially Chicago and New York after 1890—and the perspectives of writers whose work illuminates those sites—Theodore Dreiser's *Sister Carrie,* Upton Sinclair's *The Jungle,* Hart Crane's "The Bridge," John Dos Passos's *Manhattan Transfer,* and Richard Wright's *Native Son,* among others. Despite recent concern with historic and environmental preservation, gender equity, and multicultural pluralism, we have only begun to explore evidence that our urban literature in fact challenges our skyscraper assumptions. Besides codifying alienation, our urban literature constructs experiences of "urban pastoralism" (Machor

1987), "cities of sisterhood" (Squier 1984), and "ancestors" in ethnic neighborhoods (Morrison 1981b).

This book seeks to further our recovery of literary resources that open up historical, regional, residential, and neighborhood dimensions of urban life at street level, as additions to those that elaborate the economic and megalopolitan aspects of skyscraper alienation. I have included, along with the standard urban tunes, literary voices from times and places not conventionally catagorized as urban—in James Fenimore Cooper's *The Pioneers,* the *Narrative of the Life of Frederick Douglass,* Kate Chopin's *The Awakening.* I have also heightened the voices of racialized ethnic groups and women writing about street life and home in skyscraper cities—in Clara Laughlin's *"Just Folks,"* Elia Peattie's *The Precipice,* Langston Hughes's *The Weary Blues,* Nella Larsen's *Quicksand,* Anzia Yezierska's *Hungry Hearts,* and Henry Roth's *Call It Sleep.* I do so not only to give diverse voices a hearing as a matter of social justice but to give our literature its full cultural resonance as a matter of aesthetic concern. This book seeks to fill in major gaps in some of our primary cultural beliefs about the urban thrust of U.S. history and the urban imagery that Joyce Carol Oates (1981, 11) calls "an archetype [for] the human imagination." It also seeks to extend literature's power to take each of us into experiences not our own—down "streets you fear or streets who fear you" in the "grids of Them-and-Us experiences" that writer Marge Piercy (1981, 209–10) says constitute today's urban culture. It seeks to expand the range of literary resources by which our citizens and urban planners can translate "the cities of our minds" (Chmaj 1976) into the cities of our lives.

The intersections of urban life and literature are abundant. They occur whenever a city setting and a writer's creative experience meet, in various dimensions. They occur in the streets of the cities our writers know and in the texts they create, the "writing itself...a practice located at the intersection of subject and history," as cultural critic Trinh T. Minh-ha reminds us (1990, 245). Intersections also occur in our reading and response to literary texts and to the urban contexts they illuminate. In every case diversity, in historical period and region, in gender, in race and ethnicity, enters into these intersections.

Certainly, new scholarship has pointed us toward urban cultural diversity far beyond the measure of popular skyscraper iconography or studies of "classic" American literature (e.g., Marx 1964; White and White 1962). The "mythologic" that equates the city with the machine and spells out its conceptual opposition to nature and community[1] does not even account for the resonant ambiguities and affective dynamics that distinguish any work of imaginative literature from discursive ideas, as Alan Trachtenberg points out (1967, 283–85). Literature's "reasonable criticisms" of cities cannot be dismissed as Romantic "prejudice," despite the Whites' argument (1962, 231–38); they cannot simply be dismissed as anti-urban either. Attention to a broader range of literary works, to their multivocal resonances and historical contexts, reveals a wealth of symbolic construction. This wealth offers valuable insights and resources on which city planners can indeed (again, despite the Whites) "rest or depend" when launching their "campaigns in behalf of urban improvement" (13).

To tap literature's diversity we need to allow our inquiries to be "informed and conceptualized" by history and other disciplines beside literary analysis. We need to take a contextual, cultural approach to urban literature. Only then can we "plunge more deeply"—in Clifford Geertz's terms (1973, 25)—into the "interpretation" of our urban literary culture.

In particular, we need to pay attention to the contexts of intellectual, urban, social, and biographical history. Without denying the transformative power of creativity, we must acknowledge that writers' experiences, visions of what could be, and texts are shaped by these historical contexts. U.S. urban literature varies as different cultural ideas and traditions, different "social constructions of reality" (Berger and Luckmann 1966), inform writers' expectations. Literary changes also depend upon the cities writers have known in different times and regions, upon the writers' diverse social situations and group identities, and upon their personal and aesthetic development.

Simply put, every human being is situated to discover some threads of human experience and to miss others. Any human statement, any book, whether fiction or nonfiction, whether considered a classic or not considered at all, is situated, too. It is a *qualified* truth. Its author's situation has vantage points and horizons that qualify its claim upon what we call reality. By pressing down on one point or another in the fabric of human experience, we test and stretch the whole and establish our biases (cf. Gunn 1982, 61; Albanese 1988, 279–83). Such biases doubly qualify what any author has to say, both justifying and limiting its truth claims at the same time. We cannot escape this human partiality. To use Ralph Ellison's terms (1963, 322), the "universal" in any human life or statement lies in its "specific circumstance." Specificity is the crux of what is universal in our human situation, and no one human's situation can encompass it all. Hence we need to entertain diverse perspectives to stay alert to the range of our humanity.

The situational diversity of U.S. urban literature is not, however, shapeless. Seen in the contexts of intellectual, urban, social, and biographical history, textual images of cities reveal recurrent, if divergent, patterns. If we attend to the intersections of literature with both intellectual and social history, we can delineate the biases that qualify our standard literature of urban alienation, and we can discover the lineage of a countertradition extending in markedly different directions. If we attend, as well, to the intersections of literature with urban history and biography, we can highlight significant variations in both traditions as they deal with the changing forms of cityscapes, power relations, social heterogeneity, and urban dreams.

Closely examined in the contexts of intellectual and social history, then, the imagery of urban alienation that has built up around the skyscraper is heavily conditioned—by mid-nineteenth-century Romanticism, post–Civil War nationalism, and the early twentieth-century social experiences of white, male, mobile, professional writers. Intellectual history reminds us that alienation has not always defined cities for us. Urbane federalists preceded the anti-urban Romantics; European colonists who envisioned America's future as "a city upon a hill" preceded them. Cities as expressions of human choice were well established in North America before the advent of urban alienation. Social history reminds us that physical, social, or psychological alienation had little to do with the experiences of Native Americans inhabiting cliff cities; nor does alienation account fully for the urban experiences of women and ethnic minority people denied middle-class white men's more individualistic prospects. By looking beyond the antinatural, anticommunal assumptions of the skyscraper city, we can see that a different urban tradition exists, one of communal forms enriched by nature and grounded in native and colonial experience. It is still being developed by many women, working-class ethnics, and people of color.

Much of the imaginative literature of cities in the United States builds on native and colonial ground that we do well to remember. Recall the preprint traditions of our earliest urban dwellers: the Anasazi spinning the threads of an urban organicism in their Southwest cliff cities. Although their oral literature may seem lost, Native Americans argue that the expressive traditions of tribal nations are continually maintained and renewed as their stories are passed along. These are spirit stories that also mean bodily " ... life here / for the people." Speaking thus, a twentieth-century medicine man "rubbed his belly" to affirm his spiritual pregnancy with life-sustaining stories from "time immemorial" in Laguna Pueblo Leslie Marmon Silko's *Ceremony* (1977, 2). Reflecting on the communal and organic elements of traditional stories, Anglo Gary Snyder's *Turtle Island* (1974, 3) roots its ecological vision in an Anasazi cliff-city:

> Anasazi,
> Anasazi,
>
> tucked up in clefts in the cliffs
> growing strict fields of corn and beans
> sinking deeper and deeper in earth
> up to your hips in Gods...

As invoked here, the Anasazi represent a communal experience of city building "tucked," even "sinking," into an organic ground (see Long House, Mesa Verde, fig. 1). Their city is an ongoing, "growing," "sinking" communal action, not the object of an outsider's observation. As Vincent Scully explains (1975, 9–38), native cliff dwellers like the Anasazi built their cities to echo the sacred shapes of surrounding land forms, as do the Pueblo peoples today; the community itself, engaged in ritual activity, was an essential part of the symbolic city thus composed. Into the twentieth century Zuñi women, descendants of the Anasazi, have continued to grind corn together within the city walls and to address their grinding song to the sacred mountain, Toyallanne, whose shape Zuñi Pueblo mirrors: "Elu homa Toyallanne!"—"O, my lovely mountain, Toyallanne!" (Nancy Curtis 1923; quoted in Jensen 1981, 18–19).

The Puritan dream of a city *upon* a hill has helped to reinforce the tradition of urban organicism embodied in Anasazi cliff cities *in* hills. Before John Winthrop had even set foot on New England's shores, he proclaimed an urban pastoral challenge and promise to "be as a city upon a hill" in his shipboard sermon, "A Model of Christian Charity" ([1630] 1978, 78). Specifically, Winthrop called for a communal enterprise supported by a redeemed and fruitful land. The Puritans envisioned the city of America as an "organic" community that grew out of the people's common execution of God's will (Baritz 1964, 13–24; Carroll 1969, 131–59). It offered each person a part in a "federated liberty" (Winthrop [1653] 1978, 92), and required from each a civic responsibility based on his or her place in the "little commonwealth" of a family (Demos 1970).

City was plantation, too. Although the Puritans' enclosures eventually

Figure 1. Long House, Mesa Verde (ca. 1250), photograph by Jerrold C. Rodesch. Courtesy of the photographer.

transformed the wilderness into real estate (Nash 1973, 8-43; Cronon 1983), they were intended to fulfill nature's fruitful potential and to support the city upon a hill by realizing God's design for the New Jerusalem. The Puritans shared this urban vision with colonial Virginians, too, who were also charged—by an Anglican cleric in 1662—to promote "the building [of] Towns in each County" so that "the poore Church" might "become like a garden enclosed" to tend its "Sheep...by night" and feed them "by day." Thus the European-American colonists sought "the promised fruits of well ordered Towns" (quoted in Machor 1987, 45). They sought to transform nature from a "barren Wilderness" into both "a fruitful Land" and a "well-ordered Commonwealth"—as Puritan Edward Johnson combined these key terms in *Wonder-Working Providence* (1654; quoted in Nash 1973, 37).[2] They sought an urban "middle way" (Levin 1978, 264) that would reconcile artifice with nature, community with liberty. As they built Boston and other seaboard cities, they continued to strive, in Cotton Mather's phrase, for an "American *Jerusalem*...America, *the holy City!*" (Mather [1702] 1975, 200; cf. Bercovitch 1975, 89, 107).

These native and colonial visions of urban settlement in harmony with nature were only gradually undermined by the anti-urban ideas of agrarians and Romantics. During the revolutionary and federalist periods, the savvy example that Benjamin Franklin presented in his urban *Autobiography* (Machor 1987, 102-20), supported by Enlightenment beliefs in an open, urbane order, successfully countered Thomas Jefferson's fear that U.S. cities would repeat European patterns of crowding and thus destroy the landed basis of the new republic. The Romantics refused the idea of the city upon a hill, however, splitting the "middle way" into a polarity of extremes; they rejected the mechanical artifice and conformity of mid-nineteenth-century cities and embraced wilderness and individualism as the mythological bases for "Nature's Nation" (Miller 1967). Yet even at the height of Romantic nationalism, the dream of urban community in harmony with nature continued to exercise a compelling power. In 1832 Hudson River school painter Thomas Cole offered a philosophy for his series of five canvases, called *The Course of Empire,* in line with that Romantic dichotomy. He proposed his paintings to idealize "Savage" freedom and "Pastoral" arts and community while warning against the eventual "Destruction" and "Ruins" that the "Consummation of Empire" threatened with its urban crowds and architectural "piles" (quoted in Davidson 1957, 58; see fig. 2). Yet New Yorker Cole also promoted the ideal of a built environment informed by spiritual values in harmony with

Figure 2. Thomas Cole, *The Course of Empire: Consummation* (1835–36), oil on canvas, 51¼ × 76 in. 1858.3. Courtesy of the New-York Historical Society, New York City.

natural forms in *The Architect's Dream* (1840, fig. 3). The painting's homologous church spire and evergreen tree complement each other and balance the horizontal reach of a more thickly built city—much as an anonymous landscape painting from a century earlier (fig. 4) balances its urban and rural halves.

Similarly, Henry David Thoreau beat a daily path between Concord and his pond while writing *Walden, or Life in the Woods* (1854), and he berated the nation's failure to realize community more than he disdained the ideal itself. Although his 1851 essay "Walking" discusses city and wilderness within the dichotomous framework of "progress from east to west"—that is, from European city to American wilderness—Thoreau locates the beneficence of history and art and literature on the city side of his mythic map ([1851] 1968, 218). Ralph Waldo Emerson (1909–14, 5:310–11) also appreciated the "varieties" of the city and its capacity to exercise the analytic powers of understanding, although he reified city and country as antithetical ideas and affirmed the moral superiority of the country's "uniform . . . monotony" for nurturing reason's integrative vision. His prototypical Romantic essay "Nature" ([1836] 1960, 22–24) even modifies his philosophical dichotomy by insisting that nature includes "both nature and art" and that it can be contemplated "in the streets of cities" as well as in the woods.

The Anasazi-colonial and Romantic lines of thought have continued to inform imaginative literature in the United States. The image of "Nature's Nation," (Miller 1967), with its ethos of Romantic individualism and its anti-urban dichotomies of country and city, came to dominate urban literary culture only late in the nineteenth century, as chapters one and two of this book demonstrate. Even then the earlier ideal of an organic urban community, even in its Anasazi forms, lived on—albeit obscured by the industrial machinery of skyscraper imagery. Thus the first Chicago skyscraper novel, Henry Blake Fuller's *The Cliff-Dwellers* (1893), echoes images of the Southwest cliff cities to suggest what the turn-of-the-century economic city perverted, as I point out in chapter three. If we recover works by marginalized women and ethnic writers, we discover more. Willa Cather's heroine in *The Song of the Lark* (1915), the best known of the mostly lost Chicago novels by women (which I discuss in chapter four) looks specifically to the Anasazi as inspiration for an urban pastoral art. Following these, moreover, important bodies of African- and Jewish-American literature written between World Wars I and II seek a union of spirit and body much like the Anasazi's, in the neighborhood

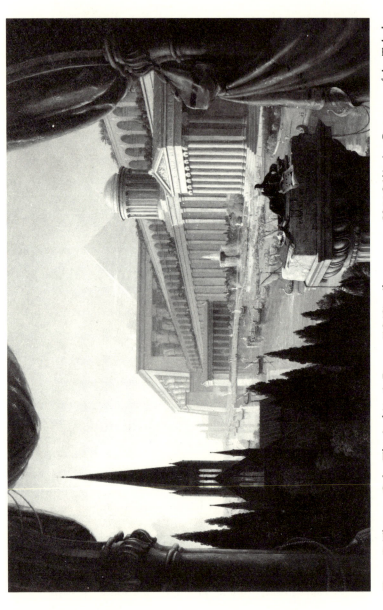

Figure 3. Thomas Cole, *The Architect's Dream* (1840), oil on canvas, 53 × 84 1/16 in. Courtesy of the Toledo Museum of Art; gift of Florence Scott Libbey.

Figure 4. Unknown artist of the American school, *Landscape* (eighteenth century), oil on panel, 27¼ × 51¼ in. Courtesy of the Worcester Art Museum, Worcester, Massachusetts; gift of Dr. and Mrs. Roger Kinnicutt.

dreams I explore in chapters six and seven. Together, works by ancient cliff dwellers, New England colonists, turn-of-the-century Chicago women, Harlem Renaissance writers, and Jewish New Yorkers reveal a long-lived tradition indeed, a worthy alternative to the dominant chorus of skyscraper works that culminates in megalopolis (chapter five).

What needs equal emphasis here is that literary imagery out of both these traditions has developed significant variations over time. Bringing urban as well as social history and authorial biography into play highlights these literary variants. Their branching lines of development, moreover, correspond closely to the physical and social shifts that have structured urban experience and the national culture that major cities have helped to form. But we need to remember that all of urban history does not run at a uniform speed any more than it runs along a single track. Instead our literature reveals a mixture of changes and continuities—toward more literary activity here, more industry there, denser residential experience here, more intensely bound neighborhoods there, more extensive mass marketing elsewhere; different cities and different social sectors of the same cities pose different configurations at different times. Indeed, the uneven public power associated with various phases of urban development helps explain how our dominant literary culture shifted to a Romantic emphasis on urban alienation, how it obscured alternative understandings, and how women and ethnic minorities nonetheless developed an organic vision. In turn, imaginative literature from both dominant and marginalized traditions helps us understand how Americans have responded to diverse phases in U.S. urban development.

Changes in the dominant imagery of nineteenth-century urban literature feature historical innovations in large U.S. cities, with somewhat of a time lag—for example, mechanized streetcars appearing on city tracks in the 1870s, then as an organizing symbol in literature in 1890. The strong alternative imagery found in women's residential literature and the literature of marginalized ethnic neighborhoods, however, makes clear that the "walking city" did not disappear with the advent of the "streetcar city" (Weber and Lloyd 1975).[3] Comparing the dominant urban literary conception with previously overlooked texts shows that urban changes do not cancel out urban continuities. This more comprehensive literary sampling thus modifies the single line of development that traditional histories trace from "polis" to "metropolis" to "megalopolis" (Phillips and LeGates 1981, 81–105).[4] Nonetheless, urban literary imagery generally does fit into three such stages, and the neglected texts help embody the social heterogeneity that largely distinguishes one stage from another.

During the pre–Civil War period in which fairly homogeneous, powerful mercantile elites dominated the economy and society of U.S. cities, culture and community were usually central to literature's urban images. What I call the city-town model in literature is thus presented as a direct expression of human capacities—for good or for evil, in that period's frequently moralistic language. The city-town's political and aesthetic spaces may be easily accessible to all—as in Cooper's *Pioneers* and in the open rationality of William Penn's seventeenth-century plan for Philadelphia; or they may be hidden in labyrinthine mazes—as in Hawthorne's "My Kinsman, Major Molineux" and in the unplanned twists of Lower Manhattan's eighteenth-century streets. In either event, the city-town's spaces form an environment that is shaped by human choices more than it shapes them. The city-town's community is primarily voluntary, too, based on extensions of private family relationships. It involves both a strong sense of history and an open-ended future. Above all, there is plenty of room to move in and out and around in literature's city-town, on foot and on one's own. The city-town might be visualized as a street map of the sort that historical societies prepare for self-guided walking tours among residences, public buildings, and other landmarks located in close proximity.

Literature's city-town derives a flexible model from the pre-Romantic tradition of urban organicism. Because of its open-ended structure, it accommodates the urban liberty that African Americans like Harriet Jacobs and Frederick Douglass treasured so much in escaping slavery, as well as the civic order that relatively powerful Anglo-Americans like James Fenimore Cooper tended to uphold. It embraces the visions of both male and female authors, since family enterprises and connections figured heavily for men and women alike during the formative years of the nation. Especially for the elite, who outnumbered other American writers published before the Civil War, the city-town allowed private and familial wishes to modulate naturally into the public sphere. Neither did authors from less privileged backgrounds recognize the impending, constraining power of industrial machinery before the Civil War. Even in the face of full-blown urban industrialization later, the emphasis on art and community in the city-town model proved extremely hard to think past. Only painfully did William Dean Howells make the breakthrough to a national, economic perspective on the city in the late 1880s.

The sense of the city as a shaping environment fueled by antinatural and superhuman forces came into its own in literature only during the 1890s, when urban literature split into two branches. Howells's *A Hazard of New Fortunes* and the many novels that followed its lead mark the belated culmination of Romantic anti-urbanism. Literature's economic city thus follows in the wake of post–Civil War nationalism and the concentration of industry in cities. The machines of an increasingly intrusive public environment, rather than personal and familial sources of expressive life, define the structure of the economic city. Its society is articulated by public arrangements (such as economic classes, segregated residential patterns, and transit systems) imposed upon a heterogeneous population that apparently shares little beyond a frustrated commitment to economic individualism. Its structure might be visualized as a transit map of the sort that cities distribute to help bus riders find the set routes among far-flung residential, shopping, and industrial districts.

The rise of the economic city in literature expresses a surge in concern with urbanization, as the 1890 census marked the close of the American frontier. One especially coherent group of turn-of-the-century novels focused squarely on the economic city as a national phenomenon. So well do they fit Blanche Gelfant's definition (1954, 3–10) of "the city novel" as a work that takes the city as its subject that they have long been recognized as a kind of subgenre: "the Chicago novel." The national economic city—epitomized by Chicago's new skyscrapers and heavy industry—supplies subject and structure, not just setting or metaphor, in works like Dreiser's *Sister Carrie,* Sinclair's *The Jungle, The Pit* by Frank Norris, *Memoirs of an American Citizen* by Robert Herrick, and still others. The concentration of such Chicago novels after the 1893 World's Columbian Exposition (where Turner's frontier thesis was first presented), their documentary attention to capitalistic structures and political machines and class divisions, and the epic resonance of their rhetoric all underline their self-conscious relationship to the urban history of Chicago.

At the same time, their male-only authorship also dramatizes the increased division between the urban experiences of middle-class men and women during the period. The gender-specific patterns of collaborative experience shared by Chicago women such as Jane Addams of Hull House, Bertha Honoré (Mrs. Potter) Palmer of the fair, Harriet Monroe of *Poetry* magazine, and a number of other literary women whose names are now mostly forgotten—Edith Wyatt, Clara Laughlin, and Elia Peattie among them—explain the continuation of literature's city-town pattern in their fine novels. Their leadership in social work, civic arts, and suffrage led them to deal with increasing urban heterogeneity by developing a civic-family variant on the city-town model. While the men's Chicago novels pay attention to divisions among classes and between men's public and women's private roles, the novels of Chicago women emphasize continuities among various sectors of society and between private and public affairs. This is also in keeping with the suffragist campaign then to expand "woman's sphere" of responsibility to include "social housekeeping." The history of Chicago's reification as a symbol for the nation thus exemplifies the different ways male and female writers have engaged various dimensions of urban life, how they have expressed those differences in their literary works, and what might account for the dominance of one literary vision over another.

In the world city of New York after World War I, the pervasiveness of urban culture became a common experience among white Americans, although the increasing distance between downtown and suburb continued to affect men and women differently. Literature's megalopolitan variant on the economic city model emphasizes this "urbanism as a way of life" (Wirth 1938) beginning in the 1920s. Implicitly, megalopolis contains nearly all the U.S. population, spreading beyond city limits into the suburbs and from sea to sea. The artificiality of the economic city has sunk into the minds of literature's megalopolitans. As the media of mass culture shift from print to electronics, megalopolis produces ever more immediate mass stereotypes and manipulations. The megalopolis is as much psychological as economic in its dynamics. Its consumers are alienated conformists, and their urban environment is less spatial than synaptic—rather like a diagram of the electronic circuitry inside a radio or TV.

During the decades that established literature's megalopolis, the walking-tour map of the old city-town was powerfully reconfigured—in New York's famous ethnic neighborhoods by African- and Jewish-American writers. While they recognized the economic city as a model for Anglo-dominated structures of urban experience, they often depicted New York as divided and inserted a version of the city-town model into their works to express neighborhood life. In fact, most racialized ethnic groups have had limited access to megalopolitan dimensions of urban life. The stereotypes of mass culture have operated to exclude them, and the service sector has employed them as menial, not professional, workers. Thus literature's megalopolis arose largely without their participation. However, the New York populations of Jewish and African-American ethnic neighborhoods became sufficiently large and concentrated to support countercultural literary activity in the 1920s and 1930s. Epitomized by the Lower East Side fiction of Anzia Yezierska and the Harlem poetry of Langston Hughes, the neighborhood-city variant on the city-town model centers in an organic, connective culture that expresses its sensory vitality in streetlife, its spiritual wealth in ethnic language, arts, and dreams. At best these ethnic expressions transform ghetto enclosures into sheltering homes. They may also press beyond the boundaries of the divided city toward multicultural possibilities—as in the epiphanies that climax Henry Roth's *Call It Sleep* and Ralph Ellison's *Invisible Man*. The collective biographical experience and literary imagery of the Harlem Renaissance writers, particularly as its counter-cultural development parallels that of Jewish immigrants on the Lower East Side, exemplifies the strengths and limits of the neighborhood-city model. These two communities' urban dreams of belonging contrast powerfully with the lost generation's nightmares of megalopolitan alienation.

Models of the city-town, the economic city, and their civic-family, megalopolitan, and neighborhood variants, are depicted in many more literary works than the hundred or so discussed in this book. Their variety challenges the supposed universality of skyscraper alienation in U.S. urban culture. While the economic city continues to serve as a powerful model for political critique in literature, the city-town has been a complex, flexible model of cultural, sometimes multicultural, experience, enmeshed in the marginalization of women and ethnic minority groups. The city-town cannot be dismissed as "rural," although it is organic. Indeed, it expresses an original, regional perspective on urban experience that we would do well to honor.

The literary models I offer are not straight jackets but skeletons for viewing differing urban patterns in relationship to each other. Set within the contexts of intellectual, urban, social, and biographical history, the models represent constructions of urban experience as well as aesthetic contributions to urban culture. This approach requires attention to literary works in which the city per se is not a central theme in order to discover the diverse ways in which literature relates urban imagery to its other elements and constructs. In the work of Cooper and Cather, for example, the city is one of many expressions of society's moral choices; in Fitzgerald's works, the city is all-pervasive, as given and unremarkable as the atmosphere. Cities inform these works but are not themselves the focal subjects. That does blunt the city as a probe for locating the thematic centers of such works—but this book does not claim the city as the central subject of each literary work it examines; it is not just about "city novels" (Gelfant 1954, 3-10). It is instead an examination of the place of urban experience both as figure and as ground, in both the lives and letters of U.S. writers. Only because novels provide the fullest literary rendering of urban structures developing over time, this book emphasizes novels, although it includes other prose, poetry, and a few plays in the literature it treats.

Urban Intersections keeps its historical context thick by focusing on various kinds of authorial experience and literature written in and about Chicago from 1890 to 1915 and in New York between the world wars. While also discussing U.S. urban literature in many other times and places, it highlights the definitive skyscraper cities in order to expose the peculiar historical foundations upon which a special cohort of writers constructed Chicago as *the* American city at the turn of the century, then the equally peculiar circumstances out of which the lost generation rejected New York as an alienating megalopolis after World War I. It also recovers the alternative literary visions cultivated by women and marginalized ethnic writers in those same cities at those same times, reconstructing their "lost continuities" (Bremer 1981) with pre-Civil War literature's city-towns. *Urban Intersections* thus places Chicago and New York skyscraper literature on a long chronological line overlaid with a broadening cultural criticism that traces not one but two traditions in U.S. urban literature—as branching, sometimes interlacing lines of development. It demystifies and challenges the dominant skyscraper imagery by placing it in historical context.

The purpose of this study is to expand, not further dichotomize, our literary resources for urban life and culture. The branching in U.S. urban traditions, ironically, was caused by the push to create a monolithic America. That push has polarized urban literatures, subordinated one to the other, and obscured the variety of U.S. experience. I question throughout this book the part that nationalism played in bringing the economic city and its megalopolitan variant into the literary limelight. My concluding chapter pushes beyond any either/or dichotomy to open up the multiple possibilities of regionalism. That brings us full circle to our embodiment in situations—in historical times and places with their own cultural codes, in social and personal circumstances, in various "regions" of human experience—that qualify our constructions of human reality in literature.

No one model for the city will do—either to help us interpret the range of our experiences or to help us imagine the variety of urban and literary possibilities. Thus implicit in this study is a plea, to all of us as citizens, and especially to those among us who study cities and seek to plan or manage them, to recognize what literature has to offer our urban understandings. And implicit in this study is another plea, to all of us as readers, and especially to the writers, critics, and teachers among us, to acknowledge that every work of literature is historically situated and to make the full range of literature's diversity accessible.

1
Pre–Civil War City-Towns

The city-town, as a center of culture and community, is one of the oldest treasures of human civilization. Its power is encoded in languages, the built environment, history. Linguistically, *polis* means a place of art as well as discourse, George Steiner (1973, 3) reminds us, and it is properly translated as "communion," "communication," and "community." Its earliest manifestations in North America are the major pueblo cities built in Chaco Canyon and into the cliffs of Mesa Verde (see fig. 1) in the tenth and eleventh centuries, ceremonial and clan centers for the Anasazi tribe in the Southwest (Ferguson and Rohn 1987, 193–96). As late as 1862, a Wisconsin newspaper appealed with confidence to the historic Puritan version of the city-town as an established American tradition; Appleton, Wisconsin's civic spirit made it "a city set on a hill, whose light cannot be hid," the local *Motor* declared (Merrell 1975, 9). Even after the economic city had changed this image of America's urban promise into a symbol for amassed individual wealth, Ronald Reagan invoked the "city on a hill" in his 1984 presidential campaign (*Time* 1984).

John Winthrop coined that resonant phrase aboard ship heading toward the New World in 1630, when he shared his vision of the future with the Massachusetts Bay colonists. He said, "we must consider that we shall be as a city upon a hill, the eyes of all people are upon us." Calling them to put aside "ordinary" private interests and societal divisions and to build a settlement that would display their virtue to "succeeding plantations," Winthrop essentially defined the concept of the city-town that would last, in literature and in life, until the time of the Civil War.

Winthrop's "city upon a hill" was to be a future-oriented expression of communal virtue rooted in the New England region. It affirmed open-ended promise, moral community, and organic regionalism as urban characteristics. These three themes comprise a flexible city-town pattern that bends to interpret many kinds of urban experience, cultural beliefs, evaluative stances, historic patterns of settlement, social backgrounds, and personal histories. It is the flexibility of the city-town image that held back the development of the economic city's dominant, adversarial, and antinatural image for so long, despite Romanticism's thrust in that direction.

Before the Civil War cities belonged to Europe, and "city" had yet no clear definition that distinguished it from "town" in the United States. Both were concentrations of settlement—hence my label "city-town"—on a continuum with villages, other dwelling places, and even domesticated farmlands. In New England, the word "town" meant both "a nucleated urban-type settlement" and "the entire community of village lots and farm fields," according to John W. Reps (1965, 120). A place might be called a "city," "town," and "village" indiscriminately—as was James Fenimore Cooper's fictional Templeton, which "resembled a city" (*The Pioneers* [1823] 1959, 91) but could also be called both "town" and "village" in a single short sentence (*Home as Found* [1838] n.d., 243).

In general, any settlement—even a paper plat—might have been a city in the making. What became of it depended upon what its citizens made of their regional setting and history. Even the largest cities did not achieve a status clearly differentiated from towns or other forms of settlement. Cooper's *Home as Found* presents New York of 1820 as "a commercial town," its best features recalling "some country town" in Europe, its lack of social depth "resembl[ing] an encampment," its clamor proclaiming it a "city" (132, 111, 55, 330).

City-towns did not represent any unique phenomenon or object of concern. They stood among many measures of human achievement and aspiration, and city histories and potentialities were indeed diverse. The Puritans' embryonic Boston had not been the only colony along the Eastern Seaboard, nor was theirs the only religion that sought a place in the so-called New World. Anne Hutchinson and Roger Williams rejected the Puritan vision as overly constrictive and founded the colonial city of Providence, its very name forward looking. Spaniards established Catholic St. Augustine primarily as a military outpost. Philadelphia, with its park-centered squares, physically symbolized the rationality of the Quakers' moral vision. Elsewhere fortress settlements gave way to plat book townships and street grids in the name of growth as soon as Native American opposition was decimated.

As the colonists joined into a loose federation of states, the openness of city growth and change was tempered somewhat by a rationalized federal architecture, but this constricted each city's uniqueness only slightly. America's sense of local history was strong, and Washington Irving made it the motivating joke for *A History of New York*—the grandiose title of which continued, *from the Creation of the World to the End of the Dutch Dynasty* ([1812] 1984, 17–19). His *History* burlesques Diedrich Knickerbocker's worries that "the early history of this venerable and ancient city . . . will be buried in eternal oblivion . . . for want of a historian." Nonetheless, uncertainties about the futures of early American cities did affirm interest in the multiplicity and productivity of their pasts. From a unique and continuing history built upon communal choices and regional roots, each settlement was expected to generate its own urban future.

This is the central urban motif in *The Pioneers* (1823). Although primarily a wilderness novel, it expresses Cooper's hope for "the City of the West"—which Ralph Waldo Emerson also looked for when he dubbed the nineteenth century "the Age of Cities" (Emerson 1909–14, 7:525; qtd. in Cowan 1967, 1). Cooper's city resolves a set of early Romantic conflicts between individual and society, nature and art, in this first famous Leatherstocking tale. The beginning of *The Pioneers* establishes the Romantic paradigm by setting the lone frontiersman Natty Bumppo at odds with a land-owning magistrate, Judge Marmaduke Temple. Natty and the Judge are the older generation in a novel that concerns itself primarily with the new nation taking shape in the hands of the younger generation. The new synthesis is symbolized by the love affair between Judge Temple's daughter, Elizabeth, and Bumppo's young forest companion, Oliver Edwards. Each inheriting the strengths of the past generation in new form, Elizabeth comes from the city and Oliver from the woods to meet and marry in a wilderness town that promises to become a city. They embody both the historical connections and the future concerns of Templeton as city-town.

The "unfinished" houses of Templeton lack the permanence and developed taste of a mature city, but they offer promise for the future. Though the streets have been cruelly carved out "by the compass" in disregard of nature's "trees, hills, ponds, [and] stumps," Templeton has been designed for "posterity." It is a pledge to its pioneering inhabitants, for whom "nothing could look more like civilization, than a city, even if it lay in a wilderness!" (180, 47–48, 5). Its fifty buildings were intentionally "grouped together in a manner that aped the streets of a city, and ... looked far ahead." Templeton's rough-cut streets "lay like a map" (33), clearly centered around the judge's home, an inn, and an academy doubling as church and courthouse. Yet the map is open to expansion. Templeton's physical arrangements epitomize the city-town's ad hoc gathering of residential, commercial, cultural, religious, and governmental structures. Its layout closely resembles Boston in 1657, when the governor's house, the market place, a church, and the town hall were all located at the main intersection, as described by John W. Reps in *The Making of Urban America* (1965, 141).

Templeton's open-ended physical form derives from a social order and institutions that express its citizens' personal values and talents. Indeed, literature's city-town was such a flexible and enduring model before the Civil War precisely because it expressed the voluntary community of its inhabitants. Like the Temple family that defines Temple-ton (or the Cooper family founding Cooperstown), an active, expansive joining of individuals creates each literary city-town. Human characters define the city's character. A fertile bond between individual and society ensures the future.

Thus Templeton's social arrangements express the intersections of individual and collective, private and public, motives. Comparable to a "king" as Templeton's founder, Judge Temple has a preeminence in keeping with his civic energies and personal qualities of rectitude and learning. Templeton's otherwise democratic hospitality expresses the heterogeneity of its population of Native Americans, free African Americans, and others from "half the nations in the north of Europe" (118). Templeton closely resembles historical early American cities in its mixed social order, too. A "natural" aristocracy of elite families with private businesses and exclusive education dominated the postcolonial leadership of most cities. Even during colonial times, the largest cities—New York, Philadelphia, Charleston, Boston—were ethnically heterogeneous (McKelvey 1973, 8). In fictional Templeton, all share a collective building spirit despite their differences, in the spirit of John Winthrop's conception. The judge's "will" accords with "the wishes of his followers" (Cooper [1823] 1959, 29), and social activities express individual desires in forms appropriate to communal harmony and future life. The marriage of Oliver and Elizabeth, which predictably ends the novel, patches up old feuds and promises to generate a new order appropriate to Oliver's natural virtues as well as Elizabeth's urban refinement. At base, the city-town grows out of just such voluntary, familial joinings as theirs. It does not force a choice between individual and social priorities. Indeed, the definitive institution of literature's city-towns is the family.

Other urban institutions are likewise expressive of human talents. Instead of industrial and political "machines" externally controlling their lives, as in literary portrayals of turn-of-the-century economic cities, citizens express their own social intentions in a city-town's private homes and churches, commercial inns and markets, schools and museums, and governmental assemblies. So "meeting [house] ... museum, and ... both Legislaters" (Smith [1830–59] 1978, 1151) make up the character of the "great town" of Portland, Maine, in Seba Smith's *Jack Downing Papers*. Fictional rustic Jack Downing goes to stay with relatives, market, and see the sights there in 1830. The carryings-on in these nodes of urban life are deliciously irrational to him because Portland's citizens are so.

Nathaniel Hawthorne's "My Kinsman, Major Molineux" also shows that the city-town is not a preformed entity but an evolving expression of its inhabitants. Social gatherings hold the key to the character of Boston just before the Revolutionary War, when Hawthorne's proto-American Robin Molineux seeks his uncle in that "little metropolis" (Hawthorne [1832] 1965, 230).[1] Although Robin eventually rejects the family-based colonial society to "rise in the world without the help of [his] kinsman, Major Molineux," his conversion is a social "contagion" he catches from other citizens there (230–31). Their gatherings—in a tavern, a shopping street, and a political mob (pointedly not in a deserted church)—simultaneously develop and reveal Revolutionary Boston's violently contentious character.

The compounding of citizens yields city-towns with diverse natures in pre–Civil War literature. Portland's comic irrationality and Boston's violent contentiousness are only two possibilities, each presented as belonging to a very specific time and place. The several city-towns depicted in African American Harriet Jacobs's nonfictional *Incidents in the Life of a Slave Girl* (1861) express yet other collective characters. Edenton in North Carolina, Philadelphia, and New York are certainly not like Templeton, Portland, and Boston in any particular. Nor does Jacobs, a Southern-born woman escaping from slavery, share much social background with free white male Northerners like Cooper, Smith, and Hawthorne. But the communal dynamic that shapes their urban imagery is the same. The concentration of people is for Jacobs too the defining characteristic of a city-town. Being "in the midst of people" makes Edentown a safer place of enslavement than "a distant plantation," because social acquaintance and reputation moderate her master's rapist intentions into less physical forms of human violation ([1861] 1987, 53, 29). For her, the differing characters of citizens explain urban variety, and each city-town centers in private associations epitomized by families—the interracial family connections that crisscross Edenton, the "many [new] friends" that transform Philadelphia from a "city of strangers" into a sheltering haven, and the black and slave-holding family members, "all from my grandmother's neighborhood," who make New York both homelike and dangerous (158–59, 165).

Literature's city-town imagery can contain such variety because it derives from family-like associations of individuals into communities. Family was centrally important to social status for slave and free women and men alike before the Civil War. Only gradually was that common denominator displaced by the growth of public and economic institutions outside the home along with the political extension of the vote to all—but only—white men by 1840 (Lerner 1969).

Family-like gatherings—including city-towns—are not, of course, always happy. And because its associations are not forced, the city-town figures as a moral expression of its inhabitants' choices. Indeed, slave narratives like Jacobs's and the *Narrative of the Life of Frederick Douglass* (1845) derive much of their moral power from slavery's offense against the model of voluntary community undergirding public life throughout the United States. As a rule, the city-town poses neither more nor fewer restrictions on its inhabitants than any other form of settlement, and it proves more or less good or evil as its inhabitants prove so. "If ours the faults, the virtues too are ours": so trumpets the prologue to Royall Tyler's *The Contrast* ([1787] 1990, 1091), the first U.S.-authored play, which takes "the circles of New-York" as its subject. The city-town does not even limit choices to come, to stay, or to leave. In contrast to the economic city as "an inescapable controlling force," a "problem" in much urban literature written after the Civil War, the communal city-towns of pre-Civil War literature are conceived "in more moralistic... terms," as Janis Stout also argues in *Sodoms in Eden*. A city-town is a symbolic, moral community subject to human choice, "an essentially controllable rather than controlling entity"—especially since, as she explains, city and country "are taken to be viable (that is, equally available) alternatives" (Stout 1976, 2–3).

City and country are even taken to be interrelated in most pre–Civil

War literature. Both are organic constituents, like the family, of a regional reality powerfully situated in place and time. Organic regionalism is, indeed, the third critical element in city-town imagery. Thus the regional distinction between the slave South and the free North overrides any distinctions between city and country in slave narratives like Jacobs's. Massachusetts citizens express their "love of freedom" in Boston no less than in the Berkshires; the immorality of slaveholders enforces "stagnation in our Southern towns" no less than on distant plantations (Jacobs [1861] 1987, 189, 183).

As city and country are of a piece, moreover, so there is no sharp line of demarcation between nature and culture in the city-town. The relationship is flexible. Authors as diverse as traditional Zuñi singers making "their prayer sticks into living beings" (Zuñi [1929–30 trans.] 1978) and Ralph Waldo Emerson praising poetry as nature's song ([1841–42] 1957) embrace the arts and other social institutions as expressions of organic community while criticizing as fakery only that which does not grow out of the common expressive impulse joining city and country.

Even the centuries-old pastoral dichotomy between city and country does not operate fully in city-town literary works. Although our early authors often "perfunctorily" invoke the familiar pastoral "scheme of rural virtue and urban vice," as Janis Stout points out (1976, 23), such an invocation is more often than not ignored or contradicted by the overall thrust of the literary work. Melville uses the pastoral convention ironically to mislead his readers in *Pierre: or, the Ambiguities* (1852). Easily misinterpreted as anti-urban, *Pierre* sets up conventional contrasts between city and country only to collapse them. The innocence of Pierre Glendinning's rural family home and the lifeless selfishness of the city turn out to be two faces of the same coin, both projections of Pierre. The city is only more honest than the country in expressing "that darker, though truer aspect of things" and Pierre's own metaphysical isolation (Melville [1852] 1957, 94).

Like Pierre Glendinning, most characters in pre–Civil War fiction move easily between city-town and country, as did their authors. The rural-urban boundary is very permeable. Oliver Edwards moves back and forth between Templeton and the woods; other members of the Temple-Edwards-Effingham family move between New York and Templeton upstate—between the "city" that "resembled an encampment" and the wilderness settlement that "resembled a city." Such diverse settings are equally available, while each differs from the others in degree rather than in kind. New York has more cultural and material advantages, Templeton more public acquaintance and quiet, the woods more physical excitement; but none wholly lacks the attributes of the others. Thus Templeton is not "dispersed" enough for "purely a country population," and New York is not "regulated" enough for a true city, in the Effinghams' European-tutored eyes in *Home as Found* (Cooper [1838] n.d., 133, 122). Country and city differ no more than their inhabitants do.

All told, pre–Civil War city-towns were unbounded by any preestablished fate as "city," as antagonist to the individual, or as opponent to nature. They could therefore take many forms in literature. Because citizens might make so many different things out of so many different regional circumstances, there was a tremendous variety in urban imagery: utopian dreams and gothic horrors; Philadelphia's New World opportunities for the shrewd youth in *The Autobiography of Benjamin Franklin* (begun in 1771) and Philadelphia's Old World pestilence in *Arthur Mervyn* (1799–1800) by our first recognized novelist, Charles Brockden Brown; the popular "mysteries and miseries" of early nineteenth-century sensationalism and the fond foibles of Washington Irving's Knickerbocker New Yorkers; the openness of frontier Chicago as visited in Margaret Fuller's *Summer on the Lakes in 1843* (1844) and the restrictions of slaveholding Baltimore in the *Narrative of the Life of Frederick Douglass* (1845); New York's materialistic indifference in Melville's "Bartleby the Scrivener: A Story of Wall Street" (1853) and its lecherous vices in *The Newsboy* (1854) by Elizabeth Oakes Smith; Boston's engaging masquerades in Hawthorne's *The Blithedale Romance* (1852) and New York's equally engaging transparencies in Whitman's "Crossing Brooklyn Ferry" ([1856, 1881] 1965a). Ranging from New Jerusalems to Sodoms, U.S. literature's city-towns eluded any more constricting *a priori* placement.

The various circumstances of city-towns could even, moreover, evoke diverse evaluative responses from the same authors, and these might be colored by changing personal circumstances. Harriet Jacobs was positively or negatively disposed toward different cities at different times in her life's journey from slavery to freedom, as was James Fenimore Cooper as he traveled through different stages in his professional life. At different times, Cooper expressed significantly different attitudes toward the same features of the same city-town. He wrote *The Pioneers* while enjoying cultural prominence in New York; fond memories of his childhood in Cooperstown inspired him to create a positive image of the wilderness city-town of Templeton. However in *Home as Found,* published fifteen years later, Cooper cast a bitter light over Templeton. After returning from five years abroad, he found literary disputes and unpopularity awaiting him in New York and retreated to unhappy privacy in Cooperstown. The two novels have remarkably similar plots (involving conflicting land claims, recovered family members, and promising marriages) and emphasize similar features of city-town life, but *Home as Found* despairs at the very lack of historical depth and finality, social divisions, and distinction from country life that *The Pioneers* finds promising. Changes in Cooper's life experience and biographical perspective appear to have made the difference. To a man who felt cut off from social success and thus less able to secure society's appropriate privileges, the American future was less promising and provincial taste less wise. Attuned to the shadow side of the United States, Cooper's later novel reminds us that city-towns were not utopias, only free from the machinery that eventually trapped the economic city.

Importantly, adopted European standards lend particular force to Cooper's change in attitude. In *Home as Found,* his own perspective on American urban life, like that of his main characters, is based on the admired "tastes, tone, conveniences, architecture, streets, churches, shops, and society" of European capitals (Cooper [1838] n.d., 132). In general, however, literature's city-town imagery blunted the cultural inferiority complex from which Americans generally suffered. Because U.S. city-towns centered in communal values and expressive culture, they had the potential to embrace the best of art and refinement that European cities had to offer. Conversely, the very potentiality of U.S. city-towns and their organic continuity with nature exempted them from the "course of empire" that seemed to have driven many European cities to tyranny, corruption, even extinction. For U.S. writers, as for Hawthorne in *The Marble Faun,* Rome epitomized the fate of cities in Europe. Most writers emphasized the exemption of American city-towns from European standards. Whatever critical concerns they had about the city in general focused on Europe.

In fact, it is European cities in U.S. fiction to which cultural critics most often turn for examples of pre–Civil War writers' supposed anti-urbanism: London in Poe's story "The Man of the Crowd" (1840), Liverpool in Melville's *Redburn* (1849), and Rome in Hawthorne's *The Marble Faun* (1860). In her book *Sodoms in Eden,* Janis Stout dwells on the city of "bizarre actions and . . . tormented consciousness" in "The Man of the Crowd"; "indignation at the cruel social problems created or exacerbated by. . . . 'the City' " in *Redburn;* and the city "as a symbol of the past and of evil. . . . of threat and nightmare" in *The Marble Faun* (Stout 1976, 61–63, 122–24, 113–15). Stout gives a negative spin to her analysis by emphasizing the same three works—about European cities—that dominate Morton and Lucia White's discussions of Poe, Melville, and Hawthorne in *The Intellectual versus the City* (White and White 1962, 47–59), despite her insightful objections to their anti-urban thesis. In fact, Melville did implicate United States cities when he criticized the economic forces binding Europe and America, country and city, into a single exploitative system—in "The Paradise of Bachelors" and "The Tartarus of Maids" (1855), for example. But the other two authors posed the United States apart: "so vast a difference is there between a London populace and that of the most frequented American city," according to Poe ([1840] 1956, 136).

European cities evoke positive literary images only insofar as they partake of the positive characteristics of the city-town: a sense of historical continuity; a society based in private, family associations and cultural refinement expressive of communal values; and compatibility with natural settings, such as U.S. designers began adopting from English urban garden layouts in the 1830s (Reps 1965, 325). But American writing usually qualifies even these positive opinions of European cities with concerns about crowding, inequality, and decay. Thus in "The Paradise of Bachelors" ([1855] 1949, 187), Melville's privileged narrator finds his way through the "surrounding din" of Fleet Street to the garden "oasis" and urbane apartments of London's historic Temple Inns only with difficulty. The Inns are a "city with all the best appurtenances"; but the "perfection . . . of good living, good drinking, good feeling, and good talk" (187–88, 193) that he indulges in there turns out to be an impotent, vicarious, and ultimately parasitic existence. Melville makes his critical point by pairing "The Paradise of Bachelors" with "The Tartarus of Maids," where U.S. factory "girls" engage in a perversion of procreative labor to support the "appurtenances" of European privilege.

Hawthorne is only somewhat more ambivalent in his criticism of such European privilege on American soil in "My Kinsman, Major Molineux" ([1832] 1965, 210). His Robin enters colonial Boston "with as eager an eye as if he were entering London city" only to find the promised patronage of his Tory second cousin undone by a Revolutionary mob. As an alternative to the anarchic form of democracy that Hawthorne's story offers, the colonized European version of the city-town that Major Molineux represents is appealing, even if morally compromised. It has proved similarly attractive to other U.S. writers over the years, particularly in contrast to later forms of urban materialism. It is the "aristocratic spirit," an updated version of Melville's all-male "paradise" of good taste and "monasticism," that F. Scott Fitzgerald treasures behind the "great barricades of books" in Edmund Wilson's New York apartment over sixty years later in "My Lost City" ([1934] 1945a, 25, 23). Just as Melville's narrator gets physically ill when he has to relinquish his belief in the goodness of the bachelors' life, so Fitzgerald plunges into the drunken "hysteria" of the Roaring Twenties when he loses the seclusion of cultural privilege (30) that the city-town's communal, organic order supported.

Historical continuity, an orientation toward future generations, the centricity of familial and other private associations, concerns with social expression of individuality, a regional consciousness, a vulnerability to natural forces—and all the possibilities and difficulties that go along with these—were major aspects of urban experience in literature's pre–Civil War city-town. Indeed, they remain so, especially for the majority of Americans, whose color, gender, class, or regional location has limited their participation in national public life. City-town imagery was not wishful thinking then, before the Civil War, and for most of us, it is not now. But we have learned to think about the city in ways that make the communal organicism of the city-town seem unrealistic, even sentimental and utopian. In doing so we have lost valuable dimensions of consciousness that can still serve us, despite the intrusions of industrialization, cultural nationalism, and Romanticism.

Nonetheless industrialization did put increasing, palpable pressure on the attitude Americans would take toward their cities' futures. Paradoxically, material reality seemed to limit potentiality as progress seemed to break away from the past. The War of 1812 having proved the need for industrial independence, the earliest U.S. factories relied on water power and were therefore located at the rushing narrows of rivers—usually in the country upstream from major urban harbors. Yet "The Tartarus of Maids" makes it clear that the machinery of industrial progress threatened the nature of social life from the first. Even along the edges of Walden Pond thirty years before the peak of national railroad construction and twenty years before the advent of urban street cars, Thoreau ([1854, 1906] 1968, 128–31) warned that the railroad's mechanical ties would strangle human individuality and reduce community to conformity. Literary urban imagery took a predictable turn for the worse once industry began to center in cities. Rebecca Harding Davis was profoundly prophetic in equating a factory in an American city with the city itself, "a city of fires," in *Life in the Iron Mills* ([1861] 1972, 20). A thirty-year-old middle-class woman who had not yet found a husband and home of her own, Davis experienced the constraints of antebellum southern femininity while being poorly served by the under-developed social resources of a new industrial town in West Virginia. She understood that the new industrial urban environment did not express but instead controlled its human inhabitants: "the makers of things were being ridden" (Olsen 1972, 164). Her *Life in the Iron Mills* was immediately "recognized as a literary landmark" (88–89). But its deterministic viewpoint remained anomalous—a "preseason flowering" of naturalism (Langford 1961, 15) and of the economic city—until the symbolic ascendency of industrial Chicago over thirty years later. Until then, the city-town's orientation toward human agency in history and toward an undetermined future, which accorded with the structure of Judeo-Christian beliefs (Eliade 1959, esp. 102–12), held sway.

The expressive regional grounding of city-towns was further weakened by cultural nationalism. The "first new nation" (Lipset 1963) sought to legitimize itself with concepts of natural rights, individualism, and democracy, while limiting any conflicting cultural values. Having separated church from state, it also separated from public affairs other voluntary social units that had impacted colonial government, such as families, plantations, and tribal nations. Of course, women, children, slaves, and Native Americans were all excluded from the new ethos of democratic individualism. Thus townships and urban governments were divided from the fabric of regional society.

The postfederal classical style in urban planning and architecture also served to disrupt regional dynamics and undermine distinctions between U.S. city-towns and European cities. Rome became the new nation's dubious touchstone, monumentally displayed in the architectural plans for the Capitol (Cowan 1967, 124–79, esp. 133). Simultaneously, "Nature's Nation" began to replace the city upon a hill as the metaphorical ideal for the nation as a whole in the Hudson River school of art and early Romantic literature (Miller 1967).[2] Paintings like Thomas Cole's *The Course of Empire* series (1836; see fig. 2) warned against the city's oppressive powers, while poems like William Cullen Bryant's "A Forest Hymn" ([1825] 1935, 52) romanticized the individual's direct relationship to nature. Literature's city-towns could finesse these new mythologies only as long as they embraced an undefined future, democratic community, and harmony with nature, while leaving aside the issue of "cityness" all together.

Literary Romantics did increasingly emphasize the individual's ultimate isolation from community. Hawthorne symbolized that isolation in the many masks and veils his characters wear, only less consciously in country than in city. "The Minister's Black Veil" (1836) establishes this metaphor for spiritual isolation, which *The Blithedale Romance* ([1852] 1965, 228) carries to its logical culmination in "the black veil" of death. In the smoky atmosphere of the "New England metropolis" where the *Blithedale* Brook Farmers begin and end their tragic fantasy of pastoral brotherhood (183), they use the costuming and curtaining veils of theatrical art consciously to act out their secrets and separations. No such human creativity can be found in the wall metaphor that Melville uses to represent the stony egotism of *Pierre,* published that same year, or the impersonal isolation of city life in "Bartleby the Scrivener: A Story of Wall Street" (1853). Like Pierre (Stout 1976, 132), Bartleby resembles the stone walls that surround him, standing "mute and solitary" like a "column," lost in "dead-wall reveries" in the law office where he works, then dying as a vagrant at "the base of [a prison] wall ... his head touching the cold stones" (Melville [1853] 1950, 115, 117, 130). Melville's stone metaphor for living "mechanically" (100) in isolation cannot be put on and off like a veil. It is built into the urban environment, thus pointing toward the environmental determinism that later authors found ruling cities "mechanically." But before the Civil War, city-town imagery was capacious enough to accept Hawthorne's veils as an expression of individual isolation, and its insistence on expressive agency resisted the deterministic implications of Melville's walls.

Another writer, reaching the height of his powers in the 1850s, even suggested that Romanticism and the fires of urban industry could be creatively joined with city-town imagery. Walt Whitman's poetry sings of the "self" and utters the corporate "word democratic" in the same breath ([1867, 1871] 1965b). It bursts the limits of other Romantics' nature to make room for mechanization, movement, diversity—for change itself—as part of its organic dynamism. It realizes a transcendent union of past, present, and future in a pastoral myth with a city setting.

Perhaps Whitman's marginalized social status as a bisexual bohemian (Chase 1961, 6) motivated his radical democracy and empathy with people from diverse social backgrounds. Probably his early childhood in "the activity and noise of [Brooklyn as] a small city" and his family experience of moving frequently back and forth between the rural and urban ends of Long Island (Allen 1967, 2–16) nurtured his comfort with both the dynamic vitality and organic continuities of city-town life. (Rebecca Harding Davis was, by contrast, closed out of the industrial sector of her provincial town and into a static, privatized sphere of homemaking, and she viewed the industrial city's beginnings as alienating.) In any event, Whitman's poetry presses the continuities of city-town imagery into radical, totalizing unities. In his great poem "Crossing Brooklyn Ferry" ([1856, 1881] 1965a), the city upon a hill fuses with Romantic individualism, the prehistory of tribal Mannahatta with "years hence," the massing "crowds" with the ever-present "I," the "ample hills" of residential Brooklyn with the commercial "streets of Manhattan," the flashing sunlit gulls above with the flashing red and black foundry fires below.

Like many of the other poems that Whitman wrote and rewrote for *Leaves of Grass* between 1855 and 1892, "Crossing Brooklyn Ferry" is simultaneously modern and archaic. As Langston Hughes believed, "Whitman's 'I' is.... the cosmic 'I' of all peoples who seek freedom, decency and dignity, friendship and equality between individuals and races all over our world" (Hughes [1945]). The unities of Whitman's poetry countermand all separations. Its organic dynamism shakes the most rigid physical structures, prefiguring John Marin's 1910–13 etchings of *Brooklyn Bridge* (fig. 5). Yet it also constructs a balanced world not unlike that depicted in the eighteenth century's anonymous *Landscape* (fig. 4). Just as the people of that eighteenth-century city-town can cross easily back and forth over the little stream that separates settlement from countryside, Whitman's modern crowds steam back and forth between Brooklyn's countryside and Manhattan's commerce. In literal detail, in fact, "Crossing Brooklyn Ferry" is the first poem for urban commuters. Structurally, it also claims the future as part of its timeless energies. Playing the puckish bard, Whitman manipulates his readers into proving his own impossible point: that the "I" of there and then is with the "you" of here and now. In this radical fusion, all walls and other barriers dissolve in a brilliant kaleidoscope of light and color.

Speaking first to the "Flood-tide below me" as he looks west and crosses east from Manhattan's business day to Brooklyn's residential night, at first Whitman insists only on a rather conventional Romantic communion with nature—"face to face" (stanza 1). But then he looks forward in time to recognize "others" who "will" gaze at these waters in the future; and he takes upon himself their future perspective (stanza 2). He shifts pronouns and tenses to draw grammatically near to those others and to insist that "your" experience "is" what his own "was," as his

Figure 5. John Marin, *Brooklyn Bridge* (1913), etching, printed in black, plate: 11¼ × 8⅞ in. Collection of the Museum of Modern Art, New York; gift of Abby Aldrich Rockefeller. Courtesy of the museum.

hypnotic repetitions of "others," "you," and "I" weave together his catalogues of sights and feelings until "Just as you ... I too" am "dazzled" by the "glistening ... oscillating ... swinging ... serpentine ... tremulous" movement that brings together earth, air, fire, and water, and reader and author (stanzas 3 and 5).

Whitman assumes that all these fascinations "were to me the same as they are to you," that "just as you ... I too ... loved well those cities" (stanza 4). He pushes beyond that to pile up a list of shameful desires, affirming that "I am he who knew" all the varieties of evil that are in "you," too (stanza 6). Nothing and no one are left aside. His vision embraces sunlight and foundry fire as equally dazzling, love and lust as equally known. His is a specifically urban setting, where crowds of strangers repeat one another's experiences of beauty and tempt one another to forbidden familiarities. Whitman teases the reader as "closer yet I approach you" (stanza 7), then quietly, almost in a whisper, indicates the final fusion: "I" and "you" become "we." "We understand then do we not?" (stanza 8). And we join him in the collective voice of this final fusion, commanding that all the variety and movement of this natural, vital, urban crossing keep on varying and moving, that the rivers "flow" and life "live" and cities "thrive" forever (stanza 9).

Admittedly, Whitman's poem has largely failed as prophecy—certainly for many Anglo-American male writers. Henry James seems to be taking Whitman specifically to task as he enters New York harbor in *The American Scene* ([1907] 1968, 72–74). James remarks the "splendid light" that suffuses the scene "as if ... nature and science were joyously romping together." He exclaims over the vibrant activity that "might have been" symbolized in "some collective presence of great circling and plunging, hovering and perching seabirds" if "the intellectual extravagance of the given observer" "is open to corruption" by such large-scale vitality. James will admit only the superficial appearance and imaginative possibility of what was ultimately real for Whitman. Although James had expressed nostalgia for pre-Civil War Boston's cultural vigor and hope for postwar New York's cosmopolitan spatiousness in *The Bostonians* (1886), by the beginning of the twentieth century he wanted to keep his distance from the American city. A "restless analyst"—and anti-Semite—he despised the "alien" immigrants and the "monotonous commonness" of moneygrubbers he found in New York (82–86). He disdained the city itself as a "monstrous organism" whose "scattered members" only seemed laced together by "steam-shuttles or electric bobbins." He abhorred the "pincushion" skyline of office buildings that "overtopped" the churches and "usurped" the old "harmony" of sea and ships (75–78).

Whitman saw this ugliness, too. His vision, which James dismissed as "extravagant," was so only in its radically democratic spirit of unity. Whitman did not paint U.S. cities simply in rosy hues any more than other pre–Civil War writers. Their cities had many "darker" shades, like the red and black of Whitman's foundry fires. But even when ugly or dangerous, the city-towns of our early literature were not cut off from hope. For every sinful, sinking "City in the Sea" (1831), there was a golden "Eldorado" (1849), to borrow the titles of two poems by Edgar Allen Poe. Open-ended like Whitman's "Song of the Open Road" ([1856, 1881] 1965b), literature's city-towns encourage us to think about the future, physical order, and social commonality of our cities in ways that support a sense of continuity with the past, nature, and diversity.

2
Toward a National Economic City

Historians agree that the Civil War marks the great divide in nineteenth-century urbanization. The city-town model held less and less interpretive power in the face of changes that began occurring in urban life. The mercantile economics of colonial and pre-Civil War cities, which complemented rural productivity, finally gave way to large-scale urban industrialism. Three of the four major ports that still figured among the country's six largest cities in 1850 were industrializing heavily. Only New York returned to its original orientation toward trade—as a world center with finance and service in the forefront—after it lost an economic lead in manufacturing around 1880 (Willis 1973, 923–24). Most cities whose populations topped 100,000 after 1850 were developed as industrial from the start. By 1900 about nine-tenths of U.S. manufacturing was done in cities (Trachtenberg 1982, 114). Since many began as "railroad cities," located track-side for access to raw materials and markets, they were linked historically as well as economically to the machine. Thus the man who coined the term "city planning," Robert Morris Copeland, envisioned the city as a "great railroad or manufactury" (quoted in Jackson 1972, 132).

Daily living became more and more dependent on industry, especially in the cities. Preindustrial modes of home production largely disappeared—first spinning and weaving, then food processing, cabinetry, and the like. The family's primary homemaker became its primary consumer. Retail joined wholesale enterprises as the advertising and distributing arms of industry in major urban centers. Street railroads were introduced in the 1870s, and new residential districts were extended to ever more distant suburbs. Suburbs and cities—and the lives of their citizens—became interdependent. By the turn of the century, the independence of private homes was breached at its physical foundations by utility networks for gas and sewage, as later for telephone and electricity. Increasingly (exempting the rich from the fate of others), private homes gave way altogether to apartment and tenement flats in semipublic buildings. Jacob Riis estimated that tenements housed fully half of the population of New York City by the 1890s (cited in Trachtenburg 1982, 128).

Riis's famous photographic exposé of *How the Other Half Lives* (1890) was necessitated by a new scale of economic and ethnic division in urban populations. Various sectors were becoming strangers to one another as the second industrial revolution moved into high gear by 1880. Creating machines to make machines, rather than simple products like textiles and shoes, required tremendous capitalization and concentration of labor, making the rich much richer and the working-class poor much more numerous. The poor also became more visibly distinctive as immigrants from eastern and southern Europe and even from Asia—people whose languages, religions, customs, and skin colors exceeded the old scale of urban ethnic diversity—entered cities in large numbers. Freed from slavery, African Americans added to the darkening of urban populations. As these diverse groups were physically segregated from each other, the social heterogeneity of industrial cities became economically, ethnically, and racially discontinuous, and the literate public's "sense of the urban menace increased in proportion to middle-class withdrawal from urban centers into the new suburbs and segregated neighborhoods" (Kaplan 1988, 45).

The walking city became the streetcar city as industrialization transformed the nation. The machine seemed to unite the United States from East to West when the Union Pacific Railroad was completed in 1869. By 1883 the whole nation ran according to railroad standard time, which replaced local solar timekeeping. During the Civil War the Sanitary Commission had shown the effectiveness of national organization for nonindustrial purposes (Frederickson 1965, 98–112). In effect, the war itself represented the ultimate breakdown of community, and organization took its place. Whereas pre–Civil War nationalism had promoted expansion, post–Civil War nationalism consolidated and centralized.

The nation thus managed to bind up its wounds—technologically—and cities were a part of that process. The entire continent was made an "instrument of corporate business," organizing cities into imperialistic manufacturing centers and transforming the countryside into "a market colony," as Alan Trachtenberg explains in *The Incorporation of America* (1982, 115–17).

Increasingly urban growth was seen to hurt the countryside, where cities had once spearheaded regional health. Increasingly urban affairs were seen to overwhelm the individual, who had once loomed large in the urban community. As cities developed a critical mass that weighed on the nation's mind, the United States was plunging into a sea change in its perception of them.

Sheer numbers account for part of this. Even in the first half of the century, the percentage of Americans living in cities over 10,000 grew steadily from 3.8 percent in 1800 to 12 percent in 1850 (McKelvey 1973, 52). It was a time, however, of steady growth everywhere. The gradual expansion of a single city to 10,000 or even 50,000 did not seem particularly remarkable, nor was the short-lived burst of a speculative town likely to prove significant. Only nine cities had reached the 100,000 mark by 1860. Of these, only Cincinnati, St. Louis, and Brooklyn had ever doubled in size in a single decade. Large urban populations began booming during the Civil War. Despite the disruption and killing, Chicago and San Francisco doubled to over 100,000 in the 1860s, and Pittsburgh and Washington, D.C., came close. Similar booms occurred in Denver, Kansas City, Minneapolis, Milwaukee, and Buffalo between 1880 and 1890. By 1900 the populations of thirty-nine cities had topped 100,000, four of them passing a million (McKelvey 1973, 24, 37, 73).

Such cities were ascribed a new national status as part of the popular symbolism of the Civil War. Symbolizing the victory of the industrial North over the plantation South, cities were identified with industry and the Union, ranked against agriculture and regionalism. Urban characteristics were being defined and boundaries fixed. A special urban perspective, a perspective *on* cities, was being established, too. Cities were becoming "spectacles" (Trachtenberg 1982, 104), subjects of national observation more than centers of local participation. In place of the particularity and regional diversity of city-towns, "the city," once associated only with Europe, became American. By the turn of the century, Americans were debating whether the city was the nation's "shame" or its "hope," in the terms set respectively by Lincoln Steffens (1904) and Frederic Howe (1906). The city, especially as an economic phenomenon, was a "challenge" to the nation and to Americans individually, Josiah Strong (1911) added.

We can see the equation of cities with factories, their identification with the nation, and their juxtaposition to the individual much more easily in hindsight. At the time, however, the picture was not so clear. In part, that was because the United States did not vest economic and political and cultural primacy together in any one city, so it lacked a city to exemplify *the* city. The United States had no London or Paris or Vienna, and indeed, a national city would have made no sense during the pre-Civil War era of regional particularity. Americans would "not even bear the ascendency" of one capital city then, Cooper's Europeanized Effinghams had complained in *Home as Found*. We need not accept their grumbling explanation—that Americans are obsessed with equal rights—in order to recognize some truth in the effects they pan: "Formerly, Philadelphia, then the largest town in the country, was the political capital; but it was too much for any one community to enjoy the united consideration that belongs to extent and politics; and so the honest public went to work to make a capital, that would have nothing else in its favor but the naked fact that it was the seat of government, and I think it will be generally allowed that they have succeeded to admiration," John Effingham explains (Cooper [1838] n.d., 335-36).

After the Civil War, the abstract city called for exemplification. U.S. authors began to introduce cities as national centers. Among major cities in the latter half of the nineteenth century, however, Philadelphia proved too old, Washington too merely political, Boston too merely cultural, and New York not sufficiently industrial to sustain symbolic status as *the* American city. *Waiting for the Verdict* (1867) by Rebecca Harding Davis, *Democracy* (1880) by Henry Adams, and *The Bostonians* (1886) by Henry James—while concerning themselves primarily with social caste, political power, and cultural reform—dramatize the respective inadequacies of Philadelphia, Washington, and Boston as national cities. None has held a prominent place in national literary imagery since then. As an alternative to cultural Boston, commercial New York seemed more promising at first—in *The Bostonians,* then in the work of William Dean Howells. Indeed "the Dean of American letters" contrasted the old city-town and the new economic city with almost schematic precision in *The Rise of Silas Lapham* (1885) and *A Hazard of New Fortunes* (1890). But even though New York City has figured prominently in our imaginative literature from Washington Irving to Grace Paley, *A Hazard of New Fortunes* set the stage for Chicago, not New York, to gain the title of national city. It was Chicago, a new industrial city, that proved most compelling for a nation using technology to reunite after civil war. New

York would have to wait to take center stage as a cosmopolitan world city after the First World War.

As a nineteenth-century candidate for national city, Philadelphia was too bound to its past. It failed to dramatize any generative links between the past and the present, and thus toward the future. It won the competition against Washington, Boston, and New York to hold the first American world's fair because its Independence Hall had an unbeatable historical claim on the 1876 Centennial. But history played little part in the exposition itself. The fair officially started up with the Corliss steam engine and announced its closing on telegraph keys in Machinery Hall, where technology and individual inventiveness were celebrated as the main attractions in Fairmont Park. One wonders at the failure to make more of Philadelphia's civic tradition, which had constructed that major urban park and its pioneering public waterworks in the 1820s in keeping with William Penn's founding ambitions for "generous . . . open spaces," "a green country town," and a "healthy" city (quoted in Reps 1965, 141); but Penn's original plan had been distorted beyond recognition. One wonders, too, at the failure to make more of the Liberty Bell, which symbolized the city's claim to national preeminence; but liberty may have been too controversial to celebrate so soon after slave emancipation. Philadelphia may also have been hampered by the political associations of its local origins as "the Quaker City"; in the shadow of the Civil War, Quaker pacifism had become as unappealing for the North as Quaker abolition for the South.

Precisely those national issues and local associations set the uneasy terms for Rebecca Harding Davis's mixed novel of social realism, melodrama, and protest. *Waiting for the Verdict* (1867) focuses its plot and thematic structure on matters of Civil War and "blood" discrimination North and South, and it introduces Philadelphia as "the Quaker City" on the first page. Davis ([1867] 1968, 99) is quite explicit about offering the city as a microcosm for the nation: "The face of a great city compacts and reflects like a convex mirror the feeling of a country." She also recognizes the popular equation of such a "great city" with the Union (365), while reflecting as well the newly separated terminology for city and town. She contrasts "Northern cities" to the "town" of Richmond "with its country . . . houses," and the North's "market" and "mills" to the South's agricultural "supplies" and "customers" (340). Clearly Davis's novel participates in the emerging mythology of the industrial city's national dominance. It focuses on the heterogeneity of the new city, too. The intertwined careers of mulatto physician Dr. John Broderip and bastard white artisan Rosslyn

Burley question what is to be the future of newly freed black Americans and of working-class white Americans who lack family credentials. Davis implicates both groups in a striking protonaturalistic metaphor for urban vitality: the "swarming" street hucksters among whom Rosslyn Burley starts her life (1); the "swarming" downtown crowds toward whom her Southern fiancé feels an ennobling pull (102); the "swarm" of debased blacks in whom John Broderip recognizes "his race" when he acknowledges his black brother and gives up his white fiancée (295); and "the steep manufactories swarming with human life" that this second young woman observes dispassionately just before she meets the doctor (66). Although insect-like, these "swarming" crowds promise a public energy, an urban counterpoint to the individual growth that the novel locates in a family farm house in the New Jersey suburbs.

What is therefore especially remarkable—and unpromising—about Davis's image of Philadelphia is its lack of industrial dynamism and public consciousness. It stagnates in privatism. Although Davis had pioneered urban industrial imagery in *Life in the Iron Mills*, *Waiting for the Verdict* develops no sustained sense of the emerging forces of industrialism. The "steep manufactories swarming with human life" that it locates close by the depot of "rushing trains"—thereby calling attention to the huge locomotive works that gave Philadelphia a jump on the second industrial revolution—are *Waiting for the Verdict*'s only manifestations of Philadelphia industry, "the city's chief boast" during the centennial decade (Clark 1975, 62). Instead of an industrial present, a fifteen-year flashback to the old port city's wharves begins the novel and sets the terms for its urban structure. Philadelphia is a "dull town" with a "deadening" milieu, "the great flat Quaker City locked in by the two lazy rivers, going off into a sleep" (Davis [1867] 1968, 1–2). This deadening dullness enfolds the city throughout the novel.

Moreover, Davis never manages to bring the vitality of her "swarming" crowds into the plot. As metaphors in the novel, they serve only to reveal the characters of the four individuals who respond to them; they do not develop a new foundation for the city itself. For all of Davis's declared concern with discrimination as an institutional, public, economic issue, the novel is a drama of individual, private, attitudinal change. Davis paints Philadelphia as a city-town crossroads of rural-urban exchange with a cultural expressiveness that is based in private family associations, but unlike Cooper's Templeton, these cultural exchanges, expressions, and associations generate no civic life. The city is frozen against change and rigidly privatized in its old hierarchies. *Waiting for the Verdict* points clearly toward the movie era's snob city in "The Philadelphia Story" when its "wooden" and "rock"-like embodiment of old-family high society, one Mrs. Van Fitter, objects to the nameless "merchants" and "tradeswomen" who threaten to turn high society into an "asylum" (130–32).[1] Davis's novel offers several melodramatic incidents in which individuals transcend such personal and familial prejudices—including, miraculously and momentarily, Mrs. Van Fitter—but it provides no way to generalize such change to the city as a whole.

Rigidity is even worse than the loss of civic purpose that Sam Bass Warner discovers in his history of Philadelphia's industrial age, *The Private City* (1968). In *Waiting for the Verdict,* the industrial age is hidden in the grip of the past, and the past is ingrown—not just private, but privatized, dead. In Davis's novel, Philadelphia's residential streets are "dull" (66); even its market is "tiresome" (27). The only civic institution mentioned is the Academy of Science, described as a storehouse of dead stuffed animals, mummies, and human skulls (99–102). When John Broderip sails away from Philadelphia to lead a black regiment into the Civil War at the novel's end, the scene is as "gray and dull" (326) as the opening at the city's port fifteen years before.

In historical point of fact, as Warner (1968, 71) notes, "the whole city was a mix of old and new," as indeed any city is. Davis knew the old, residential side of Philadelphia best, having moved there and become a middle-class wife and mother since writing *Life in the Iron Mills.* She wrote the rest of her books from a home that she and her husband called "the Centre of the Universe" (quoted in Langford 1961, 41). While continuing her intellectual interest in reform, she did not even manage more than "one evening" at the Centennial Exposition, as she wrote the wife of her publisher, "tho I believe my name was on a committee" (letter to Annie Fields, quoted in Langford 1961, 61). Davis was constrained by a middle-class married woman's status in a city of rigid class distinctions before the era of feminist social expansion. Whereas turn-of-the-century Chicago's women novelists would nurture what Jane Addams called the "civic family" in clubs, settlement houses, collaborative enterprises, and literature, Rebecca Harding Davis ensconced herself and her fictional Philadelphia in a stifling privacy.

In contrast, privacy was the last word to describe Washington, D.C., particularly as depicted by Davis's male contemporaries. Here the publicity of politics reigned—manipulated in the *Congressional Record* and trumpeted in newspaper stories of the scandal-ridden Grant administration. Here society was public and open to the currency of the present: "It doesn't need a crowbar to break your way into society there as it does in Philadelphia. It's democratic, Washington is. Money or beauty will open any door," proclaims one of the cast of corrupt speculators in *The Gilded Age* by Mark Twain and Charles Dudley Warner ([1873] 1968, 138). The idealistic heroine of Henry Adams's *Democracy* ([1880] 1908, 46) generalizes her Washington social observations to the nation: "'Society' in America means all the honest, kindly mannered, pleasant-voiced women, and all the good, brave, unassuming men, between the Atlantic and the Pacific. Each of these has a free pass in every city and village, 'good for this generation only.'"

Along with *Honest John Vane* (1875) by John W. De Forest, *The Gilded Age* and *Democracy* evidence the imaginative pull that Washington exerted for the reunited nation.[2] As Chicago's fame would compel the attentions of major writers in the 1890s, so Washington in the 1870s incited their hunger to find typifying dramas for the age ("gilded"), the body politic (a "democracy"), and the American ("honest"). Washington's novelists agreed on the primary literary components of their subject: at least one speech-filled session of Congress, an awkward calling-card exchange among provincial ladies and polished diplomats, prying newspaper stories, concerns with lobbying and bribery, and a thematic focus on the displacement of public by private interests (e.g., Twain and Warner [1873] 1968, 218–23, 224–38, 322–24, 301–2, 358). *Democracy* probes these components most deeply. Indeed Adams's novel fully develops several underlying mythic issues for urban culture, although its Washington finally proves more concerned with political culture.

Democracy is the story of a young wealthy widow's search for purpose in Washington, D.C. Adams ([1880] 1908, 1–10) introduces Madeleine Lee's "experiment" with the "machinery of society," "the heart of the great American mystery of democracy and government," in a broad but specifically urban context. Before turning to her adventures in "the political world" of Washington, D.C., a capsule biography describes her exploring the other major urban centers that were candidates for the national city. Born to "social position" in Philadelphia, Mrs. Lightfoot Lee had accompanied her Southern husband to New York to find their "fortune." But as a widow, she "had lost her taste for New York society; she had felt no interest in the price of stocks." She found nothing of vital consequence for society in the educational interests of "her Boston friends" either.

Thus characterized and dismissed, well-born Philadelphia, commercial New York, and intellectual Boston are noted again when Adams later specifies the districts represented in Congress and, still later, the crowds at a diplomatic ball. *Democracy* contrasts the capital city's political vitality to these other cities, as also to the peaceful countryside of Mt. Vernon and Arlington. From the perspective of the countryside's park-like settings where the heroes of the past are entombed, Washington is both "dreadful" and "idealised" (132, 219), but it belongs emphatically to the living present. Although its "ordinary people" can make New York seem "in comparison... a New Jerusalem" and Boston's "Broad Street a grove of Academe" (11), Washington's currency and political energies hold "what she wanted... POWER" (12).

Disallowed the direct exercise of power as a woman before the passage of the Nineteenth Amendment, Madeleine Lee looks for a worthy man to join. Specifically, she seeks a Washington hero who is both an "engineer" strong enough to wield "the machinery of society" (12) and "a tree" tall enough to "cast a shadow" in the "wilderness" of the common crowd (2). Such human power is exactly what she fails to find in *Democracy*'s Washington. Instead she finds the "great machine" of Washington clogged by the "mire of politics" (195) and out of human control. This is *Democracy*'s metaphoric breakthrough in urban imagery. Adams's novel weaves into its text a pair of logically antithetical metaphors—the city as machine and wilderness—that would become critical to literature's economic model of the American city. The two images point toward Upton Sinclair's later novel about Chicago meat packers as cogs in a machine and beasts in *The Jungle* (1906). The dichotomy appears for the first time in *Democracy*.

The Romantics laid the groundwork for seeing people trapped by mechanization, especially in cities, and Melville and Davis applied that idea to factory settings. Adams works out the machine image as a metaphor for a city in fiction, embodying the illusion of human control that covers up the machine's dominance. Even the president and first lady are "mechanical figures," "toy dolls," "automata" controlled by the machinery they seem to run (86). Thinking herself in charge of her own affairs, Madeleine Lee also begins to act "mechanically" (321). She just barely escapes Washington before "being dragged under the wheels of the machine" (341).

Simultaneously Washington is a "wilderness of stunted natures" enmeshed in social disorganization and political corruption. Like New

York City—which is given meaning only by the mechanical accumulation of "numbers" and also called a "wilderness" because of its crowds—Washington lacks any cohering "aspiration" toward the "public good" and thus breaks the old promise of organic community (174, 2–3). Its most powerful men are animals, like the corrupt Senator Silas Ratcliffe, who woos Madeleine Lee and nearly wins her. They appear foolish to her at first, like fish and birds that one can bait with flies and worms (35, 48); then domestic, like the dogs and mice that cats can toy with (96, 100); then deceptive, like "wolves in sheep's clothing, or asses in lions' skins" (182); but finally dangerous, "a whole pack of political hounds" (333, cf. 205, 232). Having read Darwin, Madeleine Lee recognizes them as evolutionary throw-backs, suffering from "atrophy of the moral senses" (352–53). Henry Adams brings urban imagery into the realm of determinism. Whether machine or wilderness or paradoxically both, Adams's Washington is dehumanized and dehumanizing.

Even when introduced in relationship to other cities and made to bear such powerful metaphors, however, Washington stands for the urbanizing nation more than for the American city in *Democracy* and other novels. Even with "a whole continent centering at Washington," it is more a "political prairie" for folks from far away (342) than a city in its own right. People who live elsewhere come to do political business, stay until that business is exhausted, then return to their elsewheres. Adams's fictional Senator Ratcliffe will eventually go home to Peonia, Madeleine Lee is reminded, and she herself is expected to return to New York, not Washington, after a sojourn in Europe to escape the capital's newspaper gossip.

City planner Pierre L'Enfant had laid Washington out along the double axis of White House and Capitol malls, splitting it off from the residential and commercial streets that became its backyard. It was established by governmental fiat as an administrative district, rather like the French *cité* and the Italian *città*. It also resembled old Southern cities imposed on the plantation colonies to centralize British political and economic control. What Washington didn't resemble in its origins was other Northern cities. It began neither as a communal religious project like the Quakers' Philadelphia or the Puritans' Boston nor as a speculative enterprise like Dutch New Amsterdam (Reps 1965). And despite the mechanical imagery that Adams brought to bear on its politics, Washington was certainly not industrial.

Boston and New York were likewise not industrial cities, but they had established several other claims to national status in pointed competition with each other on civic, economic, and cultural grounds (as also discussed in Green 1967). It was Boston that John Winthrop envisioned as the "city upon a hill," and it was Boston that tradition identified as the birthplace of the United States. That historical claim depended, however, upon a city-town community that was highly homogeneous with a thoroughly Brahman leadership well into the nineteenth century. To the extent that Boston became more heterogeneous it lost that foundational power. The ascendancy of New York's Tweed Ring and Tammany Hall epitomized the new civic alternative, and a similar victory of new Irish-Americans over the old guard occurred in Boston. New York's Castle Gardens and later Ellis Island came to symbolize the United States to its increasingly diverse urban populations.

Just when Boston shifted its mercantile energies into manufacturing and gained new economic momentum, moreover, the completion of the Erie Canal in 1825 isolated it. The canal undermined Boston's chance to establish national economic leadership and sent New York State trade to New York City. After the Civil War, Boston lost still more economic power to the railroading West, while New York City consolidated its economic base around trade, finance, and administration. In the process, New York dropped out of the race for industrial primacy, denying that especially potent economic and symbolic base to its immigrant population.

As a result of these economic shifts, New York became the nation's publishing center in the 1880s. Many writers came to live there, making New York the stuff of their own lives and fictions. This dealt a serious blow to Boston's status as "the chief literary center of America" (Garland 1930, 6). Its intellectual reputation lost its clout when New York made a national business out of literature, and, as Martin Green has argued in *The Problem of Boston* (1967, 108), "the idea of culture [as the basis of Boston's special status] swelled as it grew emptier, acquiring even more charisma as a symbol while its content as an experience lost the old firmness and fullness."

Importantly, New York publishing helped to define other cities in literature. All writers, no matter where they themselves lived, had to pay attention to New York expectations if they wanted national publication and recognition. Eventually a corps of mostly male authors would develop a national perspective on other cities—most significantly, Chicago—for New York-based publications. Literary versions of cities even "a continent away" began to fit "the New York truth," Chicagoan Edith Wyatt objected

(1914b, 17). San Francisco, for instance, still belonged to the Gold Rush in the stereotyped "standard patterns"; not even the 1906 "earthquake [had] shaken the New York San Francisco." From the new national literary perspective of New York, moreover, a city's regional dynamics tended to freeze into static, one-dimensional stereotypes of provincial peculiarities. The focus on Boston in 1880s literature thus looks like a rear-guard attempt to make it an archetype of the nation's cities despite its loss of power. The best known Boston novels of the time—James's *The Bostonians* (1886) and Howells's *The Rise of Silas Lapham* (1885)—in effect usher it towards a provincial backseat and bow towards New York's national ascendancy.

Along with Howells's *A Hazard of New Fortunes* (1890), these fictional depictions of Boston and New York also bring into focus an increasing concern with the relationship between the so-called public and private "spheres" in urban literary imagery. Although recent feminist thinkers have fully demonstrated that public and private experience are always intimately intertwined, it is not the case that "no distinction can finally be made" between them, as Irving Howe overstated in his 1956 introduction to *The Bostonians* (vi). We do distinguish between home and market, family and government, personal friends and anonymous crowds—in our actions, institutions, and understandings. And we often attribute primary power to one or the other dimension of this dialectic. The literary imagery of city-towns and the economic city divides at just this point: private choices express themselves in public life in city-towns, while public arrangements mold private affairs in the economic city.

Concern with the balance between private and public life runs throughout much urban fiction in the late nineteenth century. Davis's and Adams's works share in it. Catching its full force, Howells's city-town Boston centers on private relationships and a cultural expressiveness that generate public life in *The Rise of Silas Lapham,* while his economic New York subordinates private relations to constricting and disruptive public forces in *A Hazard of New Fortunes.* Contrarily James's *The Bostonians* explores the extent to which Boston isolates and New York integrates the private and the public arenas. Indeed, James's novel builds its thematic structure precisely on the private/public issue of the relationship of personal feelings to political movements, within the context of regional and national affairs.

At the outset *The Bostonians* makes a regional claim to national status for Boston. Its title asserts its regional focus on an urban society that

James promotes as "the New England capital" ([1886] 1956, 105). He depicts Boston's historical continuities and residential dynamics as the expression of an entire region's social character. The city's proud roots certainly reach much deeper than Washington's "invented" society, as the opening dialogue makes clear (8). Simultaneously, James offers Boston as *"American,"* as "very national, very typical," specifically in its regional concerns with "those friendships between women so common in New England," as his 1883 notebook explains (quoted in Howe 1956, xi). James's Boston bids for national attention based on its internal, regional dynamics and specifically its reputation as "a city of culture" (James [1886] 1956, 16). Conceding economic leadership to New York from the outset, it stakes its claim on something much larger: "it's humanity" (21).

The central private/public conflict of *The Bostonians* follows this emphasis on region and nation. It picks up precisely those regional lines that Americans found culturally most powerful—and most divisive—after the Civil War. James pits southerner Basil Ransom against New Englander Olive Chancellor in a battle (the military metaphor is used repeatedly) for possession of Verena Tarrant. Basil wants Verena to mind the private sphere of his domestic life while he pursues his professional "desire for public life" (193). Olive wants Verena to be her public voice in the women's rights movement, since she is too shy "to speak herself" (101). At issue between them, Verena is "a simple American girl" (63), a kind of literary stand-in for the nation. Nothing less than the national importance of region—and of Boston as a regional city—hangs in the balance.

The Bostonians is profoundly antiregional in its final thrust. The juxtaposition of Olive Chancellor to Basil Ransom exposes Boston's regional identity as no less "provincial" and decadent than the "reactionary" South (11, 194). In particular, the three-part plot portrays Boston as split, its reform traditions maintained only in narrow privacy and cut off from its public life. This was not so in the "heroic age of New England life," when private "plain living" and public "moral passion" complemented each other (408, 183), as they still do for old Miss Birdseye, a remnant of that time. Even Basil Ransom "found himself liking" Miss Birdseye (220), having recognized "the city of reform" as his worthy antagonist at the start (7), but she is dying. The modern Bostonians of the title dishonor the banner of "the city of reform" in a feminist battle that James portrays as personal, not civic. As Olive's sister insists, the reform movement "isn't the city; it's just Olive Chancellor" (7). Characterized with homophobic undertones in a perverse masquerade, Boston has shrunk into a "sister city" (214) that commands no respect.

Olive maintains the moral essence of Boston only artificially, privately. She closets it in what James dubs "Miss Chancellor's interior" (99)—in her painfully shy character and the "narrowness" of her parlor's "organized privacy" (15-16). In two passages that contrast old Boston indoors to contemporary Boston outdoors, James makes it clear that Olive's parlor windows separate her self-indulgent beliefs from Boston's public concerns and misrepresent the city's "inexorable ... poverty" as "very picturesque," even "lovely" (15-17, 178-79). Such "organized privacy" lacks power to generate civic life quite literally; Boston's female reformers are split off from the male cohort of commercial publicists who dominate the public world. The reformers include only two married couples, one without children, the other estranged from their daughter, Verena. Verena herself eventually rebounds from the public exposure of newsstories and speeches directed by Olive Chancellor into the privacy of domestic procreation subservient to Basil Ransom.

Between the exposed Bostonian privacy of Olive Chancellor and the domestic southern privacy of Basil Ransom, *The Bostonians* unfolds a superior alternative: New York City, "a larger world" (155). There is "a sense of vastness and variety, of the infinite possibilities of a great city" in New York (297). New York can turn a Bostonian's "local reputation" into "a first-class national glory" (208). The home of parents with children and of married couples who combine their cultural and economic resources, James's New York offers an integrated context for expressing personal power socially and seeing public realities clearly. In the home of her New York suitor and his mother, for example, Verena can speak "personally, individually" to an audience of publicly influential people (274) without having to choose between promiscuous publicity and selfish privacy; Henry Burrage is willing both to marry her and to support her lecturing career. In the "narrow inclosure" of Central Park (333), she can conduct her private affairs with Basil openly, "sequestered" but not hidden (335) nor insulated from the "near neighborhood" of commercial New York (189). The simultaneous protection of private affairs and access to public contexts extend the city-town into a cosmopolitan setting—even more open than that suggested in Cecilia Beaux's 1914 painting *After the Meeting* (fig. 6). James gives every reason to regret that Boston lacks the larger range of integrated cultural expression that New York offers.

Figure 6. Cecilia Beaux, *After the Meeting* (1914), oil on canvas, 40 15/16 × 28 1/8 in. Courtesy of the Toledo Museum of Art; gift of Florence Scott Libbey.

An expatriate for ten years before he wrote *The Bostonians,* James was a bit out of step with growing perceptions of cities as dominant rather than expressive. From his lionized position among the elite, he found cosmopolitan New York more attractive than provincial Boston because it seemed "larger" without being too large for human control. His good friend William Dean Howells differed with him on that critical point. As a working editor, Howells found New York not more attractive but more powerful than Boston. A midwesterner who treasured his acceptance into literary Boston in the 1860s and considered New York City only "the next best thing" even after he moved there in 1888, Howells characterized regional Boston as fundamentally private and New York as fundamentally public. He did not see a private/public split in the former and private/public integration in the latter, but rather an imbalance in each. Personally, Howells preferred the private skew. Although he severely criticized Americans who failed to recognize their "complicity" in others' lives and in public affairs, he never lost his emotional attraction to "home itself" (Howells 1917, 23). In articulating New York's ascendancy as a public environment, he wrote with a critical edge that proved compelling for others, too.

The eclipse of regional Boston by the large-scale public economy of New York becomes clear in the pointed contrasts between *The Rise of Silas Lapham* and *A Hazard of New Fortunes.* Despite omens of the rising economic city, Howells's Boston centers on a homogeneous, largely private society of well-born families, mercantile gentility, and cultural refinement. His New York emerges as a heterogeneous, public society shaped by economic interests and mechanical transit networks. Just five years, yet worlds of difference, separate the two urban novels.

"Money is to the fore now. It is the romance, the poetry of our age," laments Bromfield Corey, the male representative of refined Boston in *The Rise of Silas Lapham* ([1885] 1957, 52). His statement identifies the primacy of economic forces in the postwar nation, invading even Boston. The self-conscious aging of Bromfield Corey, whose inherited fortune derives from colonial sea trade, and his son Tom's decision to work for Silas Lapham's paint manufacturing company signal Howells's recognition that the nation's urban economy was shifting from a mercantile to an industrial base. Within this context, Howells introduces the entrepreneur as the characteristic "type of the successful American" (4), for so Silas Lapham seems through the public clichés of a newspaper interview. His credentials are money, not family membership in society, and his move to Boston from Vermont enacts the Horatio Alger myth of urban opportunity.

But Boston is not yet the entrepreneur's domain. Silas Lapham's factory is squeezed in among the "narrow ... crooked" streets down by the old port city's wharves. His money is not enough to ensure his acceptance into the city's inbred society nor the social fortune of his marriageable daughters. "Oh, it isn't what you've got, and it isn't what you've done exactly. It's what you are," his wife, Persis, explains in despair (98). Private social matters of family, education, and taste are primary in Boston. They even affect economic affairs. Thus Silas's "rise" is morally, not economically, motivated when he refuses to enter into a sleazy railroad deal. His reward—since even such good "qualities" as honesty don't count for as much as "manners" in old-family Boston (296)—is a chance to return to his family homestead in Vermont and to market the top-quality paint he has named after his wife. *The Rise of Silas Lapham* is, as Edwin Cady (1957, xii) has noted, "the first important novel to deal with ... the businessman," but it subordinates "Silas's business activities to the Lapham family's efforts to breach the walls of Boston society," as Kenneth Lynn (1971, 279) has demurred.

The central metaphors and shaping incidents of this 1885 novel reflect the preindustrial city-town, though without the old city-town's concern with the future. In particular, private homes epitomize their inhabitants' cultural taste and the family base of the city's social structure. Detailed descriptions contrast the "quiet old ... stately ... seclusion" of the Corey home on Bellingham Place with the Laphams' "unfashionable" Nankeen Square home and the Beacon Street "house in the style" that they are building, showing the differences in family background and aesthetic taste that separate the "offensively aristocratic" Coreys from the nouveau riche Laphams (Howells [1885] 1957, 153, 20, 33, 74–75). The Laphams' upward mobility depends on others' advice about home libraries, house decor, and private etiquette. Their social failure is climaxed by homey catastrophes. First Silas gets drunk and spoils a private dinner party at the Coreys' home, then the Laphams' ostentatious Back Bay house is destroyed by fire. These catastrophes also frame the novel's essentially private crisis, the moral "rise" that precipitates Silas Lapham's economic fall. Although Silas's economic activity is deeply involved in the moral dilemmas he faces, private matters—his wife's unfounded jealousy, his daughters' confused marital prospects—are much more critical to their resolution. Thus *The Rise of Silas Lapham* bases even the city's economics in family relationships, private social affairs, and expressions of taste.

It is hard to resist the idea that Howells created *A Hazard of New Fortunes* as a counterpoint to his Bostonian parable of individual moral success. Certainly his first New York novel offers analogous metaphors and key incidents. In place of Boston's private family homes, New York offers apartments, rented rooms, and a commercial "house." Part I is organized around the hunt for a New York apartment by the primary observers of the novel's events, Basil and Isabel March from Boston. Basil declares that the typical New York "flat abolishes the family consciousness" while it gives "artificial people a society basis on a little money" (Howells [1890] 1965, 58-59). No one lives in a private home; several characters live in a boarding house that one runs, and another sets up his quarters over the offices of the magazine, the "house" that brings them all together. Not the family but money underlies the structure of this city.

Public economic catastrophes replace Boston's familial, private crises. Whereas Silas exposes his personal lack of refinement at the Coreys' family dinner party in *The Rise of Silas Lapham,* a whole economic consortium exposes its lack of social cohesion at a business dinner in *A Hazard of New Fortunes.* Class conflict erupts between an oil tycoon who finances the magazine and a German-born socialist who translates for it. That class conflict causes private crises within the tycoon's family and for the socialist's editor-friend Basil. A public streetcar strike climaxes the unrest, as the burning of the Laphams' house had in the earlier novel. The strike's violence kills the tycoon's son and the socialist, precipitating yet further public and private events that end the novel. Whereas the loss of a house confirms Silas Lapham's private tragedy in Howells's Boston, a public labor dispute confirms the social disintegration of a magazine, a family, indeed the whole urban society in his New York.

A Hazard of New Fortunes is not any particular individual's story at all. In this lies its most fundamental contrast to *The Rise of Silas Lapham* and its greatest breakthrough in urban literature. Here the city is, for the first time, the subject rather than the setting of a U.S. novel. The great flat hunt of part I introduces the city itself as the main character. Mapping out the city's economic divisions, "the line" of "respectability" between tenement districts downtown and mansions on parade uptown, the novel traces the city's divided character. It establishes both the shape and the limits of the Marches' urban comprehension (Kaplan 1988, 48-49). It makes it difficult for "comfortable people [like them to] understand how the uncomfortable people live" (Howells [1890] 1965, 51, 128)—as Jacob Riis also argued when he published *How the Other Half Lives* (1890) the same year.

Within that context of divisions, the magazine embodies the economic interests that bring "the singular incongruities" of people together in this city (Howells [1890] 1965, 281). It defines the heterogeneous cast of characters who have all left homes in other regions to hazard their fortunes in the "only...city that belongs to the whole country" (12). They comprise a social anatomy of oppositions along regional, ethnic, occupational, familial, and ideological lines: genteel Bostonian and unreconstructed southerner (as in *The Bostonians*), immigrant and native, aesthete and public relations specialist, homemaking spouse and widowed boarding-house manager, socialite and reformer, capitalist and socialist. Without any "brincibles"—to use the German immigrant's word (255)—to join them, they struggle at odds with each other. Echoing urban imagery from Davis's Philadelphia, Adams's Washington, and James's Boston, Howells presents New York as a "vast wilderness" of economic selfishness, its inchoate life "swarming" in poverty so alien as to seem "picturesque" from the vantage point of the old city-town (38, 158, 56).

And over all rides the el. It is Howells's metaphoric discovery, the mechanical trope that brings the new city's public order and heterogeneity together. Howells explicitly offers the economic machinery of New York's elevated roads as a metaphor for the city itself. Like the el, the city "shrieks and yells with ugliness here and there; but it never loses its spirit." The Marches are fascinated by the el, built in the 1870s but still unique in American cities in 1890, because it focuses their ambivalence about the city—their proclaimed "satisfaction" and their repressed horror (54).

To their "satisfaction," the el organizes the city, indeed "aggressively composes the fragments of urban life," as Amy Kaplan argues in her excellent analysis of its significance (1988, 49ff.), and presents it to them as the "superb spectacle" of a

> track that found and lost itself a thousand times...the moony sheen of the electrics...and blots of gas far and near; the architectural shapes...rescued by the obscurity...and the coming and going of the trains marking the stations.... They often talked afterward of the superb spectacle, which in a city full of painters nightly

Figure 7. John Sloan, *The City from Greenwich Village* (1922), oil on canvas, 26 × 33¾ in. Courtesy of the National Gallery of Art, Washington, D.C.; gift of Helen Farr Sloan.

works in unrecorded miracles ... but for the present they were mostly inarticulate before it. (66–67)

It was almost three decades before one of the city's painters, John Sloan, confirmed this literary discovery of the el's power to organize the city, in *The City from Greenwich Village* (1922, fig. 7). U.S. painting in general lags just about that much behind literature in its urban imagery after the Civil War, as if the thing needs to be named before it can be seen. *A Hazard of New Fortunes* names the economic city in the flats and commercial houses that display its socioeconomic divisions and in the el's mechanical organization.

To the Marches' horror, however, the el trains are also "atrocious" "monsters" (54), and their mechanical organization imposes an "organized lifelessness" on the city (67). The el symbolizes three deadening effects of technological organization. First, while it displays the "heterogeneous" city (267)—"even better than the theater" for the middle-class voyeur (66)—it also embodies the power that private monopolies like the traction companies then exercised over poor lives. It disrupts their homes by "kill[ing] the streets and ... triumph[ing] over their prostrate forms with a savage exultation" (54). When the city's workers strike against the surface street-car lines, the elevated overrides their efforts and ensures their failure.

Second, and more fundamentally, the el epitomizes Howells's vision of the city's increasingly powerful physical environment. As the el kills working-class street life, so flats "abolish" middle-class family life (59). The tenement districts are "establishing conditions of permanency to which human life adjusts itself as it does to those of some incurable disease, like leprosy" (56), while "the virus of commercialism" infects the comfortable (151). Basil is firmly convinced that "conditions *make* character" (380). As the shift in Howells's titles implies, the city is becoming resistant to human control: the moral base and controlled direction suggested by "rise" give way to the social chaos underlying the "hazard" of individual fortunes. In *A Hazard of New Fortunes* the city no longer expresses human capacities, it shapes them. The economic city had arrived and established itself as the national city, to be studied from a psychological distance.

Finally, the el makes it clear that the "violent invasion" of private life by the city's public machinery will not stop at the city limits. The West Side lines show the Marches "the city pushing its way ... into the country" (264). Dryfoos, the tycoon from Pennsylvania's natural gas country, laments, "We *can't* go back! ... There's no farm anymore to go back to" (201). New York stands for a city that lacks a regional connection with the surrounding countryside and even threatens the country's very existence nationwide. Unlike Boston, New York offers an "immense, friendly homelessness" (267) and no chance to retreat to some nearby country homestead.

The paradigmatic contrast between the city-town in *The Rise of Silas Lapham* and the economic city in *A Hazard of New Fortunes* dramatizes a profound reorientation toward the entire world by Howells himself. Howells felt the very foundations of his worldview give way while he was writing *The Rise of Silas Lapham:* "the bottom dropped out."³ He had a serious nervous breakdown as he confronted Silas's moral example and his own inability, by contrast, to act on his deepening convictions about the inequalities of society. Even after he had risked his national reputation by defending the Haymarket anarchists in the *New York Tribune* in 1887, he had to admit to his father that he was only a "theoretical" socialist (2 Feb. 1890 letter in Howells 1928, 2: 1) and to Henry James that he was well wrapped in an aristocrat's "fur-lined overcoat" (10 Oct. 1888 letter in Howells 1928, 1: 417). He castigated himself for failing to move his convictions beyond "words, words, words!" (28 Oct. 1888 letter to Edward Everett Hale in Howells 1928, 1: 419). He felt trapped in his habits of upbringing, class, and comfort. At the same time, the family responsibilities that might have justified his maintaining these comforts collapsed when his daughter Winifred died (Twain and Howells 1960, 579).

When Howells transferred his own base of action from Boston to New York, the move involved much more than a physical change. In fact, the physical change may have seemed minimal to him. His notebooks and travel diaries record few differences other than the el. Mostly similar details of street-car exposure, ethnic variety, and poverty fill the Boston and New York scenes in his personal records. But he felt "at home" with friends in Boston (Cady 1956, 163) and "homeless" in New York (1896 letter to Samuel Clemens, quoted in O'Connor 1974, 6). He had written his old Boston publisher only a few years before that he was "thoroughly 'wonted'" to Boston after living there fifteen years and would "rather not leave" (16 Dec. 1882 letter to James R. Osgood, Howells Papers). Howells seemed to approach New York willfully in a spirit of "intellectual decision which ran counter to his ... pleasure," as Leo F. O'Connor (1974, 6) has also concluded. He forced himself to leave a house on the waterside of Beacon Street, such as Silas had lost in his moral rise, and the security of Boston, such as Basil and Isabel March left when they moved to New York from Nankeen Square, where Silas had also lived.⁴

Howells's discomfort with his move to New York is evident in the fact that he lived at thirteen different addresses there between 1888 and his death in 1920, while his novels turned inward toward domestic and psychological themes after *A Hazard of New Fortunes*.⁵ But his novel of the city as subject struck a chord in the national literary consciousness.

Edward Bellamy, of utopian *Looking Backward* fame, told Howells: "You are writing of what everybody is thinking and all the rest will have to follow your example or lose their readers" (17 Oct. 1889 letter to Howells, Howells Papers).

Bellamy's prediction held. Authors found it hard to turn away from Howells's economic city imagery, which was both symbolically coherent and congruent with much of their own urban experience. The set of structural elements in *A Hazard of New Fortunes*—its heterogeneous cast of characters, its narrative line shaped by public events, its mechanical metaphors, its thematic focus on economic power and conflict—recurs in many novels that follow. They articulate powerful insights into the political economy of the city, its challenges to the individual, and the limits of individualism. They confirm the economic city as powerful subject matter for literary analysis.

The shift proved as uncomfortable for others as for Howells. Authors otherwise radically different from each other, like Dreiser and Wharton, dramatized alienation—from others and from self—as a consequence of confronting the city as an external phenomenon. The economic city broke down continuities in the human "life-world" (Gadamer 1975, 218), obscuring and thus diverting human beings' expressive connections to the city's social, physical, and cultural environment. Lost was the collective psychological power that the city-town fostered by maintaining a sense of continuity and community.

Literature's imaginative shift to "a public world that is an economy rather than a polis" was not, however, "inevitable"—contrary to Philip Fisher's claim (1985, 16–17)—even when industrialism, the postwar urban boom, and nationalism had made "the primary plane of social life [seem] economic rather than political . . . focused on money rather than power, and based in the lives of individuals rather than families." Indeed, as Fisher himself argues in *Hard Facts* (1985, 4), the belief that a particular version of reality is "obvious" and without possible "alternatives" only proves the "highest" success of the cultural act of symbolic construction. Although Howells's contemporary Bellamy also implied that the economic city model was inevitable, elements of the old city-town continued to infuse many aspects of everyday urban experience—in homes and neighborhoods, with weather and play. But they were so common that they were taken for granted. In line with Bellamy's words, popular consciousness focused on the then new developments in urban history as these converged with other circumstances of intellectual, social, and biographical history. The economic city in U.S. literature ascended to represent "the city" in mainstream consciousness, while women and ethnic minority and regional writers quietly continued to explore those common urban experiences that did not fit with the alienation of middle-class mobile white male writers like Howells. It is here that urban literary imagery divides, and no better example of this can be found than in turn-of-the-century Chicago literature.

3

The Standard Chicago Novel

Congress took a critical step toward settling the post–Civil War search for a national city in 1892, when it named Chicago to host the 1893 World's Columbian Exposition. Incorporated for just over half a century and nearly destroyed by fire in 1871, Chicago won a cut-throat competition with Washington, St. Louis, and New York for the privilege. Chicago was to represent the nation in celebration of its "discovery," insofar as the United States had no established national city (Badger 1979, 19), as so many writers before Howells had found. Singled out at the fin-de-siècle watershed for all Western civilization, Chicago was sure to attract global limelight—even more than London had when it hosted the first great world's fair in the 1851 Crystal Palace. Indeed, the 1893 World's Columbian Exposition became the "Chicago Fair" that its *Tribune* boastfully dubbed it (quoted in Burg 1976, 113). Chicago's complex population, physical form, and institutional structures, no less than its world's fair, "needed explanation" if the city was to provide Americans like Henry Adams ([1907] 1961, 339, 343) the "education" they sought there for the nation's future. "One must start there," he said.

Chicago epitomized the new concentration and diversification of urban populations in the United States. In general, the nation's cities had been populating faster than the countryside ever since 1790, and most newer Midwestern cities had grown faster than their Eastern elders during the mid-1800s. Even against this background, Chicago's growth was phenomenal. During the three decades following its chartering in 1837, Chicago's population multiplied sixty-seven times over, doubled again in the 1870s, and grew to over a million by 1890; it would double once more to over two million by 1910, making it the fourth largest city in the world (Still 1973, 123, 133n; Ginger 1965, 95). During the turn-of-the-century decades, people were "pouring in at the rate of 50,000 a year," as Dreiser correctly noted in *Sister Carrie* ([1900] 1959, 13).

English-speaking newcomers often commented in local newspapers on the strangeness of Chicago's people, for the tremendous urban population explosion was complicated by ethnic diversification. African Americans numbered fully 15,000 by 1890. Immigrants recruited by factories added up to many more. Poor Irish and darker skinned Italian Catholics, Eastern Europeans, Russian Jews, and (from the West Coast via the railroads) Chinese all challenged the numerical dominance of WASP residents descended from earlier immigrants. The 1890 census defined over three-quarters of the city's inhabitants as foreign-born or as children of foreign-born parents. In its heterogeneity, Chicago even outstripped the nation's gateway city of New York, where immigrants and their children made up about half of the population in 1890. By World War I a Chicago literary man reported that Chicago had as many Poles as Posen, as many Bohemians as Pilsen, and as many Germans as Danzig (Chatfield-Taylor 1917, 65–66).

But not everyone in Chicago was newly arrived and alone in a Babel of unfamiliar languages, customs, and complexions. During the post-Civil War period, old-stock Germans, no less than old-stock Britons, established tightly knit, elite social networks on the North Side. Families followed the single men who came to do heavy labor in the depression years just after the fire, and new immigrants congregated in various ethnic neighborhoods where their "lands-people" and relatives often awaited them. By 1890 Maxwell Street was the lively marketing center of a Jewish ghetto; the Irish had turned Bridgeport into a residential community and had organized an effective political machine. Chicago also included "an Italian city, a city of Russian Jews, a city of Greeks ... and so on." Writer Clara Laughlin (1912, 12–13) remembered Chicago's diverse population not as an accumulation of discrete numbers but as collectivities all connected by "the main artery of Chicago life," Halsted Street. Architectural competitions also highlighted these neighborhood communities.

The population of Chicago formed other kinds of collectivities as well: white and black women's clubs, City Beautiful associations, unions, and settlement houses. Jane Addams, seeking to bridge what she considered an artificial gap between rich and poor, founded Hull-House in 1889 to provide civic activity for both young middle-class women fresh out of college and immigrants fresh off the trains near Halsted Street (Addams 1893).[1] Chicago's population was a microcosm of the centripetal and the centrifugal forces at work in growing U.S. cities at the century's turn.

Chicago also epitomized the physical consolidation and expansion of cities during the latter half of the nineteenth century. As the "railroad capital" of the United States, it already had more interurban trunk lines than any other city by 1854, and the arrival of the Union Pacific Railroad ensured Chicago's primacy after the Civil War. In the wake of the 1871 fire, new intraurban streetcar lines advanced Chicago's rapid growth beyond walking distance, quickly making it a far-flung "streetcar city" with classic "streetcar suburbs" (Weber and Lloyd 1975, 187 ff.; Warner 1962). By the end of the century, Chicago had the most complete transit system in the United States, including the nation's second elevated line (after New York) (Mayer and Wade 1969, 37–38, 120–22, 206–16). Streetcars helped to intensify the concentration of new commercial development downtown, where the tracks' "Loop" emphasized the expansion of Chicago upward at its center.

In fact, Chicago had the nation's tallest buildings. The demand for rapid, large-scale construction after the fire had attracted talented engineers who eventually devised the floating foundations and iron-framed skeletons needed to raise multistoried buildings on Chicago's swampy base (Condit 1964, esp. 79–85). When the Monadnock Building reached the sixteen-story limit for masonry construction in 1893, the tall office buildings and department stores in downtown Chicago were unprecedented in size. Then came the steel-beamed skyscrapers, with seeming disregard for the forces of mass and gravity, boosting Chicago's technological reputation for defying nature. Meanwhile, large windows displaying structural elements, as well as commercial goods, added to Chicago's reputation for defying taste.

But Chicago had also developed strong means for preserving its natural surroundings, and its most innovative architects often concerned themselves with aesthetic and civic principles. The city that jacked itself up above the mud of Lake Michigan and reversed the flow of its main river to drain its sewage was also the city that had made "Urbs in Horto" its founding motto and forest preserves part of its first planning efforts, long before New York established Central Park. Major roadways both traced the routes of commerce and outlined the beauty of park-bordered Lake Michigan—which became the primary line of reference for Daniel Burnham's most famous contribution to City Beautiful planning, the 1907 Plan of Chicago.

It was the beauty, not the technological achievement, of Louis Sullivan's Auditorium Building that first "secured" the nation's attention for Chicago architecture in 1889 (Condit 1964, 69). Its entrance arch displayed an "organic" yet geometric decoration, which Sullivan would later articulate as his *System of Architectural Ornament* ([1924] 1967). Sullivan put technology in the service of artistic and civic, as well as commercial, purposes, when he designed the Auditorium. He maximized the theater's acoustical space and sight lines, taking into account even the lowest-priced seats, and designed rental space for offices and a hotel in the same building to provide financial support for the theater. The Auditorium Building exemplified the union of aesthetics and function that distinguished Chicago architecture, successfully elaborating the modern principle that "form follows function."

Fundamental to the economic grounds from which Chicago's architectural aesthetics rose, Chicago epitomized a major shift to industrial capitalism in the institutional base of U.S. cities. Of course, its origins were mixed—although blatantly economic from the start. Fur trading established Chicago's location; real estate speculation fueled its incorporation then made good its headlined promise to "rise again" like a Phoenix from the ashes of the fire (Medill 1871). But because of that fire, Chicago blatantly displayed the increasingly common reliance of U.S. cities on heavily capitalized industry. Post-fire Chicago was designed—much of it literally from the ground up—to accommodate the expansion and consolidation of modern economic ventures. Surrounding prairie spaces as well as whole city blocks razed by the fire provided the acreage needed to site large manufacturing and processing plants, "union" stations for railroad transfers, warehouses and department stores for marketing, and centralized "exchanges" for trading stocks and commodities.

Although New York was the capital of high finance in the late nineteenth century, Chicago brought finance and industry into obvious combination. Many of Chicago's leading speculators such as Philip Armour and George Pullman also headed major factories, while others such as Charles Yerkes and Samuel Insull controlled the city's mechanized transit and utility systems. They became prime targets, as well, for working-class protest during the heyday of industrial capitalism. When workers congregated to promote a general strike in 1885, they met outside the new Board of Trade building during its inaugural banquet (Pierce 1957, 192–233;

Lewis and Smith 1929, 156–58). A year later the Haymarket Affair called the nation's attention to the gathering power of organized labor and the police power of capital, in direct and particularly violent conflict. The grand display of the 1893 World's Columbian Exposition itself threw into vivid relief the paroxysms of industrial capitalism: the national depression; the assassination of Chicago's mayor Carter Harrison; the organization of Eugene Debs's American Railway Union and its strike on George Pullman's Parlor Car Works, his "model" company town, and the entire Chicago railroad system.

The display was nonetheless grand—and only part of an impressive cultural expansion that blended industrial and aesthetic materialism, bending individual wealth to civic benefit. The years 1891 to 1893 saw the founding of the Chicago Symphony Orchestra and the Museum of Natural History; the opening of the University of Chicago; the ground breaking and building of the new public library, the Art Institute, the Newberry Library, and the Academy of Sciences; and the dredging, filling, landscaping, designing, and building of 686 acres for the exposition (Condit 1964, 95–96; Badger 1979, esp. 131). Recitals of these achievements alongside depression, assassination, and strike tap the heart of Chicago's mythology. Apt to be compressed by poetic license into a single year, an "annus mirabilis" of civic virtue and vice, the litany of these events obscures the complexities of Chicago's local history. It emphasizes instead the stark contrasts between idealism and conflict during the nation's Gilded Age of big business. The wonders of 1893 Chicago were recalled during the second Chicago world's fair in 1933 as the turning point between the nation's frontier and modern periods in *Chicago: The History of its Reputation* (Lewis and Smith 1929) and in Edgar Lee Masters's epic *Tale of Chicago* (1933). The achievements of 1893 provided evidence for proclaiming Chicago "the most American city and yet unique" (Duffey 1956, 69; Burg 1976, 72).

Chicago remained the nation's representative city long past the world's fair not because it was seen as average but because it was promoted as an epitome. The publicity surrounding the fair established the grounds on which writers built. Following the lead of Howells's *A Hazard of New Fortunes,* Chicago was presented as a city of national interest by mostly male writers, often from other parts of the country, and now best known for their Chicago novels: most famously Theodore Dreiser's *Sister Carrie* (1900) and *The Titan* (1914), *The Pit* (1903) by Frank Norris, and *The Jungle* (1906) by Upton Sinclair; from local pens, Henry Blake Fuller's *The*

Cliff-Dwellers (1893) and *With the Procession* (1895) as well as Robert Herrick's *Memoirs of an American Citizen* (1905) and other Chicago novels. Hamlin Garland's *Rose of Dutcher's Coolly* (1895) and Willa Cather's *The Song of the Lark* (1915), by authors best known for other Midwest writing, also remain available to readers, as does Frank Harris's minor work, *The Bomb* (1908).

But what about Edith Wyatt's *True Love* (1903), with a collective narrative structure that represents as remarkable an aesthetic achievement as Dreiser's well-known documentary style? Or Clara Laughlin's *"Just Folks"* (1910), equal in quality to the works of Norris and Sinclair? Or Wyatt's and Laughlin's several other lesser Chicago works, to cast light on these major achievements? Or Elia Peattie's *The Precipice* (1914), only just given the reprint recognition long ago accorded Herrick's and Fuller's similarly modest achievements in social realism? Or Clara Burnham's *Sweet Clover* (1894), as historically interesting about the 1893 world's fair as Harris's novel about the 1886 Haymarket bombing? Or *The Glory of the Conquered* (1909) or *Unquenched Fire* (1912) by accomplished playwrights Susan Glaspell and Alice Gerstenberg, arguably deserving the kind of literary historical attention paid to Hamlin Garland's Chicago novel? These distinctively residential novels by women range in quality—as do the far better known standards—from excellent to merely curious. Yet only *The Precipice* comes easily to hand now, and none come readily to mind.

Chicago's links with the city-town tradition—the families, neighborhoods, parks, arts, and civic affairs that many women's novels depicted—took a back seat to the ways in which the standard novels written by men displayed Chicago as the "first," "most," or "greatest" example of the new economic city. Chicago's mixed population, bristling cityscape, and industrial enterprise told only part of the U.S. urban story, but they triggered powerful ambivalences about ethnic diversity, family privacy, women's rights, technological progress in "Nature's Nation," rugged individualism, trusts, unions, and democracy. Such ambivalences arose just as Chicago was loudly insisting on its status as a city and as the United States was seeing its future not in forests and farms but in cities. Reporters covering the exposition's scholarly congresses told the entire nation that Frederick Jackson Turner had declared the frontier closed there (Burg 1976, 238). Chicago dramatized the ascendance of city as the age of discovery came to an end.

Dichotomies of virtue and vice had been part of Chicago symbolism at least since the Great Fire, when Chicago was mythologized as born anew out of ashes (Miller 1990, esp. 1–37). Thus dichotomies of virtue and vice were easily developed around the newness and hugeness of turn-of-the-century Chicago and its fair. About twenty national magazines devoted special issues to the World's Columbian Exposition and its Chicago setting. They had the cumulative impact of establishing the fair and its city as the nation's spiritual and material vanguard—while also splitting the one from the other. The "good family" social elite honored when Bertha Honoré (Mrs. Potter) Palmer was selected to head the Board of Lady Managers, the triumph of beaux arts aesthetics when Daniel Burnham was appointed chief architect, the monumental style of the exposition buildings under his charge, and the civic spirit of bond drives to underwrite the immense project were presented as part of the same Chicago spirit that erected libraries and museums and university buildings elsewhere in the city. Paradoxically, however, while the fair provided a focus for such civic qualities it simultaneously isolated them from the rest of the industrial city. The fair, not Chicago, emerged as a civic enterprise.

The policies and publicity of the fair also trivialized or obscured important elements of the new urban experience in Chicago. It collapsed all of Chicago's immigrant richness into ethnic "days" and Midway concessions—where each ethnic group "had its place," as the *Tribune* put it (Denton J. Snider quoted in Miller 1990, 238). African Americans found "Colored American Day" particularly demeaning given the exclusion of their cultural accomplishments from all national and state exhibits. Ida B. Wells-Barnett had to station herself at the Haitian pavilion headed by Frederick Douglass (Thompson 1979, 77–90) to distribute her pamphlet, *The Reason Why*. It protested that "the progress made by the race in 25 years of freedom as against 250 years of slavery" had not been exhibited as "tribute to the greatness and progressiveness of American institutions" (Wells-Barnett 1893, 1). The fair organizers paid no such tribute to the new urban diversity that Chicago epitomized—nor, except in exhibits of technology, to the new impact of industry on its cityscape. The Illinois Central Railroad delivered people from the nation's "railroad capital" to a pedestrian city at the fair. The fair ignored the unsettling, skyscraping aspect of Chicago—what Henry Blake Fuller in 1897 called Chicago's real "upward movement." With the towering Ferris Wheel relegated to the Midway, Louis Sullivan's Transportation Building stood as the lone example of the innovative Chicago school of architecture on the exposition grounds. Even better hidden was any divisive evidence of the city's new capitalist economy. While the fair conspicuously consumed wealth and variously recognized Chicago's financial leaders, its working-class leaders were excluded from the programs, and unseemly controversies about blue laws and bribery were hushed up (Badger 1979). Given a good-family, beaux arts, civic profile, the fair would not contain the richness of the city, and Chicago itself became vulnerable to contrast with its own celebration.

In the December 1893 issue of *Cosmopolitan* magazine, French littérateur Paul Bourget (1893, esp. 135) used the conventional image of the neoclassical exposition as a white city to create a split that Americans were quick to deepen: the fair was a perfect but temporary "White City by the Lake," he wrote, "while the black city, which will endure forever, is only at its commencement." The Fair expressed Chicago's civic achievement only in temporary honors, monuments, and holiday "cooperation." Other contributors to *Cosmopolitan* (e.g., Howells 1893) confirmed the "dreamy" artificiality of this vision. Idealizing the exposition as an inverted double for Thomas Cole's old nightmare vision of empire (fig. 2), writers envisioned the organic, open-ended communalism of the city-town being replaced with hierarchical classicism. Simultaneously, White City/black city rhetoric condemned the heterogeneity and commercial enterprise of modern urban development. The dichotomy cut two ways: it limited Chicago's virtues to the whitewashed artificiality of the fair, already passing and easily dismissed as a sentimental standard for the everyday city; and it left the "real" city growing outside the purview of human values, trapped in the soot-stained blackness of its vices.

Literary Chicagoans as well as commercial boosters helped to develop the White City symbolism. As a burgeoning literary center, Chicago had the country's largest book publishing business beyond the East and a diversity of local talent including railroad novelist Opie Read, historical romancer Mary Catherwood, journalist Eugene Field, and poet Harriet Monroe, who wrote the fair's dedicatory "Columbian Ode" and would later found *Poetry* magazine. Some residential novelists, like Clara Burnham in *Sweet Clover: A Romance of the White City* (1894), presented the White City as outgrowth, not antithesis, of Chicago enterprise. Its plot follows the evolution of the fair from the application of Chicago "pioneers" to host it, through the summer of its glory, to marriages that grow out of its decay and destruction. Affirmation of Chicago's social continuities also informs some of the Chicago novels by Monroe's childhood neighbor Henry Blake Fuller and by Harvard-educated Robert Herrick, who was imported during the year of the fair for the new University of Chicago.

These Fuller and Herrick novels, however, also confirm the vision of fair and Chicago as White City/black city, thereby laying the local groundwork for the Chicago standard novel. Fuller's novel of Chicago's family-based society, *With the Procession* (Fuller [1895] 1965, 72–73), strikes a skeptical note when a young man "met half-way the universal expectation that the spirit of the White City was but just transferred to the body of the great Black City close at hand, over which it was to hover as an enlightenment." Even skeptical hope gives way, however, in face of the black city's substance: "The great town, in fact, sprawled and coiled about him like a hideous monster—a piteous, floundering monster, too." Herrick uses a powerful fire and ice version of the same black/white dichotomy to structure *The Web of Life* (1900). He places Chicago and his doctor-hero in an untenable conflict between the ruins of the idealized fair on the icy shores of Lake Michigan and the "blast furnaces" of class "war" during the Pullman Strike; Dr. Howard Sommers must break away to the East for several years before miraculously finding a "home" back in the "human factory" of Chicago (Herrick 1900, 77, 188, 283). No such wishful ending mars Herrick's masterpiece, *Memoirs of an American Citizen* (1905). It presents the fair as mere puffery manipulated by Chicago's robber barons of industry. Undercut by the split between city and fair, and consequently vulnerable to the intervention of social Darwinism, skepticism and wishful reaction collapse into cynicism about Chicago.

Moreover, Fuller's first Chicago novel, *The Cliff-Dwellers*, focused the nation's literary attention on the threatening side of the Chicago/fair contrasts, even though its preparation and publication in 1893 was treated as one of the important cultural events of Columbian Chicago. The news that Fuller's novel would center on "a tall building in the heart of the city" overshadowed word of the long-awaited completion of the fair's Manufactures and Liberal Arts Building in the first "Chicago Letter" that Harriet Monroe's sister Lucy wrote for the New York weekly *The Critic* (L. Monroe 1893a). Lucy Monroe kept the nation's readers posted on the progress of *The Cliff-Dwellers*, its serialization in *Harper's Weekly*, and its exposure of "a section of life in Chicago as it is, without idealization" (Monroe 1893b). Chicagoans were both proud and dismayed. As late as 1917, Harriet Monroe felt it necessary to point out that Fuller's depiction of the city's economic energies was "not Chicago complete, not her whole self...not quite the whole story." Regionalist Hamlin Garland (1 January 1895 to Fuller, Fuller Papers) probably fingered the precise point at issue. He did not object to the critical edge in either *The Cliff-Dwellers* or its successor, *With the Procession,* having just made his own literary reputation on bleak portraits of Wisconsin coolly country. But he preferred *With the Procession*'s more intimate, residential representation of personal relationships and local ways, as "*the* book of Chicago. No outsider could write that book," he declared, implicitly suggesting that an "outsider" could have written Fuller's first Chicago novel. In fact, an "outsider" perspective is the source not only of *The Cliff-Dwellers*'s harsher critical edge but also of its national appeal and its inauguration of the standard Chicago novel.

The Cliff-Dwellers uses a single urban structure, the skyscraper, to identify its characters and events. While Howells's fictional characters in *A Hazard of New Fortunes* create a New York magazine, Fuller's fictional Chicago imposes a rigid mold of economic enterprise upon its workers and visitors. The skyscraping Clifton becomes a microcosm of a city determined by its economic structure. The skyscraper's upper stories provide, like Howells's el, a vantage point for viewing the city. The panorama exposes the economic power of this strange new cliff town as a matter of national concern. *The Cliff-Dwellers* devotes its entire first chapter to that view.

In the objectifying language that was then being used to describe Mesa Verde (Nordenskiold 1893),[2] the voice of an "explorer" discourses here on the exotic "geology" and primitive "tribes" of Chicago's western "cañon." Its skyscraper-lined streets appear so unfamiliar that they need to be located—"between the former site of old Fort Dearborn and the present site of our newest Board of Trade"—then studied in detail and in terms of a new vocabulary. In this "restricted yet tumultuous territory," the narrative explains with elaborate seriousness,

> during the course of the last fifty years, the rushing streams of commerce have worn many a deep and rugged chasm. These great cañons—conduits, in fact, for the leaping volume of an ever-increasing prosperity—cross each other with a sort of systematic rectangularity, and in deference to the practical directness of local requirements they are in general called simply—streets. (Fuller [1893] 1968, 1)

Fuller's narrative thus attempts intellectual control over a natural panic in the face of the unnatural erosion that has created Chicago. This cliff town is the opposite of the ancient Pueblo's communal cities in harmony with nature. Fuller's narrative makes any heavenward admiration for the "towering cliffs" impossible by looking from the Clifton roof down on the "seething flood" of commerce—not life-giving water—that has "devastated" the land and "worn its bed" to a depth measured by sixteen "of these stories... until some of the leading avenues of activity promise soon to become little more than mere obscure trails lost between the bases of perpendicular precipices" (1–2). Continuing for five pages, Fuller describes Chicago as a world likely to overwhelm any walker in its streets and as a subject requiring comprehensive study, preferably from a safe distance.

The Cliff-Dwellers reinforces its national, rather than native perspective by placing an eastern newcomer to Chicago in the midst of its multiple plots. Unlike Howells's urban newcomer and fictional editor Basil March, however, George Ogden is a bank clerk near the bottom of the Chicago skyscraper's economic hierarchy—on the ground floor, to be exact. There his own career is jostled by the "sudden falls, unexpected rises, precipitous dislocations" of a ruthless real estate "hustler," a banker who totally neglects his family for business, a rough-and-ready Irish working-class parvenue, and others in this unfinished city where "the high and the low are met together. The big and the little alternate in a rapid and illogical succession" (Fuller [1893] 1968, 3; cf. Fuller 1897, 542). Thus the novel anatomizes the materialistic ambitions that drive Chicago's natives and eastern transplants alike—including a visitor from the central Boston office of the Massachusetts Brass (not Bay!) Company, so far has the nation moved away from the Puritans' city on a hill.

All participate in the proud Chicago spirit of "I will" and in the underlying egotism that Fuller exposes beneath that spirit. None has any "sense of... right relation to the community" (38) or much awareness of how his or her individualistic ambitions might injure others, "like a child lighting a match" (27).[3] Even the Clifton building has been selfishly erected by "one man" to underwrite his wife's conspicuous consumption, without a thought for the "hundred others [who] are martyred in it," as George Ogden muses (324). Fuller's skyscraper city has the structure of a traditional Pueblo cliff town without its communal ethic.

It is this Chicago of egotistical, economic ups and downs that stands for the nation in *The Cliff-Dwellers*. Fuller makes Chicago's national status explicit when his most compassionate and level-headed character, the "oldest and most sedate" Chicagoan there, mildly asks why Illinois shouldn't "give the country the final blend of the American character and its ultimate metropolis?" Fairchild cannot be written off as a stereotypical Chicago booster, even when he asserts (in almost Biblical terms) the superhuman power of Chicago to define itself, to compel the faith of its inhabitants, and to realize its destiny on a national scale: "Chicago is Chicago," he said. "It is the belief of all of us. It is inevitable; nothing can stop us now" (242–43).[4] *The Cliff-Dwellers* does not discount Fairchild's prophetic vision of Chicago as the nation's "ultimate metropolis." It expresses reservations about the ambiguous character, not the inevitable realization, of the future that Chicago promises to the nation.

While also playing out an urban melodrama and displaying local color, *The Cliff-Dwellers* distinguishes itself from previous Chicago fiction in its concern for Chicago as a new form of society "crystallizing into a compound" (229) for the nation. Despite Fuller's long-term Chicago residency, his first Chicago novel takes a new observer's perspective and self-consciously addresses a national audience. It calls attention to Chicago's socioeconomic structure as its determinative reality and as the nation's business. It also introduces the features that most literary newcomers and visitors to Chicago, including literary naturalists like Theodore Dreiser,[5] would employ time and again over the next two decades: metaphorical and documentary seriousness; emphasis on contrasts, alienated characters, antinatural settings, and economically delineated plots; and—underlying all—a profound critique of the individualism and lack of local community that all of this embodies. The standard Chicago novels extended until World War I the explosion of Chicago-watching that erupted nationwide around the fair and established the nation's definitive cityscape in their terms. Dreiser, for one, acknowledged Fuller as the Chicago novel's "pioneer" (Dreiser 1928, viii).

Theodore Dreiser's *Sister Carrie* ([1900] 1959, 16) is only the best and most famous literary testament to the "many and growing commercial opportunities" that helped to make Chicago "a giant magnet" for Carrie Meeber's real-life counterparts, including novelists. *Sister Carrie* warms up to its Chicago theme more gradually, but no less deliberately than most. By quietly contrasting the "small ... cheap ... small ... scrap" of Carrie's resources and "the great city" toward which she travels, Dreiser's opening paragraphs point toward Chicago as a threatening phenomenon. The novel then builds metaphoric intensity by generalizing about "the city" as a "superhuman" seducer and by prefiguring Chicago in the person of Charlie Drouet—both a commercial "drummer" for Chicago's goods and an amoral "masher" like Chicago itself (Dreiser [1900] 1959, 5–7). After Carrie gathers her first disoriented impressions of the city itself, Dreiser abruptly interrupts the plot line: "Before following her in her round of [job] seeking, let us look at the sphere in which her future was to lie." Several pages of exposition follow this self-conscious break. Emphasizing Chicago's "magnetic" power to attract new adherents and thus to expand itself, Dreiser links his metaphor of superhuman seduction to a detailed mapping of the city's "vast wholesale and shopping district" (16–18ff.).

Also following "pioneer" Fuller's *The Cliff-Dwellers,* other Chicago novels similarly include extended documentary descriptions of the city in their introductory pages. They swell with metaphoric, even mythic resonance whenever their narratives or dialogues bear on Chicago's prototypical status. Chicago is described as a "gigantic and portentous presence" rising "like an [American?] eagle" in *Rose of Dutcher's Coolly* (Garland 1899, 156), as a "gigantic beast" wound around "a modern inferno" in *The Web of Life* (Herrick 1900, 77, 338), as an "immeasureable colossus . . . Titanic" in *The Pit* (Norris 1903, 50–51), and as "the fire of the ages . . . perpetual . . . inexhaustible" in *The Jungle* (Sinclair [1906] 1960, 30).

In combining empirical reportage and exclamatory metaphor, Chicago novels echo reports in the national periodicals of the building and "mythmaking" of Chicago's fair (Boyesen 1893, 173) and the Chicago boosters who wooed hard-nosed investors there. In novelistic context, however, that journalistic rhetoric expresses tension more than enthusiasm.[6] The documentary distance of the novelists' narrative stance asserts a structural "control" over the city, as June Howard (1985, 104ff.) perceptively demonstrates, while their mythic metaphors imply that the city's meaning ultimately defies comprehension and control. Both documentary detail and metaphoric elaboration, moreover, show Chicago's power to compel attention to itself, even when that means awkward intrusions into the novel's story. Although they make little reference to the fair itself after 1900, the standard Chicago novels also take a structural lead from White City/black city rhetoric, articulating Chicago by contrasts. Contrasts—like Dreiser's "small" and "great," like Fuller's "high and . . . low"—structure not only documentary and metaphoric descriptions, but the very plots.[7] A main character's career is usually opposed to another's, caught between two others, or self-divided—and subjected to ambiguous moral valuations on both sides. So Carrie Meeber rises while George Hurstwood falls; Howard Sommers is caught between icy idealism and fiery conflict in *The Web of Life;* and Curtis Jadwin ricochets between the social arts of his wife and the warfare of the commodities market in *The Pit* until his supposed power collapses into antithetical enslavement.

Unlike most fair publicity and Chicago boosting, the novels that insist on Chicago's national power also refuse to simplify it into unity. They discover both fascination and fear in face of Chicago's strangeness. They expose Americans' deep ambivalence toward modern cities—combining, like Robert Herrick, "moral shock with a half-suppressed feeling of exhilaration" (Szuberla 1971, 152).[8] By the same token, they split up urban society and discourage wholehearted identification with any one side or other. Theirs is a bifurcated world where an observant newcomer "perceive[s] only contrasts," as in *Rose of Dutcher's Coolly* (Garland 1899, 179), and only the beguiled feel "a part of it all," as in *The Jungle* (Sinclair [1906] 1960, 45). Standard Chicago novels thus pit the individual against "it all," against the urban world as a complex external phenomenon, in stark contrast to the city-town as an expression of communal character. When they bring the city's structural contrasts to bear on individual careers, they also challenge the integrity of the individual, simultaneously the source of their distant perspective and the burden of their concern. Indeed, an uneasy critique of individualism informs the novels' cumulative patterns of characterization, setting, and plot.

Lone newcomers figure as the main characters in most standard Chicago novels. Even when they arrive with other family members, most soon find themselves on their own—like runaway Carrie Meeber. Thus translating the general statistical growth in Chicago's population into individuals' separate encounters with the city, the novels present an atomized image of Chicago's new inhabitants. Unlike the immigrants who in fact swelled Chicago's population, in fiction most of Chicago's new arrivals come from small U.S. towns. They share the national values and beliefs associated with individualism, yet their stories dramatize the impossibility for even acculturated Americans to manage Chicago's massing energies. As the typical newcomer approaches Chicago by train, the city's "enormous" power and "perplexing" mystery (Payne [1898] 1970, 1; Sinclair [1906] 1960, 29) evoke utter confusion, deepening the danger of being thrown upon one's own resources, as these characters inevitably are, within the city.

Each stands alone against the city. But the city itself is socially divided as well. The novels portray Chicago as an ethnic wilderness without any shared cultural basis for community. They often describe ethnic diversity at a public distance that implies alienation—as when immigrant types are catalogued impersonally, "chattering unintelligible languages" on the streets in *Rose of Dutcher's Coolly* (Garland 1899, 195–96).[9] The novels treat ethnic pluralism as chaotic and alienating. This contrasts sharply with the local color sketches from that time, which elaborate ethnicity as a source of community ties and valuable perspectives on a shared democracy. Occasionally in Chicago's residential novels, but never in a standard Chicago novel, does the equivalent of Finley Peter Dunne's delightful Mr. Dooley, who made his Chicago newspaper debut the same year as the fair and *The Cliff-Dwellers,* deliver "th' rale message" to "Dimmycrats an' Raypublicans" and "pluthocrats" in a cozy community setting (Dunne 1962, 63–69).

The standard Chicago novels focus much of their attention on economic divisions in Chicago society. With poverty on "that side of the city" and wealth on "this," Chicago seems like "a battle-field" to the title character in *Rose of Dutcher's Coolly* (1899, 170, 179). In emphasizing contrasts, standard Chicago novels juxtapose the extraordinarily wealthy and the extraordinarily poor—as in the opening of *The Pit* (Norris 1903, 11), when a "prolonged defile of millionaires" enters the Auditorium's overheated lobby under the gaze of "a crowd of miserables shivering" outside. The contrast between rich and poor always threatens Fuller's "precipitous dislocations." Nonetheless the rich and the middle class encounter the poor only occasionally and their differences rarely explode into direct conflict. They are not groups, they are divisions—divided internally, too. They are competitors in "the vast web of petty greeds and blind efforts," from which Herrick's novel *The Web of Life* (1900, 316) takes a paradoxical title that seems to affirm commonalities.

Both rich and poor are alien, moreover, to the novels' usually middle-class perspective. The central characters are concerned with individual upward mobility rather than class membership. They especially feel "no kinship" with the poor (Garland 1899, 224). In marked contrast to residential novels by Chicagoans like Edith Wyatt and Elia Peattie, affirming allegiance to "the People" is an unusual mark of altruism in standard Chicago novels (Lovett 1907, esp. 203–5; cf. Chatfield-Taylor 1895, Herrick 1900). Their imagery of ethnic wilderness despairs of any cultural community; their socioeconomic contrasts deny any common interest at all.

The supposedly "good, new Western fashion which finds the unit of society ... in the individual" (Fuller [1893] 1968, 39) even infects families. They are reduced to "companies" of willful individuals whose economic interests can divide at the drop of a dollar (Fuller [1893] 1968, 7). Husbands and wives are alienated from each other, only partly because of the urban gender split between masculine production and feminine consumption in the Gilded Age. In these novels, wives pursue the ethic of individual interest no less than husbands. The only difference is that the wives are excluded from direct business activity even when they affirm marriage as a "partnership," as does Adela Anthon Wilbur in *The Gospel of Freedom* (1898, 108), Herrick's anatomy of marital alienation. Subordinating herself to what must finally be "her husband's interests" does not satisfy Adela's desire for independent "freedom" (105), so she takes up artistic interests that compete with her husband's and deplete the economic capital they share. Breaking their "partnership" dissolves their marriage. A similar split in *The Pit* (Norris 1903, e.g., 184) is mended only when Curtis and Laura Jadwin retreat to country life.

Such fictional Chicagoans form no sustaining allegiances, just temporary alliances. With only personal ambition to guide her, a Chicago newcomer like Dreiser's Sister Carrie moves all too easily and alone from one sector of urban society to another, "a Waif amid Forces" of wealth and poverty ([1900] 1959, 5). Carrie cuts off all contact with her family when she moves out of her sister's flat and into Charlie Drouet's, and she loses touch, in turn, with Charlie and his successor, George Hurstwood, as she moves economically upward, finally into the more closely knit "Walled City" of New York (273). She even changes her name as she goes. The multiple roles taken on in Chicago by Sister Carrie—alias Carrie Meeber, alias Mrs. Drouet, alias Mrs. Wheeler, alias Carrie Madenda—are neither bent toward nor supported by any social community. As a result, she has no continuing identity. And her unnamed yet poignant dissatisfaction, as she repeatedly sits in rocking chairs at windows, alone and disconnected from the city she overlooks, reflects psychic dissociation as the ultimate cost of such individualism. Relying only on herself, Carrie becomes separated from herself. Individualism threatens psychological alienation as well as social collapse in this and other standard Chicago novels.

Reckless individualism is also embodied in Chicago's built environment in these novels. Skyscrapers flaunt individual ambition, while streetcar monopolies deepen social divisions by oppressing labor and segregating residential districts.[10] The upwardly and outwardly expanding structures induce psychological distress. Skyscrapers and streetcar lines create a sense of powerlessness. Their enormity dwarfs ordinary people, despite being manifestations of humankind's soaring imagination and technological know-how. Their physical extension is unsettling, pointing toward a future of "indefinite continuation" (Fuller [1895] 1965, 8), of constant expansion "in anticipation of rapid growth" (Dreiser [1900] 1959, 17).[11] Most importantly, they seem to defy natural laws without expressing any alternative, communal order.

It is on the built environment that standard Chicago novels concentrate their metaphors. At best, their fictional Chicago embodies a perverse substitute for nature. *The Cliff-Dwellers*'s skyscraper-cliffs and street-canyons carved by economics instead of nature become a cliché. In other novels, Chicago's vaunting downtown evokes images of a wasteland: "a vast and fantastic formation of rock . . . in a forgotten place" (Payne [1898] 1970, 173); "mountainous masses . . . as desolate as a burnt-out volcano" (Garland 1899, 182); and "sphinx"-like monoliths "without sign of life" (Norris 1903, 35, 306). Human life may figure as "minute larvae" (Garland 1899, 182), ants, flies, spiders, and moths there (Dreiser [1900] 1959, e.g., 6, 43–44, 106). Even the city's parks are described as a "hothouse" growth perversely "made into nature by a *tour de force*" in *The Gospel of Freedom* (Herrick 1898, 103).

Herrick describes the transformation of the Chicago wasteland into a hothouse in a telling context: as his central character enters the city by railroad. In fact, the railroad, Chicago's first point of national pride, triggers the most negative images of the city in standard Chicago novels. Chicago, the railroad capital, is seen as antinatural, invading the countryside and threatening all life. Railroad metaphors are dynamic and monstrous, such as Dreiser's "giant magnet" spreading and drawing people to the city depot or the "ample stomach" of Herrick's "Tartarean . . . beast" (Dreiser [1900] 1959, 16; Herrick 1900, 77). Railroad scenes regularly introduce the novels—and are ubiquitous in popular histories (e.g., Lewis and Smith 1929, v–vi). *The Gospel of Freedom* thus declares that a railroad approach is the "best" way to see the city as "a stupendous piece of blasphemy against nature." Chicago parches outlying fields with factory smoke (Sinclair [1906] 1960, 29), gathers its energies in multiplying rails and telegraph poles (Dreiser [1900] 1959, 11), and becomes "hotter and fiercer mile by mile" as the trains plunge into its clashing, crashing, grinding, mechanical core (Herrick 1898, 101–4). Where horizontal rails meet vertical buildings, Herrick's most hellish metaphor describes Chicago as the "animated circle of a modern inferno," in *The Web of Life* (Herrick 1900, 338). "Large and vague," "gay" and "grim," with all the inchoate contradictions "of a city of shades," Chicago's "cross-streets intersecting the lofty buildings were dim, cañon-like abysses" seen through "the suffused splendor" of "myriad lights" and "foul" vapors from the Twelfth Street depot.

It is not the artificiality, per se, of the city's built environment to which standard Chicago novels object; it is uncontrolled growth and lack of informing unity. Underlying the development of skyscrapers and streetcar systems is the same neglect for communal values that divides urban society. Unregulated speculation shapes the physical environment. In *The Gospel of Freedom* unregulated speculation prompts John Wilbur both to invent a beneficent irrigation system and to cheat the public in a streetcar traction scheme. Once the city rejects all limits on what its self-serving citizens can freely attempt, it loses communal power to choose progress over degradation. Ultimately, then, Chicago's forced growth turns upon itself, like a cancer. Thus "the great sore of a city" has dumped its garbage to create " 'made' land," where pools "of stinking green water" fill the streets and "swarms of flies" fill the air around the stockyards in *The Jungle* (Sinclair [1906] 1960, 33). Thus privately owned streetcar lines manifest tyranny in Dreiser's fictional biography of Charles Yerkes, *The Titan* (1914). Fuller's 1897 essay on Chicago culture makes the message explicit:

> Nowhere is the naif belief that a man may do as he likes with his own held more contentiously than in our astounding and repelling region of "sky-scrapers," where the abuse of private initiative, the peculiar evil of the place and time, has reached its most monumental dimensions.... [The] extent of our failure in the art of living together is fully typified by our obvious failure in the art of building together. (541–42)

The novels' insistent metaphors—irresistably quotable—emphasize the antinatural and apocalyptic implications of such a failure.

Inevitably the novels' concern with the "abuse of private initiative" turns attention to tycoons. As the supposed leaders and beneficiaries of the city's economy, rugged individualists like Yerkes and Armour (the model for Herrick's *American Citizen*) personified the industrial capitalism of Chicago for the popular imagination. Tycoons figure prominently, from the first, in Chicago melodramas such as *The Colossus* (1893) by railroad writer Opie Read and *The Social Lion* (1901), pseudonymously published by Chicagoan Margaret Potter. Tycoons only loomed in the background of the first standard Chicago novels (like the mysterious owner of Fuller's Clifton) until a minor 1898 novel linked a tycoon to the resonant standard imagery of skyscrapers and machines, thereby pressing his significance beyond sensation. Dubbed the Duke of Gas, Will Payne's fictional double for Samuel Insull in *The Money Captain* is himself a civic monument, an "edifice" that seems as "immutable" as his bank (Payne [1898] 1970, 317, 303). Other human beings are to him "only so many rods and blocks in the big machine [he] contrived and operated" (101); but he turns out to be "a sort of machine" himself (56), indeed only a "shadow" of forces beyond his control (217). Both tycoon and bank collapse in *The Money Captain,* making it the first of many Chicago novels to depict the destruction of tycoons by the political-economic machinery they think they control. These novels' plots demonstrate that individualism is factually and ethically inadequate as a guide to urban life.

Standard Chicago novels devote so much attention to documenting the details of finance that they often read like business primers. Such documentation asserts the centricity of economic individualism and the economic machinery it masks in Chicago. The novels do not demystify the economic base of the city in exposing its power and destructive effects, however. Instead they further its mythic dominance by personifying it in the tycoon, weighting him with all their exclamatory and explanatory rhetoric, and embedding his story in their contrasting structures. Only Herrick's *The Memoirs of an American Citizen* exhibits baldly—without elaborate commentary—the emptiness of the tycoon's identification with the city environment ([1905] 1963, 266) and the demoralizing impact of his material grandiosity and Chicago's upon the entire nation's civic life. *The Pit* is far more typical in raising the voice of the standard Chicago novel to its "epic" pitch.[12] Using monopolistic capitalism as a vainglorious assertion of individualism, "Napoleonic" Curtis Jadwin's dealings on the Chicago Board of Trade unleash a "mighty" and unnatural whirlpool that swirls "far out through the city's channels" to move "grain in the elevators of Western Iowa" and carry "men upon the streets of New York ... bewildered and unresisting back and downward into the Pit itself" (Norris 1903, 192, 62). Its "undertow" leaves Jadwin himself financially and psychologically ruined. "I corner the wheat!" he finally explodes. "Great heavens, it is the wheat that has cornered me!" (207). The city machine runs the rugged individual, not vice versa.

The perverse domination of Chicago by economic machinery is clearest, however, when Upton Sinclair turns attention to the poor. *The Jungle* differs from other standard Chicago novels in its focus on an immigrant and his family rather than on a lone Anglo-American. Its setting in

Chicago's outlying slums and factories rather than in its railroading, skyscraping center and its dramatization of a struggle for survival rather than a battle for success also set it apart. Although nearly all the residential novels articulate grounds for communal life in Chicago, only *The Web of Life* and *The Common Lot* among standard Chicago novels share this focus with *The Jungle*. Sinclair's depiction of Chicago as the great and awful, national economic city prevents his work from breaking away from a divisive, dehumanizing portrayal. First alienated as a group by language and customs, Jurgis Rudkus's Lithuanian immigrant family is eventually broken apart by meat packers, realtors, criminals, and politicians. "Blind and insensate Greed" (311) simultaneously separates and enslaves them all to a vast interlocking trust—a mechanized, monopolized version of Herrick's "web of petty greeds and blind efforts." Initially enthusiastic about becoming part of the slaughterhouse operation that efficiently turns sheep and hogs and cattle into canned meat and sausage and glue, Jurgis finds that he, like the animals, marches naively toward death (36–40, 311). Weakened by overwork, he is discarded like the other "worn-out parts" of the great machine (Sinclair [1906] 1960, 126).

So strong is the Chicago belief in individual will, moreover, that Jurgis does not see himself as oppressed until his wife is raped and allowed to die along with his son, his sister-in-law becomes a prostitute and drug addict, and he and others are blackballed, jailed, and hospitalized by industrial forces. His eventual affirmation of the proletariat does not offer a clearly positive alternative, however; the collectivity he joins screams in the "voice of the wild beast, frantic, incoherent, maniacal" (304). Indeed, that voice represents a politically logical but structurally discordant answer to the standard novels' questions about individualism. Like *The Web of Life*, *The Jungle* exemplifies critic Amy Kaplan's point (1988, 160) that such wishful endings "embody the desire to posit an alternative reality" outside "the novel's construction of the real," namely, the economically divided and mechanized city. In fact, *The Jungle*'s socialist resolution exceeded the limits and energies of this Chicago novel genre. Although Sinclair's muckraking spurred legislative action on the Pure Food and Drug Act and the Beef Inspection Act in 1907, eight years elapsed before the publication of another major Chicago standard novel. Based then on research that Dreiser undertook at the Newberry Library, *The Titan* has a déjà vu effect.

No passive part of Chicago's ascendancy as a national city, the standard Chicago novels essay a powerful critique of the city's meaning for the nation. Their alienated characters, unnatural settings, and economically enslaving plots demonstrate that belief in the primacy of the individual both exacerbates the excesses of modern urban life and proves inadequate to control them. Thus individualism undermines cooperation in Chicago's fragmented society, precludes any limits on how far a skyscraper or factory might flaunt its builder's pride, and masks the self-propelling forces of the city's economy. Conversely, the individual is powerless to contend against Chicago's social "battle-field," "Tartarean" environment, and economic "machine." Despite their critique of individualism, however, the novels actually reflect and perpetuate alienation through their structures. Despite the skyscraper collection of characters in *The Cliff-Dwellers* and the collectivism at the end of *The Jungle,* the novels concern themselves primarily with the individual's oppositional relationship to the city. Despite Herrick's desire to affirm interdependency in *The Common Lot* and *The Web of Life,* his emphasis remains on "individual ethical initiative" in "direct opposition to" urban industrialism (Bray 1982, 110). In his "iceberg"-cold decision to become "a part of *them,"* (Herrick 1900, 217, 194), Herrick's fictional double Howard Sommers recalls his historical precursor William Dean Howells's determination to exchange Boston's comforts for New York's "homelessness."

Within a national economic paradigm, such Chicago novels envision the city as an alien, external phenomenon. Their documentary detailing maintains distance from that phenomenon, their mythic metaphors belittle common human powers, and their contrasts preclude any human joinings. They support the "outside expert" approach to urban problems—and to cities as problems—still common to social scientific studies and governmental interventions today, and so deeply implicated in maintaining the status quo. Caught up in the national Chicago-watching that divided black city from white, the standard Chicago novels ignore the communal and organic continuities that were also a part of Chicago's story.

4

Chicago's Residential Novels and Their Social Roots

Willa Cather's *The Song of the Lark* (1915) does not fit the pattern of Chicago novels such as Dreiser's *The Titan,* published the same year. This is not because much of the novel takes place outside Chicago; indeed, the same can be said of Dreiser's *Sister Carrie,* an epitome of the type. And Cather's heroine, Thea Kronberg, is, like Dreiser's Carrie, a newcomer who remains an outsider to Chicago and treats the city as raw material for her performing career. What distinguishes Cather's novel is that her heroine never breaks her ties to family and friends; she sees Chicago as similarly bound by social ties and probes beneath material surfaces to root her art in rural and urban continuities. Along with other novels that I call "residential," generally written by turn-of-the-century Chicago women whose names are unfamiliar to us now, *The Song of the Lark* dissents from the standard image of Chicago as a national economic spectacle rent by socially fragmenting and antinatural contrasts. In residential novels, as in the lives of their white middle-class authors, Chicago is a regional base of social action, infused by the continuities of natural generation and human association. The problem is that the "social [and literary] construction" (Berger and Luckmann 1966) of the economic city in the standard Chicago novel has made it difficult for us to understand the urban bearing of *The Song of the Lark*. It has also worked to eclipse the entire set of residential novels by women, including three at least as good as Henry Blake Fuller's quasi-residential novel, *With the Procession* (1895):

Edith Wyatt's innovative *True Love: A Comedy of the Affections* (1903), Clara Laughlin's superb *"Just Folks"* (1910), and Elia Peattie's suffrage novel, *The Precipice* (1914).[1]

If we choose to limit the turn-of-the-century "city novels" of the "Chicago school" to those that treat the city as a "subject" (even a "problem") following the lead of Blanche Gelfant (1954, 2–3) and Blake Nevius (1962, 88) and to ignore the residential novels, we will continue to base our literary understandings of Chicago on works mainly by "outsiders who simply managed to capture [its national] significance," as Kenny Williams (1980, 443) notes.[2] We will continue to ignore even the novel whose publication led William Dean Howells to declare a "Chicago School of Fiction" in the first place, Edith Wyatt's *True Love*.[3] This residential novel's richly patterned plot, significant themes, and supple prose construct the city as a setting, not a subject. It is of Chicago more than about Chicago.

True Love never expatiates upon "the sights of Chicago" as a Dreiser or Herrick novel would do, although its opening scene of two cousins on a carriage tour seems set up for just that purpose (Wyatt 1903, 3–5). It does establish Chicago's historical, natural, and residential ground as Emily and Inez Marsh and their escort ride under drifting clouds, past the site of Fort Dearborn and the Stephen Douglas monument, up tree-lined streets with trimmed lawns. But the novel gives these sights no more nor less attention than its listing of "the drainage-canal, the grain-elevators, and the stock-yards" that a later visitor tours (197). Wyatt's opening mentions physical points of interest only to exemplify the cousins' subjective responses and expectations: Inez's class-conscious seriousness about working up fashionable "interests" and Emily's easy openness to "demoralized" relaxation on "home" streets (6–7). Wyatt avoids any extended, objectifying description of Chicago as spectacle and focuses instead on her characters' conversation.

True Love's opening scene is a literary precursor to Isabel Bishop's painting of two young women engaged in intimate conversation in a public subway, *Homeward* (1951, fig. 8), much as Howells's description of a view from the el and Fuller's introduction to *The Cliff-Dwellers* prefigure John Sloan's *The City from Greenwich Village* (1922, fig. 7). In Chicago's residential novels, even the arrival of a newcomer like Inez March provides an occasion for exposing the social attitudes that contribute to its urban life—whether convention-bound, familial, or even, as with Thea Kronberg in *The Song of the Lark,* "incurious" (Cather 1915, 193).

Figure 8. Isabel Bishop, *Homeward* (1951), oil and tempera on panel, 26 × 20 in. Courtesy of the Midtown Payson Galleries, New York.

Urban issues emerge as social debates within the city rather than arguments for or against it.

This does not mean that residential novels were written without regard for Chicago's cash value in the nation's literary market place. Clara Burnham's opportunistic novel *Sweet Clover: A Romance of the White City* (1894) reads like a souvenir book for the world's fair. Nonetheless, it is Burnham's early expression of the residential perspective that makes her novel "more than a literary oddity," not the (doubtful) connection to "early naturalist fiction" that critic Ross Miller (1990, 209) proposes. Whereas *The Cliff-Dwellers*, written just a year earlier, displays the "black city's" economic importance, *Sweet Clover* celebrates the lived-in qualities of Chicago and its White City. The difference between the national observer's perspective of Fuller and the local participant's viewpoint of Burnham accords with the gender-related differences between "separate" and "connected knowing" that Mary F. Belenky and her colleagues have developed (Belenky et al. 1986, 100–130; cf. Gilligan 1982, esp. 151ff.). Burnham depicts the fair as the creation of Chicago "pioneers" and a setting for residents' social interactions. "We Chicagoans aren't Fair visitors. We are Fair livers," one of her characters declares (281). Similarly, in an 1899 *Atlantic* article explaining the world's fair as proof that "the artistic sense has always existed among us surreptitiously," novelist Elia Peattie identified herself as a part of the city, a daughter of "pioneers" on the South Side (828).

In fact, the forgotten women who wrote residential novels all grew up with Chicago—like Henry Blake Fuller but unlike the other famous Chicago novelists. The residential authors did not grow up elsewhere and discover Chicago at the height of its Columbian fame as Fuller pretended to do in *The Cliff-Dwellers*. As members of Chicago's journalistic corps and contributors to its artistic and social welfare activities, the residential writers were participants in local affairs, and their novels proceed from a sense of the city as "we." They present Chicago through its inhabitants and embrace the "comedy" as well as the "glory" in the daily lives of "just folks"—as their titles suggest (Wyatt 1903; Glaspell 1909; Laughlin 1910). They accept Chicago not as a portent but as their own slice of modern life. Chicago "is simply there," implicit and pervasive, in their novels—as Wyatt could also say of Frank Norris's hometown San Francisco in *Vandover and the Brute* but not of his monumental "unrealized" Chicago in *The Pit* (Wyatt 1914c).

Accordingly, residential novels lack extended elaborations of documentary detail and metaphor. They do not employ striking contrasts to define Chicago or distance the individual spectator. They avoid the dichotomies that structure standard Chicago novels—rise versus fall, husband versus wife, rich versus poor, repeatedly. Instead, the residential novels embrace multiple life-stories as overlapping, not opposing, possibilities for urban life. Typical are the several neighboring clusters of poor families with whom the social-worker heroine of *"Just Folks"* chooses to live or the university and dining co-op women whose various responses to the woman's movement *The Precipice* anatomizes.

Henry Blake Fuller's *With the Procession* also has a decidedly residential dimension, despite its thematic concern with the economic city's "selfish" consumerism. It is organized around three families—each parental pair boxed as a unit on the chart Fuller drew inside his personal copy (reproduced in Bowron 1974, 160–61). Although alienation and distance are established at the start, that perspective is undercut as "irresponsible" by the end. The primary actor is the oldest daughter of an "old family," Jane Marshall, who refuses to be "left" out of "the town" in exercising "her office to keep the family from disintegration" (Fuller [1895] 1965, 33–34, 226, 54, 22). Although Jane is set apart from all the others in Fuller's chart,[4] *With the Procession* realizes his declared preference for studying "a group of individuals in their relation to the community" (quoted in Duffey 1956, 37) far more successfully than *The Cliff-Dwellers,* where the skyscraper arbitrarily collects characters whose stories strain against each other.

A collective structure fully appropriate to the residential novel is the special achievement of Edith Wyatt's *True Love,* however. It is an early example of what Rachel Blau DuPlessis identifies as a feminist strategy for "writing beyond" individualism and other masculine values embedded in standard novelistic conventions. Specifically, the "communal protagonist" approach presents "the group [as] the central character," and does not develop "an individual against a backdrop of supporting characters" (DuPlessis 1985, 163). Indeed Wyatt makes several family groups her characters, and the interlocking collectivity of these groups becomes her embodiment of Chicago and its social environs. The democratic Marsh family is her "central character," embodying both her understanding of the city's continuities and her urban ideal of a social ethos that embraces them. The Marshes are linked to the city's natural setting by name, to its rural environs by the family of Mr. Marsh's brother downstate, and to its past by Mrs. Marsh's aging aunt and her deceased father's old

Civil War comrade. Mr. and Mrs. Marsh's four children complete the three-generation range of this extended family, whose members all live in the grandfather's unpretentious home and regularly welcome visitors to "the kindliest intercourse" and lively group activities (Wyatt 1903, 29). Among those with whom they exchange visits are the elitist Hubbards: widowed Madame mother, her two sons, and her maiden cousin. Quite different in social style yet embraced by the Marshes' family associations and good-humored affection, the Hubbards have an elaborately decorated "sepulchral" mansion. It is a "penal spot" where visitors put their sophistication to the test by exchanging calling cards and stiff formalities (17).[5]

These two city families act out the tension in the novel between participatory democracy and elitism as alternative social ethics. The tension proves regional, extending beyond city limits to involve country families. Downstate the two social ethics are mixed: the narrowly nuclear family of Mr. Marsh's hospitable brother and sister-in-law includes their snobbish daughter Inez while the loose "family" of democratic Dick Colton, his Polish-American aunt, and their ethnically diverse friends includes his increasingly snobbish sister Fanny. Colton's figurative family congregates in the lobby and dining room of the small town hotel he runs, a "free place for everyone" to be "at ease and contented" (215, 130) similar to the Marshes' home in Chicago and pointedly unlike the Hubbard house with its "little cold, bare reception-room" (177).

True Love explores social democracy in both city and country, as well as the tension between that democracy and social elitism, most dramatically through several romances interlocking its family characters. Democratic city woman Emily Marsh finds her appropriate mate in country man Dick Colton. These two young people discover the expansive possibilities of a love that evolves through everyday interactions with others, unobsessed by display or sentiment. Emily's elitist country cousin Inez is matched up with urbane Norman Hubbard just long enough for their elaborate gestures of "true love" to expose the selfishness from which they proceed and the boredom toward which they tend. Fred Hubbard and Fanny Colton mix and mismatch "strenuous" Norman Hubbard's "unpretentious" younger brother with "commonplace" Dick Colton's "exclusive" younger sister (Wyatt 1903, 7, 96, 106, 269). They marry on the run, then are violently separated when Fred commits suicide. Fanny rebounds into the fashionable Hubbard mansion and the arms of her former brother-in-law, whom Inez has released in favor of a level-headed and distinctly unfashionable family friend from the East. The "comedy" of the whole—

its socially affirming tendencies—resides in this "common" choice and in Emily's choice of "common" Dick Colton (288).

In structure as in theme, *True Love* is an insider's story, concerned primarily with a network of ongoing overlapping relationships. It is "like one's own story in not being certain of the relative importance of its different persons and events," William Dean Howells (1903, 736) remarked—in significant contrast to his assessment of Fuller in *With the Procession* as "able to regard [his characters] sufficiently aloof to get them" despite being "himself born to the manner of the people he depicts" (Howells 1895). Specifically, Howells praised Wyatt's novel for emphasizing the daily family contexts ignored by larger than life literary conventions, which the standard Chicago novel tended to follow: "Strangely enough, the lovers and self-lovers have families about them.... [*True Love*'s families] are not treated as mere pieces of mechanism for transacting the lovers' passion." Indeed, no single individual emerges as the central character in Wyatt's novel, distinguishing it from every other Chicago novel, whether standard or residential, and marking an important breakthrough in novelistic convention generally. More fully than *A Hazard of New Fortunes* or *The Cliff-Dwellers* or *The Jungle, True Love* is successful in developing a collective form that moves beyond individualism. It characterizes citizens in terms of families and social ethics; social collectivities, not economic ambitions or machinery, define its city. In form as in content, *True Love* emphasizes not contrasts but continuities. Its continuities of time and place, among people, and within the city's social concerns, moreover, define the residential vision.

Turn-of-the-century Chicago is not rigorously separated from every other time and place in residential novels. It is an organic[6] part of a historically and geographically seamless "life-world" (to use Husserl's concept as interpreted in Gadamer 1975, 218). In residential novels Chicago is not the spectacular city that appears fullblown out of nowhere. *Sweet Clover,* for example, recognizes the "pioneer" past as part of the "cosmopolitan" present (Burnham 1894, 18, 180–81). Although *With the Procession* similarly underscores the growth of "the city from an Indian village to a metropolis ... within the lifetime of a single individual," it dramatizes—in the terms of the standard Chicago novel—the radical newness of a physically "dead," socially "rotten," "speculative" city that "assaults" "Arcadia" and reduces the old settler's "whole lifetime ... to naught" (Fuller [1895] 1965, 133, 274, 166, 225, 169, 10, 273, 264).[7] The women's residential novels insist on evolutionary continuities, drawing no such dichotomies between the modern city and a pastoral golden age, nor even between the city and its contemporary rural environs.

Whereas Sinclair's Jurgis Rudkus, Herrick's Howard Sommers, and Norris's Curtis Jadwin retreat briefly to the country for revitalization, no firm city limits define urban by contrast to rural in residential novels. They regularly present country activities as part of their city-based narratives. Fictional characters move back and forth between Chicago and its environing region. Whether going or coming, moreover, they move within familial networks without significantly altering their roles or attitudes. Generally, the city extends social possibilities that more sparsely settled rural areas constrain. The urban/rural differences amount to shadings—matters of more or less—not radical dichotomies or transformations. The heroine of Peattie's *The Precipice,* for instance, frees herself from the patriarchal "tyranny" of her childhood home in downstate Silvertree (no remote golden age there) to find greater, but nowhere near complete, equality in Chicago. Moving beyond the role of "village ... gossip" Kate Barrington is able to use her "Silvertree method" of "neighborly" dialogue in the broader field of urban social service work (Peattie 1914, 30, 183, 179). Peattie's Chicago is not antithetical to country virtues nor to country vices.

Neither is it antithetical to nature, for nature interpenetrates the city. This perception differentiates residential novels sharply from standard novels, which characterize Chicago as a willful "blasphemy against nature." In *With the Procession,* for example, the destruction of the Marshall family's currant bushes by industrial blight is a major motif marking both their father's death and their move into a showy new mansion surrounded by "dead weeds" (Fuller [1895] 1965, 244, 18, 249, 263). On a few occasions, the women's novels reject such an antinatural view of Chicago, usually expressed by male characters. When Susan Glaspell's heroine sees Jackson Park as nature's boon in *The Glory of the Conquered* (1909, 280–81) and imagines "how the earth heaved a sigh" to create its slopes, she preempts her husband's debunking: "Now don't tell me the park commissioners made them!" In *True Love,* conventional Norman Hubbard denies his own enjoyment of the city's "finest season"—which Wyatt's narrative confirms as "entirely beautiful"—in order to pontificate on the antinatural "hideousness" of urban "smoke and grime" (Wyatt 1903, 40, 38). The residential novels emphasize "the inevitable enfolding of the city & its dwellers in the elemental things of nature," as an admiring "city born & bred" reader of Wyatt's poetry put it (Alice Thacher Post 12 Feb. 1918 letter to Wyatt, Wyatt Papers).

Yet the novels do not sentimentalize nature as the standard Chicago novels idealize what the city destroys. They present nature as a real and powerful presence within the city, acknowledging both its negative and positive effects. Lake Michigan frequently epitomizes nature's refreshment, while seasonal extremes in weather epitomize its oppressive weight—often in ambivalent combination. In just these terms, Willa Cather most powerfully reinforces the novelistic vision of her "lost Chicago sisters" (Bremer 1984). In *The Song of the Lark,* Thea Kronberg realizes "the city itself" not in the railroad depot upon her arrival but in a "furious gale" "beating over the city from Lake Michigan" that she experiences after several months' residence. Chicago becomes a figurative extension of nature as the winter storm fills the streets with "streams" of "cold" and "barking" people—an organic "congestion of life" (Cather 1915, 200). And when Thea's experience of the storm climaxes in the threat of a sordid sexual assault, Cather dramatizes a sense of danger, as well as vitality, associated with the city's natural life force. She implies that a woman's ambivalence about urban nature might reflect the cultural emphasis on her own "natural" vulnerabilities.

Thea bases her artistic maturation on the fusion of city and nature. The storm comes just after a visit to the Art Institute of Chicago where she discovers Jules Breton's pastoral painting *The Song of the Lark.* She also discovers there her own responsibility to a cosmopolitan conception of art that goes beyond both the local prejudices of her country hometown and Chicago's bourgeois society. Hearing Dvorak's pastoral *New World Symphony* in the urban setting of the Auditorium Theater further strengthens this artistic commitment.[8] But before pursuing her operatic career to New York and Europe, Thea finds urban pastoral inspiration once more on a trip to the urban cliff dwellings of the Southwest Anasazi, the same trip Cather herself was making when she visited Chicago two years before publishing *The Song of the Lark*. The organic architectural expression of the communal soul of "the Ancient Ones" (see fig. 1) confirms Thea's artistic vision, as it did Cather's own.[9] Whereas Chicago perverts the Anasazi union of nature and human community in Fuller's *Cliff-Dwellers,* Chicago's urban pastoral moments complement the Southwest's in *The Song of the Lark.*

Such rural-urban continuities in time and place are intimately related to human continuities. By rejecting cities "without suburbs" and "walled cities" (1914, 85, 89–90), Peattie's Kate Barrington metaphorically rejects disruptions and limitations in human relations in *The Precipice.* In Edith

Wyatt's fictional Chicago, continuities between the city and its natural and regional setting—as well as continuities over generations—make it possible for families to sustain human connections despite Americans' increasing mobility. Indeed, Wyatt saw mobility not as a "mechanized" or divisive force (Herrick 1914, 226) but as "our largest common background" and the basis of U.S. society's "unity in variety" (1914a, viii–ix). Similarly, other residential novels present the city as an organically rooted, flexible society rather than an oppressive machine.

For the most part, they enmesh their characters in family networks—matrices of the sort that critic Christine Sizemore (1989, 11) has found also to be "especially appropriate to [modern British women writers' images of] the city because they can incorporate time as well as space and because they focus on connections." Even when a central character (regularly a woman) strikes out on her own in Chicago, a familial substitute quickly emerges for her. In Clara Laughlin's *"Just Folks,"* for example, the Irish household of an old family servant provides social worker Beth Tully with acceptance into the working-class neighborhood she serves. Often familial associations go beyond blood lines, even linking diverse ethnic groups. In *"Just Folks,"* the Caseys and Rubovitzes, Gooches, Slinskys, and Spears living on Henry and Maxwell streets become Beth's extended family, not because of an abstract ideal of "brotherhood" that treats "the poor as a theorem ... or class," but because of daily interactions that make them "familiar personalities" to her and their various stories part of hers (Laughlin 1910, 2, 104). Other residential novels establish similar networks of familiarity.

The Precipice examines most pointedly the familial substitutes and extensions that the city offers. Citing Jane Addams's concept of the city as "a great home" and "civic family," Elia Peattie's suffrage novel (1914, 181–82) examines whether such an unbounded public family can make a woman's home and what that home should be. *The Precipice* begins in the city train station, as a lonely college friend sees Kate Barrington off to her hometown: "You have a home waiting for you. You're the kind that always has a place. If it wasn't your father's house it would be some other man's" (2). But Kate's childhood home—like the marital home later offered her by a wealthy Chicagoan—is rooted in a "contempt for women" (304). She rejects that kind of "commonplace ... home" as "stultifying" and "selfish" (294, 47, 289), limiting like "walled cities." Returning to Chicago after her mother's death, Kate "could not feel that she, personally, ever had been 'home.'" She and a married college friend find a cooperative dining room a "good substitute," however, and Kate eventually takes a room at the "hospitable" Caravansary, with its precious variety of "cooperators" (67, 47). This is the home base from which she pursues her "maternal" attempts to promote "cooperation" within the wider urban family. "Laboring in behalf of the city" and particularly in behalf of "her wistful children" there (81–83, 266), she offers a powerful contrast to the competitive individuals who subordinate any "larger use" to their own "petty greeds" in standard Chicago novels (Herrick [1905] 1963, 266; 1900, 316).

But "it was not really home" (67). *The Precipice* deeply challenges Kate Barrington, a woman bearing urban burdens, with the counterclaims of personal romance. It does so through a cousinly connection that extends from Kate's married college friend all the way to Colorado and one Karl Wander, a western mining entrepreneur. In the book's penultimate chapter, Kate realizes the conflict between the instinctual "destiny" of love to which Karl commands her and her own "declaration of independence" and civic service, symbolized by a "precipice" in the Colorado mountains where she is separated from Karl by an "appallingly deep gorge" (405, 363, 414). Finally, they agree that they both need marriage and work, in a "Republic of Souls ... with equal opportunity" (416–17). Embarking on the first commuter marriage proposed in literature, Peattie's heroine claims her right to "the joy of woman" as wife while remaining true to her commitment as a "Sister to the World" (as Peattie also called Addams[10]) and "mother ... to thousands" (393, 80, 389, 405). She achieves a synthesis of domestic and urban, of private and civic families.

In place of individualism, then, *The Precipice* and other residential novels enact urban interdependence. As they neither exclude nor idealize nature, so they also present collectivity as an urban reality full of psychological ambivalences, as well as ethical tensions. Their vision has the weight of complex personal experience, the frustrations and challenges of dealing with real families, groups, and social concerns in Chicago.

Most painfully, the social bonds forming their Chicago can leave too little—never too much—room for individual achievements. Occasionally in the novels, a woman leaves Chicago's closely knit society in order to achieve individual prominence on some public stage. Kate Barrington does so to accept a national appointment for which her Chicago work has well prepared her. But family disapproval and the trivialities of Chicago's high society frustrate the local acting career of a young woman in *Un-*

quenched Fire. In this melodramatic novel by Chicagoan Alice Gerstenberg, who put aside her own acting ambitions for a playwright's career that fit better "the patterns of my home life and city" (Gerstenberg 22 July 1955 letter to W. David Sievers, Gerstenberg Mss.), the heroine must run away to go on stage in New York: "Alone, yes; but free!" (Gerstenberg 1912, 119). Gerstenberg's Jane Carrington resembles Cather's Thea Kronberg, who must also reject parochial Chicago society for New York's greater freedom in order to become an operatic performer. Both contrast with Dreiser's Sister Carrie, who finds Chicago more open to individual mobility than the "Walled City" of New York (Dreiser 1900).

Yet the residential novels affirm the compelling claims of the human family. One breaks them only with great effort and at high cost. Jane Carrington finds that she has "more to regret than she had realized" when her disregard for social conventions shames her family into disinheriting her then leads her into adultery, desertion, and despair (384). On the other hand, *The Glory of the Conquered,* by Gerstenberg's sister playwright Susan Glaspell (1909), promotes "conquered" personal ambition as a "glory," its heroine devoting her artistic skills to her husband's scientific career. But neither calamitous rebellion nor sacrificial resignation is usual among Chicago's residential novels. The greater complexity of *The Precipice* is more representative. In seeking both personal happiness and social service, Kate Barrington rejects self-sacrifice and self-assertion as equally perverse. In exercising major "personal" leadership in the field of "social" welfare, she struggles to make sure that she seeks "service" not "glory" (1914, 406). Thus *The Precipice* advocates expressing individual ambitions in communal forms to resolve the "conflict between self and other" that psychologist Carol Gilligan (1982, 70–71) deems "the central moral problem for women."

Finally, residential novels explore tensions within the social fabric itself. *The Precipice* centers on the tension between the private and the public forms of family, sampling in that context various roles for turn-of-the-century women (Bremer 1989). The familial combinations and romantic recombinations in *True Love* explore tensions between democratic and elitist ethics, open and closed forms of association. Similarly, *"Just Folks"* exposes elitist parochialism and promotes democratic mutuality between Irish and Jewish immigrant families, between the poor people and middle-class Hull-House workers, civil servants, and other professionals. Peattie's Kate Barrington and Laughlin's Beth Tully reject residency at Hull-House specifically because it is too closed, with "too much community of interest" (Peattie 1914, 95), although they follow careers as probation officers very like those of Hull-House's Julia Lathrop and the Negro Fellowship League's Ida B. Wells-Barnett.[11] While finding Hull-House attractive, Beth criticizes the "restful" "beauty of the surroundings" and the "clever conversation" there for making its privileged participants feel "many miles aloof from Halsted Street." To her, Hull-House is a "lovely spot suggestive of some ancient close or cloister from the far world overseas," like Melville's "Paradise of Bachelors" or Fitzgerald's "book-lined room" in "My Lost City" (Laughlin 1910, 1–3; Melville [1855] 1949; Fitzgerald [1934] 1945a). In response to urban heterogeneity, residential novels regularly reject the elitism of the old city-town while extending its base in voluntary associations, as when Beth Tully and her fiancé choose to make their marital home among the poor who are their "friends" (Laughlin 1910, 375).

The residential novels extend such associations most effectively by featuring urban places and activities that bring diverse people together, especially in ethnically mixed neighborhoods and social work interactions between classes. While *True Love* neglects these, Wyatt's first book does not. The short stories in *Every One His Own Way* become a loose urban cycle as neighborhood settings bring together WASPs and Jews, Irish and Scandanavian immigrants, in various combinations. The stories celebrate cultural differences, folkish wisdom, and "large and various... toleran[ce]" (Wyatt 1901, 119). In this way residential novelists often resemble pluralistic local-color humorists like Finley Peter Dunne and George Ade while also reinforcing ethnic stereotypes of, as examples, "hook-nosed" Jews, Greeks and Italians who "lie for one another," lazy Mexicans, and "darky" servants (Laughlin 1910, 58, 327; Wyatt 1903, 143, 128). Similarly reflecting middle-class white limitations, the residential heroines nearly always avoid the factory and Loop to pursue women's "business" of social activity, homemaking, art making, social work, and research: "This, too, was Chicago" (Gerstenberg 1912, 36; Glaspell 1909, 61). They are able to create "homelike" clubs for factory workers, support the families of union strikers, join with "working girls... all sorts, all conditions, black, white" in a suffrage march, but they lack the economic power to "let them *earn* enough!" (Laughlin 1912, 100; Laughlin 1910, 282; Peattie 1914, 156; Laughlin 1912, 183). While insisting that poverty does not "alter our common human nature" (Laughlin 1910, 110), the heroines do not directly challenge the structures undergirding it, and all but Beth Tully maintain their privileges of middle-class residence.

Indeed, Beth finds it difficult to share the benefits of social mutuality with her economically impoverished "friends" and the "poor rich." Just "knowin wan another"—the solution recommended in Laughlin's later novel, *The Penny Philanthropist* (1912, 173)—is not enough here. Beth must work hard to promote learning beyond strong prejudices, including her own against the birth rates and "extravagant funerals of the poor," the "heathen doctrines" of "Sheenies," the hospitals "where people go only to die," and the unruly children (16, 127, 137, 252). She succeeds insofar as she emphasizes women's shared experiences of marital and family responsibility (cf. Stansell 1986, 42) to urge "would-be Samaritans" to drop their condescension and the poor to drop their envy (108). She seeks to recover Jane Addams's original "principle" of learning from, more than teaching, those whose backgrounds differ from one's own (107–8).

Beth Tully appeals to the particularized "ethic of care" that Carol Gilligan (1982, 21) has identified as the prize of women's "different voice" in the late twentieth century. In that view,

> moral understanding is based not on the primacy and universality of individual rights, but rather on...a "very strong sense of being responsible to the world." Within this construction, the moral dilemma changes from how to exercise one's [abstract] rights without interfering with the rights of others to how "to lead a moral life which includes [particular] obligations to myself and my family and people in general."

In keeping with Gilligan's distinction between the ethics of care and justice, expressed respectively by women and men, the romantic plot of *"Just Folks"* traces the ongoing debate between Beth Tully and her fiancé about whether particular "cases" or "the abstract law" ought to guide social ethics (73). It climaxes in an argument over her responsibilities as a probation officer when the son of her beloved "Mother Casey" appears to have killed his sister's seducer. When Beth refuses "to put Mikey in jeopardy" and increase his mother's "woe" by reporting her suspicions, Hart objects in terms of the masculine ethic of justice: "It isn't in you [women] to have respect for the law as an abstract thing.... Your pity is greater than your sense of justice; you want to make an exception of each individual case" (347–48). Promoting responsible care for particular individuals instead, Beth bends rules to visit Mikey in jail in order to convince him to confess and avoid a life running from justice. Laughlin confirms the rightness of her approach—and the wrongness of her suspicions—

when Beth learns that quite another matter than murder had bloodied Mikey, and that her suspicions had derived from her failure to listen to his story earlier. In *"Just Folks"*, an ethic of justice is based on a self-righteousness of the well-to-do that keeps them from learning from others. On the other hand, Laughlin's multiple plots and central character demonstrate that an ethic of care sustains the mutuality and learning appropriate to a "civic family." The interdependence of Chicago society thus becomes, in this and other residential novels, a profound description of urban life and an ethical prescription for improving it. In the words of a dwarf, whom Beth helps to trade lessons in love for lessons in art with a wealthy widow, "We are necessary to one another, and even the—the littlest can help the strong and lovely" (270).

In their openness to different people as constituent of Chicago's "civic family," residential novels sustain the ability of the city-town tradition to accommodate diverse perspectives. In keeping with that tradition, they attend to the familial and organic, social and civic elements in turn-of-the-century Chicago's history. Structurally, too, they are profoundly regional, constructing Chicago from the inside out. The standard Chicago novels, on the other hand, construct—while seeming only to observe—Chicago from the outside. They privilege a national perspective, which reflects the special interests of their authors as economically independent, white men wrestling with the newest, most public aspects of Chicago history. The differences between the residential and standard Chicago novels belong to a more comprehensive pattern of gender-related expectations and experiences.

Gender marked a profound division within the white upper and middle classes generally during the nineteenth century, also separating them from marginalized racial and working-class groups. Especially in cities, "gentlemen" sought replacements for the physical expressions of masculinity that the frontier and soldiering had offered. "Ladies" elaborated leisure and luxury as special badges of feminine privilege (Lerner 1969) and sought urban alternatives to the productive forms of domesticity available on farms. Whereas men were challenged to confront and overcome their environment, dealing with society, nature, and technology as objects to be controlled, women were constantly reminded of their embeddedness in the life processes of society and nature. Women were consequently encouraged as women to "stay at home" in fact and to express themselves as residents in fiction.[12] Conversely, men who were similarly "stuck" in Chicago—as were Henry B. Fuller and Robert Herrick—

disappointed a masculine expectation of independence. Sometimes expressing but more often avoiding a residential posture in their fiction, they pioneered the economic and objectifying imagery that visiting men like Theodore Dreiser played out. Moreover, women's urban perspectives differed from men's in ways that went well beyond the issue of residency and mobility. Although a visitor who remained an outsider to Chicago's residential life, Willa Cather echoed the local women's perception of their city as continous, organic, and communal.[13]

Yet the structural and thematic similarities linking these women's Chicago works with each other and even with later women's "voices" in British novels and psychological development are not essentially female but are firmly based in the particularities of urban, social, and biographical history. Living and working in Chicago when it became a "literary center" (Duncan 1964), Cather's Chicago sisters shared a set of urban experiences that were significantly shaped by their feminine status. Besides remaining in the same city (unlike Cather), they had active roles (like Cather) in the male-dominated newspaper world as well the female-dominated settlement house, women's club, Little Theatre, and Little Magazine enterprises. In these endeavors, women novelists joined hands with reformers, artists, and civic leaders. They contributed to their city in more diverse and collaborative ways than did their male compatriots. As their novels suggest, they stretched and re-created their "woman's sphere" in Chicago far beyond the limits of the public recognition they have received.

Most of Chicago's women novelists were born in Chicago or, like Wyatt and Peattie and Clara Burnham, moved there before their teens. This meant that the primary emotions of childhood experience, more than abstract concepts (like alienation) that humans develop later, formed the bedrock for their understanding of the city. They became acquainted with Chicago in the textures of daily experience radiating out, step by step, from their family homes. For all these Anglo-Saxon Protestant women except Peattie, middle-class home life provided a great deal of physical and social stability. Their experiences were in marked contrast to Dreiser moving in and out of Chicago as a working youth, living at five different city addresses with various members of his struggling family, and setting out on his own to other cities (cf. Kaplan 1988, 110–17).

Middle-class security was not just a matter of finances. Although still "poor" when first married, Peattie (n.d., 40) and her writer husband "lived like people of the professional class," because they shared the aesthetic and social opportunities that had graced the other women's lives since childhood. Being raised as a "middle-class American" in Chicago during the last two decades of the nineteenth century involved no physical, social, or imaginative restrictions, Edith Wyatt insisted. Defending "The Poor Old Past" ([1935], 1-2) against the debunking of bourgeois "narrowness" during the 1930s, she recalled her "fresh green" Chicago summers of "family and ... neighbors" sharing porches, of children playing fantasy games in the streets, of "callers and visitors," of excursions to Sarah Bernhart and "Valküre" performances downtown.

Study "back East," trips abroad and "out West," enriched their experience. They hardly merited the condescension that easterner William James expressed toward Wyatt after meeting her on a camping excursion: "But where did she learn so much of life?" (8 Jan. 1901 letter to Pauline Goldmark, Wyatt Mss.). Nonetheless, even as adults, Wyatt, Clara Burnham, Clara Laughlin, and Alice Gerstenberg all maintained their Chicago residency. They lived in the same city, some in the same houses, as their parents. If they left temporarily—Laughlin, for one, to travel—they came back. After a year in New York as *McClure's* assistant editor after World War I, Wyatt returned to Chicago to live with her mother and stayed until her own death in 1958. After newlywed Elia Peattie and her husband worked together in Omaha for nearly ten years, they returned to Chicago and raised their children for over twenty years in her parents' South Side residence, which she continued to call "the old House home" when they retired to the East (Peattie n.d., 250). Such long-term residency was a world apart from the two months Frank Norris spent in Chicago studying its commodities exchange, or the six-week investigative trip Upton Sinclair made to the stockyards.

In addition to such factual circumstances, Chicago was home to its women novelists in a special, metaphorical sense. As white, middle-class women, they were expected to identify home—with all its personal and cultural connotations—as the center of their lives. "Home" was then unimpeachable as the primary cultural metaphor for a woman's sphere of activities. Chicago meant "home" to its literary women in this sense. Even traveling women who identified strongly with Chicago as a home base tended to describe it in familial terms; eastern poet Amy Lowell called Chicago "my adopted city" during the height of her association with *Poetry* magazine, which she dubbed "my mother" (quoted in H. Monroe 1938, 400).

As an epitome of woman's place, home was not coterminus with a physical house, as cultural critic Elizabeth Janeway (1971, esp. 11-26) has explained. For these Chicago writers, however, the family house was central, implicated in civic and cultural, as well as personal and domestic, activities. Alice Gerstenberg's unpublished autobiography exemplifies this aspect of their experience. It focuses on her companionship with her mother, as together they joined the supposedly leisured "wives, sisters, and daughters" who "whirled out of their houses to their clubs and committee meetings to manage benefits, or to start new goals" in the early 1900s (Gerstenberg [1962], 209). Her descriptions of these adventures regularly proceed from and return to their house, where she details the entrance hall and reception room as settings for sociable comings and goings (95–99). For Gerstenberg and other Chicago women, the family house was a domestic microcosm for—not a bulwark against—the city itself.

Far different were the movements of a native Chicago male like Henry Blake Fuller, who held both familial and social intimacy at arm's length his entire life. In place of a home, Fuller "had a room" in "his mother's house," where "no one [of his associates] presumed to call," Hamlin Garland (1930, 270) recalled. Later he became a peripatetic "roomer," frequently changing apartments that were little more than bedsteads, eating with various friends whose children called him "uncle" as he aged. Once he gave up writing as a career around 1900, Fuller was left with an "unmanly" dependence on the family fortunes of his grandfather, a Chicago railroad tycoon. Like another *fin-de-siècle* "uncle" Henry (Adams) who lived off a family inheritance, Fuller might have felt like an exotic "begonia" (Bowron 1974; cf. Adams [1907] 1961, 319); he probably experienced the paternal disdain for a son's "feeble" interest in arts that he portrayed in *With the Procession* ([1895] 1965, 118). Certainly, Fuller's family dependence and his personal preferences for noncompetitive comradeship—as a shy "Little Cyclopedia" keeping track of Chicago artists' social activities (Fuller 24 Aug. 1908 letter to A. B. Pond, Fuller Papers)—conflicted with the economic ambition that he felt expected of him as a man. The more common masculine patterns of Chicago literary life centered unambiguously upon professional associations, to which one belonged by trade rather than residency. Men newly arrived on the Chicago scene would usually "batch" with colleagues. Their social activities turned around workplace, newspaper guild, and professional clubs such as the all-male Press and Whitechapel clubs.

For women, possibilities for living and working in a milieu so clearly outside the family were just opening up before World War I.[14] Margaret

Anderson ([1930] 1971, 56–57) was understandably distressed by "word that the family was moving to Chicago," where she had come to pioneer her own bohemian way in the publishing world. "It would be assumed that I would live at home," she realized; then "mother would try to stop the *Little Review,*" her flamboyant vehicle for Ezra Pound's expatriate *vers libre* and Emma Goldman's native radicalism. In fact, Peattie's intellectual ambitions were derailed by her father's tyranny and financial irresponsibility, which required her to quit school in seventh grade and share her mother's "bitter work" at home. Even though her husband proved "absolutely unselfish" in his support for her professional work—writing stories she dictated while sewing, bringing books home for her to review, negotiating positions for them both, supporting her travel apart (Peattie n.d., 13, 198 and passim)—she continued to feel powerful conflicts regarding "woman's work." She sharply subtitled a 1910 book review on that subject "Art *or* the Home" (italics added), and repeatedly averred the primacy of her domestic commitment to her "precious babes" and the "true comrade" to whom "every cent I earned went" (Peattie n.d., 52). Whether flouting conventions like Anderson or accepting them like Peattie, white middle-class women experienced gender-role expectations that coincided with "home" as the most salient boundaries in their lives. They staked their careers on expanding those boundaries to incorporate extrafamilial associations and the city itself.

Chicago's literary women were, however, hardly isolated from money making, current political affairs, or public leadership. Wyatt worked as a teacher; she wrote numerous periodical feature stories and essays "for which I have always had some demand [and payment] from publishers" (quoted in Kirk and Kirk n.d., 22); she became so politically effective in the 1910s on behalf of working-class laborers and department store strikers, inhumanely slaughtered animals, the victims of a pleasure-boat disaster, suffragists, child actors, and African-American newsboys (even becoming legal guardian to one) that "want[ing] Edith to be satisfied" became a political test in some Progressive circles (quoted in Porter 1920); and she was recognized as a *Poetry* magazine leader in a newspaper cartoon. Clara Laughlin edited a Chicago journal, turned out advice columns for *Good Housekeeping,* wrote popular novels and over twenty travel books, then ran Clara Laughlin Travel Services. Elia Peattie scrambled to make a living as the "second 'girl reporter'" for the *Chicago Tribune* (Collins 1942, 17), was dubbed "the first Bryan man" by William Jennings Bryan himself for her political editorials in Omaha (Peattie n.d.,

102), and wrote regular reviews with which her "talents were slain, but the bills were paid" for nearly twenty years. She further profited from her position as the *Tribune*'s literary editor[15] by contracting to write local histories, coffee-table anthologies, short stories, children's books, and even plays in her determination "to improve my condition" and not to "let my family stop where I left off" (Peattie n.d., 102, 307, 50, 271–72). Other literary women also worked for various Chicago newspapers between the world's fair and World War I: African-Americans Ida B. Wells-Barnett and Lucy E. Parsons as editors-in-chief, Anglo-Americans Harriet and Lucy Monroe as art critics, Margery Currey (who would be remembered as Floyd Dell's gracious consort) as a society editor, and poet Eunice Tietjens as a war correspondant. Clearly journalism was an important context for professional gain and social activism for women in Chicago, despite its reputation as a hard-boiled male enterprise (Duncan 1964).[16]

Chicago's clubs and settlement houses were clearly not the only arenas for women's public activity; but they were especially important as centers of female leadership. The turn of the century marked the height of the women's club movement, while settlement houses headed by women stood at the forefront of U.S. social reform. In Chicago their leaders formed an interlocking directorate that spearheaded the city's involvement in women's suffrage and social welfare. Peattie's acquaintance with Addams through their mutual membership in the Chicago Woman's Club and Peattie's annual lectures at Hull-House helped to focus her work on behalf of suffrage after 1910 (Bremer 1989, xx). Hull-House helped to salve the exclusion from white women's clubs of black clubwomen, whom Addams entertained there despite the color line. Through mutual work as founders of clubs and settlements, Ida B. Wells-Barnett and Addams became co-organizers of a Chicago mass meeting in the national movement to found the NAACP (Aptheker 1977, 6–7). The clubs gained seriousness from association with reform, and the settlements gained prestige and financial support from association with high society. Although novelists rarely led them, these organizations offered collegial contacts with influential women. And because both clubs and settlements often couched their strong political thrust in literary study, they also provided professional literary women with a public forum that was associated with traditional sources of feminine "home rule."

Most of the Chicago women who wrote novels were teachers or visitors or residents at Hull-House at one time or another. All dined with political and university leaders and attended Little Theatre productions there.

Addams challenged them to offer Hull-House English classes and experimental plays that would correct urban "over-differentiation" and advance "social democracy" and to provide "artistic expression" for reform causes (Addams 1899, 333). In fact, Wyatt did teach evening classes to immigrants there, and both she and Harriet Monroe wrote one-act documentary plays pioneering a sociologically explicit, urban subject matter, not widely successful until the 1930s.[17] Both Peattie and Laughlin referred explicitly in their novels to Addams's work and ideas—which Addams, of course, also articulated to the nation in her own prolific writings. She was a spur, a model, and an ally. Through Hull-House, residential novelists came to respect the personhood of working-class Chicagoans and practiced the cross-class cooperation and collaborative work that Addams promoted.

A collaborative spirit also permeated the Little Theatre movement, which rivaled journalism in its importance to Chicago's emergence as a national "literary center" before World War I. It was another province of women, too, despite doubts about the propriety of ladies becoming professional actresses. In her autobiography *My Chicago,* Anna Morgan (1918, 44) presented her directorial leadership and dramatic coaching as an expression of the city, "worthy of record" because it involved "the earliest efforts in Chicago to produce ... The Little Theatre." Other Little Theatre pioneers included the Hull-House Players and poet-playwright Mary Aldis, at whose Lake Forest playhouse Monroe and Alice Gerstenberg also had their plays produced. When Maurice Browne later founded the famous, albeit short-lived, Chicago Little Theatre in 1912, its producer was his Chicago-born wife, Ellen Van Volkenburg Browne, and her mother was its business manager. It was mostly the fruits of women's ideas and energies that Susan Glaspell and George Cramm Cook brought to the Provincetown Players from their early days in Chicago—where Glaspell wrote her melodramatic novel in the residential mode, *The Glory of the Conquered* (1909).

The Little Theatre movement expressed an urban aesthetic of collaborative public performance that women found especially compelling. Several of the city's literary women mentioned childhood ambitions to become actresses; in fact, Wyatt, Harriet Monroe, Peattie, Glaspell, Laughlin, and Gerstenberg all acted in theatricals at one time or another in addition to writing plays and pageants for amateur groups and a few modern dramas. The best known, Gerstenberg's frequently reprinted *Overtones* ([1915] 1922) developed a model of interior/exterior dialogue that Eugene O'Neill would later use; specifically, it exposes the private thoughts behind the public personae of two society women by having their private "characters" speak out loud what their separately embodied public "characters" are thinking. As Gerstenberg's play suggests, an impetus toward making the private public, toward giving women public voice, inclined many of Chicago's female writers toward the stage.

A similar impetus proved transformative in their poetry, which can be the most intimate literary genre. Most of the Chicago women who wrote novels also wrote poems as well as plays, and they regularly linked their poetry to the public medium of drama. A poet like Harriet Monroe saw her plays as "dramatic poetry" (1938, 175), and Mary Aldis wrote her best poems as dramatic monologues. The public textures of choral speech and song inform the poetic chants that several women wrote. While Vachel Lindsay was popularizing "primitive" chants in *Congo Songs* (1914), his female colleagues were developing chants as public songs of urban unity. Even ships' sirens chant a sisterly community in "City Whistles" (1916), which Wyatt addressed to Harriet Monroe:

> Now the morning winds are rising. Now the morning whistles cry.
> Fast their crescent voices dim the paling star.
> Through the misted city mainland, wide their questing summons fly
> Many-toned—"O mortal, tell me who you are!"
> Down the Midland, down the morning, fresh their sweeping voices buoy:
> "Siren ship! Silver ship! Sister ship! Ahoy!
>   Sister ship ahoy! Ship ahoy!"

The streetmarchers' chant in a 1915 protest poem, "The Song of the Women" by Chicago's Florence Kiper Frank, a Jewish American, is similarly typical in its collective urban voice:

> This is the song of the women, sung to the marching feet,
> Mothers and daughters of mothers, out in the crowded street,
> Yea, and the mothers of mothers, white with the passing years—
> This is the chant of the women, and wise is he who hears.

In poetry and drama, as in their novels, Chicago's women writers emphasize participatory speech rather than objectifying description. In all three genres, they affirm public forms of self-expression.

The force motivating this collective affirmation is exemplified by Harriet Monroe's career as a poet and as founding editor of *Poetry* magazine. One of many women whose early ambition was to be an actress, Monroe equipped herself for a public career by "compell[ing] my shaking body to rise and speak" at club meetings. She fought hard to see that poetry was included in the world's fair and to have herself commissioned to write the *Columbian Ode,* overcoming protracted resistance from more established men of letters on the arrangements committee. As a result, she proudly claimed one of the official "seats provided for the five hundred artists of the Fair" on Dedication Day in 1892. When her ode was sung, she received a bouquet "from the ladies of Chicago" as the publicly recognized representative of poetry and women (Monroe 1938, 46, 78, 116-38). The fair's chief architect, Daniel Burnham, pinpointed her achievement: "No other woman has ever been so honored, in the way you care for, in our country and time" (22 Dec. 1892 letter, Monroe Personal Papers I).

Monroe valued public recognition for the "feminine" muse of poetry as for herself. As she explained twenty years later, in her promotional circulars for *Poetry* and in the magazine's first issue, she was determined not to have poetry "left to herself" while other arts gained public stature (1912). Monroe chose a Walt Whitman motto for the *Poetry* cover: "To have great poets / there must be great audiences, too" (Monroe 1914a), thus affirming the artist's reciprocal relationship with society. It is no surprise that most residential novelists had their poetic works published and reviewed in *Poetry* or in Margaret Anderson's Chicago-based *Little Review*.[18] Such public presentation was crucial for them as women participating in Chicago's cultural development.

Nor should it be surprising that their poems express a natural organicism and a concern with human labor when they turn to urban themes. They show the city's mechanical forces in tune with the natural and the human, as does Wyatt's "City Whistles," and focus on the workers involved in industry, as does Monroe's chanting "Workman's Song" (1895). Such poems provided a local context for the work that labor organizer Carl Sandburg first published in *Poetry* and, with his famous *Chicago Poems,* helped create a bridge between Whitman[19] and later ethnic poets' open and dynamic—often organic—expressions of human power in cities. Sandburg's "Chicago" (1914) emphasizes the human power of labor to control—even to laugh and play with—the city's machinery. As "Hog Butcher for the World / ... Player with Railroads ... / Stormy, husky, brawling, / City of the Big Shoulders," his Chicago is itself a human laborer. And although Sandburg's language is mythic and exclamatory like the standard Chicago novels, he does not distance himself from what he calls "my city," not even from its wickedness and poverty. Nor do Sandburg's female counterparts in Chicago, writing poems about prostitutes as well as sandwich servers and often taking the point of view of workers in dramatic monologues. In particular, they show the dignity of workers in the growing service sector of cities while also testing the limitations of such public service roles, which over one-fourth of the nation's wage-earning women filled by 1920 (Wilson 1979, 115). Widely admired, Peattie's pseudonymous contribution to the first number of *The Little Review* (1914) declares a milliner's painful sense of losing herself in doing this, that, and the other thing "according to the fashion, / ... according to the fashion, / ... according to the fashion, / ... in service of other women."

While the residential novelists explored new trails for white middle-class women beyond their increasingly nuclear private families, they recognized the risks involved when women left their "shelters" in search of "kingdoms," to use Monroe's terms. They sought to take the home strengths of familiarity and hospitality with them. Monroe (1938, 317) wrote of the *Poetry* offices, "I had never been the actual mistress of any home which had sheltered me, but this little kingdom was mine, and I rather enjoyed dispensing its fleeting hospitalities." Theirs was a search for urban community that would unite professional and familial strengths in collaboration. "I do very much believe in collaboration, do you?" Gerstenberg wrote to a friend and potential co-worker (18 Feb. 1916 to Kate Jordan, Gerstenberg Mss.). That search informed the novels they published, the public arts they performed, the magazines they edited, and the clubs they joined in Chicago. It was even hard to tell where one kind of activity left off and another began. In founding *The Little Review,* Margaret Anderson ([1930] 1971, 47) confessed, "what I needed was not a magazine but a club room."

One particular club that the literary women shared with men exemplified just how far they took their search and how the lack of public recognition confounded them. Nearly all of Chicago's residential novelists belonged to the Little Room, which extended into the professional arts an idea developed by women's clubs and settlements of gathering people across lines of specialization. Like the settlements, too, the Little Room rejected the conventional gender division among Chicago's social clubs and professional organizations, bringing men and women together as friends and colleagues. Lucy Monroe suggested that they name themselves after a short story about a room in a family home, a "little room" that was visible only to the imaginative eye. It was widely understood that the author of that story, Chicagoan Madeline Yale Wynne, embodied in her own person the Little Room's multimedia union of arts and commitment to hospitality. A painter, muralist, metalworker, writer, violinist, and embroiderer, Wynne was an "all-round artist," said Harriet Monroe (1938, 197), a woman who "passed no art without a salutation," said Peattie (1903, frontispiece), and "a great encourager of others," said Morgan (1918, 153). In 1898 the Little Room began meeting weekly in Chicago's new Fine Arts Building, where artists' studios, publishing houses, small theaters, women's clubs, and political associations were housed together downtown.

By 1903 the Little Room included Chicago novelists Clara Burnham, Henry Blake Fuller, Hamlin Garland, Robert Herrick, Clara Laughlin, Will Payne, Elia Peattie, and Edith Wyatt, drama director Anna Morgan, newspaper columnist George Ade, sculptor Lorado Taft, dancer Lou Wall Moore, poet William Vaughn Moody, cartoonist George Barr McCutcheon, Jane Addams, Daniel Burnham, the Monroe sisters, and other activists in civic culture (but, notably, none of the standard Chicago novelists). The Little Roomers' weekly conversations spawned collaborative work in the arts, including annual Twelfth-Night theatricals that Anna Morgan directed such as *Cap. Fry's Birthday Party* (1904, fig. 9), a take-off on McCutcheon's cartoons. Regularly the Little Room's women, acting as both hostesses and artists, managed the "entertainments." Their leadership was recognized in the informal network of male and female members, which Henry Blake Fuller helped to maintain by correspondence when someone was out of town. The Little Room's inclusivity, moreover, expressed the women's ethos and may have justified one Chicagoan's claim then that "nowhere ... is there an artistic colony so untainted by jealousy as is that of Chicago" (Chatfield-Taylor 1918). The women, for a time, had found a way to enjoy full collegiality with men and to share the home spirit in the professional realm.

But when the Little Room began to formalize its organization in 1902, a split developed between the unofficial and official workings of the club. Although woman continued to head the "entertainment" committee and one woman joined each "class" of three elected to the Little Room's board of directors, men became the officers who called meetings and kept the records and money (Little Room Papers). A 1906 decision to include spouses as associate members laced the Little Room with literal family ties, confusing the status of the professional women who were attempting an extension of familylike dynamics beyond the private home.

As the Little Room was thus domesticated under the official leadership

Figure 9. Little Room, *Cap. Fry's Birthday Party* (1904), photograph of members. (*Back row:* seated middle, Will Payne; right, Clara Laughlin. *Middle row:* 3d from left, Harriet Monroe; 5th, Clara Burnham; 7th, Anna Morgan; 8th, Lucy Monroe. *Front row:* 2d from left, Edith Wyatt; 5th, George Barr McCutcheon.) Courtesy of Little Room Archives, the Newberry Library, Chicago.

of men, a more bohemian colony of white artists was also taking shape in some old world's fair apartments near the University of Chicago. In this setting, Susan Glaspell, Margery Currey, Sherwood Anderson, Floyd Dell, Eunice Tietjens, Vachel Lindsay, and Margaret Anderson actively rejected domestic conventions for sexual freedoms. Unfortunately, the notoriety of their sexual affairs obscured the value of the women's—although not the men's—literary reputations, in a classic case of the double standard. For the bohemians no less than the more established artists from whom they were now split off, the delicate balance between family spirit and artistic commitment was upset. Either way, Chicago's literary women fell out of a vital cultural center.

Into the breach stepped Hamlin Garland, unhappily settling in his wife's hometown after years of using Chicago only as a stopover between the rural Midwest and East Coast centers of culture. He wanted a more professional organization that would associate writers like himself with the city's public leadership—"a real club like the Players" in New York (1931, 336). That meant a men's club. Working with a "complete list of men" from the Little Room's membership roster, Garland sent out invitations in 1908. Although his new club would exclude women, it would be a "widening of the scope of the Little Room," he wrote prospective members, because it would include "distinguished men of science . . . and other professions" (Little Room Papers). For the most part, Chicago's literary men welcomed his suggestion and soon installed themselves atop a Loop skyscraper, where they met to lunch together and to lionize visiting dignitaries. Appropriately, they dubbed their club the Cliff Dwellers after the 1893 Fuller novel that had established Chicago's economic image for the nation, although Fuller was a social leader in the Little Room and one of the few men who refused to join Garland's club.

Those who did join also continued their participation in the Little Room, but it and its female members took a back seat in their collegial affections. Garland's autobiography (1931, 460, 320–38, 368–75) records a few occasions when he himself went directly from the Cliff Dwellers Club to the Little Room, taking particular pleasure, for instance, in meeting visiting local-colorist Alice French there. She greeted him, he wrote, "with the directness of a man, professing an abiding interest in all that I am doing." Of course, Garland's sense of French's adulation, which he took for "directness," made her seem "companionable, a literary comrade" to be valued, but "in the way few women achieve." So when Chicago's "truly professional" women "sent emissaries to ask the officers of the Cliff Dwellers Club, if the men would be willing to accept their female confrères [sic]. ... The reply was, 'No!' " In her unpublished autobiography, Alice Gerstenberg ([1962], 262–63) goes on to tell how the women then "launched out on their own" with novelist Clara Laughlin in the lead, and founded the Cordon Club. The name "meant, shall we say, something like many ribbons, or badges of honor, roped together," a fitting emblem for the women's vision of community in contrast to the men's skyscraping imagery. Not until 1914 would the division between the men and women be healed, when the long-established male Writers Guild invited women to a dinner to found the Society of Midland Authors. All the women on the society's organizational committee were Little Roomers, and both Clara Laughlin and Alice Gerstenberg eventually succeeded to the presidency of the new organization. But it lacked the multimedia range and informality that had been hallmarks of the Little Room, where women's special strengths and vision had shone.

During their years apart from the company of the Cliff Dwellers, the women brought the Little Theater movement to its peak, got *Poetry* and *The Little Review* underway, became active Progressives and suffragists, and produced most of their residential novels, including the most politically explicit, *"Just Folks"* and *The Precipice.* They did not, however, surpass the structural innovation of *True Love,* and they never fully recouped the professional recognition that the Cliff Dwellers had denied them. The status and authority even of those women with major achievements to their credit—such as Anna Morgan, Edith Wyatt, Clara Laughlin, Elia Peattie, or Harriet Monroe—were left open to question when the home spirit they sought to develop was denied broader social significance. Sculptor Lorado Taft, for instance, rudely challenged Morgan's right to initiate a memorial book for Henry Blake Fuller in 1929, although she and Fuller had been close friends and partners in catalyzing the Little Room's collegial community. "Why the hurry? ... Do you expect to sell it as a Christmas book?" Taft asked offensively, and then went on: "I had supposed that [such a book] would be the work of Fuller's closest *literary* companions, *men* like ... Garland. ... Next Sunday Mr. Garland [who was also Taft's brother-in-law] will be here and we can have a consultation" (20 Oct. 1929 letter, italics added, Morgan Miscellaneous Papers). Taft was hardly alone in dismissing collegial friendship as unprofessional unless it was based on specialization and masculine hegemony.[20]

As a group, the women who wrote Chicago's residential novels have been remembered only as hostesses ever since. Individually each has been forgotten or viewed with wrenching, sometimes blatantly sexist, condescension. Bernard Duffey's long-respected study of *The Chicago Renaissance in American Letters* (1956, 183, 66), for example, misrepresents Harriet Monroe as a "schoolmistress" who was herself "educated" by her achievements. And although Duffey (57) and his popularizing successor Dale Kramer (1966, 99) respectfully note Peattie as a literary critic, her old *Tribune* colleague Burton Rascoe (1937, 323–31) stereotypes her as a "bluestocking," oversimplifies her criticism as "anti-Dreiserian," dismisses her civic associations as "a culture group of women" she "dominated" and a "literary [hen?] roost" she "ran," and trivializes her voluminous literary output as "some successful novels for young girls."

The women's novels received support and recognition in particular instances but were not valued as significant in their own right, comparable in quality as they were to men's standard Chicago novels. No evidence exists of blatant discrimination in their original publication and critical reception. In reaching top publishers, the women were only slightly less successful than the men who wrote Chicago novels, and no more men than women managed to place more than three volumes of fiction with any one major house between 1890 and 1915. Novels of Chicago by both men and women received about five or ten indexed reviews apiece during the decade before World War I (discounting the unusual hullabaloo that *The Jungle* stirred up and the inexplicable silence that greeted *"Just Folks"*). Edith Wyatt's *True Love* even got stronger contemporary support than Dreiser's *Sister Carrie*. Generally, reviews of the women's novels were no shorter nor less favorable in specific content than those the men received—only more tepid.

That difference in tone could not in and of itself generate the eventual eclipse of the Chicago women's residential novels. But its subtle deflation points toward underlying cultural forces of masculine hegemony far more profound—and persistent—than any particular circumstance of discrimination. Their novels were not taken seriously enough to have their various qualities debated. Even the women's most faithful male colleague among the Little Roomers, Henry Blake Fuller (1901; 1903), went on record in the Chicago *Evening Post* proclaiming, "the creative impulse is masculine and so are all the forces that organize and propel. Feminine talent may deftly refine and perfect what already exists, but plausible simulations of the real thing" must remain in the hands of man, who "sees more of life in general than woman can hope to see." He was, of course, expressing a common view.

Certainly Fuller's remarks support the hypothesis that we have forgotten most Chicago women's novels because they fail to fit our cultural assumptions about "the real thing" and "life in general." Our urban understandings, like other "maxims that pass for the truth of human experience, and the encoding of that experience in literature, are," as most literary and cultural critics have recently agreed, "organizations, when they are not fantasies, of the dominant culture" (Miller 1981, 46). Our history now shows that those constructions are "in fact based on the masculine population" even when "stated sweepingly to cover the entire society" (Potter [1962] 1970, 318–19). We now understand that even previously well-regarded literary constructions by women were left out (along with similarly well-read regional, ethnic minority, and working-class literature) when the white academic men who founded *American Literature* established our literary canon on the grounds of national identity and professional specialization as they understood them (Showalter 1988, 824–25; Howe 1983; P. Lauter 1983; cf. Franklin 1978, xiii–xix).

Standard Chicago novels have lasted because they reflect urban experiences deemed "the real thing" from nationalistic and professional perspectives constructed by white middle-class men. When we read standard Chicago novels—or those literary works that follow their leads—we have a pleasurable aesthetic experience of recognition and completion, which each new addition enriches and deepens. Their fictional Chicago translates into urban terms the nation's dominant cultural myth of a lone Adam, not Eve, seeking to conquer a new world. They critique that mythology within its own terms, as deconstructionist theory reminds us all participants in a mythology must. Emphasizing (white male-dominated) public arenas of national conflict, they expose the lack of community that results from undermining regional contexts for belonging. In the process, however, they define as "life in general" a special segment of experience unknown to many Americans—including longtime residents in any single locale, civil servants, unpaid or unemployed workers and family members, outsiders to expectations of public leadership, and most of the white middle-class women who wrote novels in turn-of-the-century Chicago.

Not substandard quality but their nonstandard qualities explain our lack of familiarity with the women's residential novels. Although we may assume that our urban categories have nothing to do with our aesthetic experience, these novels have been ignored as sentimental or trivial because they do not fit our unfocused, yet pervasive "tacit knowledge" (Polanyi 1958) of cities. Nonetheless they profoundly challenge the standard Chicago novel on its own definitive turf and impeach the supposedly universal resonance of U.S. fiction's "standard patterns," as Edith Wyatt (1914b, 17) argued before World War I. They offer a counter-formulation of human "participation in city events which are historical [and continuous] . . . in contrast to books by men which record only [current] politics and business," as Chicagoan Alice Gerstenberg noted (1 May 1965 letter to Amy Nyholm, Gerstenberg Mss.). Their emphasis on "the continuity of relationships" also challenges the Freudian norms of identity formation through separation from a background of "failed relationships" (Gilligan 1982, esp. 39). Additionally, they challenge the later work of the Chicago School of Sociology (e.g., Wirth 1938) equating "urbanism" with modern *Gesellschaft* and opposing it to rural life and traditional *Gemeinschaft* by definition. Contrary to all modernist abstraction, they convey what one of today's leading novelists has called "a very strong sense of place, not in terms of the country or the state, but in terms of the details, the feeling, the mood of the community, of the town."

Toni Morrison's experience (1976, 167–68) certainly seems to share much with that of white women writing in Chicago at the turn of the century:

> I think some of it is just a woman's strong sense of being in a room, a place, or a house. Sometimes my relationship to things in a house would be a little different from, say, my brother's or my father's or my sons'. I clean them and I move them and I do very intimate things "in place": I am sort of rooted in it, so that writing about being in a room looking out, or being in a world looking out, or living in a small definite place, is probably very common among most women anyway.

Such a "strong sense of place" can open up the "intimately experienced neighborhood" dynamics that have baffled urban research into women's residential experience (Tuan 1974, 224, 61–66)[21]—as into the social and street life of ethnic, minority, and working-class groups.

When Peattie's (1914, 85) Kate Barrington describes her preference for continuities in human relationships as a matter of "suburbs," she does not refer to the remote enclaves of the rich that exemplify economic separation in standard Chicago novels; instead she means middle-class, near "neighborhoods" that connect "outlying gardens" with "town," as friendship connects acquaintance with intimacy. *The Precipice* thus extends into modern form the agricultural "plantations" that supported the old city on a hill and prepares the way for the vital organicism of inner-city street life in the works of marginalized ethnic writers. When Kate insists that "walled cities were no longer endurable, and walled and limited possibilities [for women] were equally obsolete" (89), she prefigures the similarly metaphoric plea in Rudolph Fisher's neglected Harlem novel *The Walls of Jericho* (1928) to tear down the walls of segregation against African Americans. The informing power of the residential novels derives from their participation in this alternative urban tradition, linking the colonial city-town with ethnic neighborhood literature. Their loss represents a crippling break in our historical consciousness.

5

New York's Megalopolitan Nightmares

After World War I, even the women among white middle-class writers in northern cities found it difficult to sustain city-town imagery. The war shifted energies from the civic family and women's settlement work to the military front and men's armies. The hopes of democratic community gave way to the horrors of trench warfare, then the realization that economic imperialism had fueled the so-called war to make the world safe for democracy. The right to vote made moot a primary reason for women to organize together and took the political edge off their club movement. The Roaring Twenties' emphasis on individual success and sexual freedom undermined the ethic of collaboration for "modern women" (Showalter 1978). In place of organic "American life" in urban as in rural settings, runaway consumption trapped them in "aridities" (Monroe 1938, 157). In place of undergirding continuities, "the world broke in two in 1922 or thereabouts" nearly as often for Willa Cather (1936, v) and other middle-class white women as for their male counterparts.

Postwar urbanism overwhelmed them. The census of 1930 located over half of the nation's population in cities. Urban culture was no longer confined to city limits as connurbation made Connecticut effectively part of greater New York and the northern end of what was becoming an East Coast urban corridor. Suburbanization in the Midwest and West extended cities endlessly outward, and radio waves brought the city to the country.

Beyond the ghettos of the unassimilated in New York and other big cities, American writers formed professional organizations rather than communal associations. Separate paths crossed, but did not join, on the streets or in the mails around New York's Thirteenth Street, where magazines were housed (Bender 1987, 252). What writers' work had in common did not embody itself in personal networks so much as itself in an abstract ethos of professionalism, which Edith Wharton valued as a way to break out of the confinements of old family New York society (Kaplan 1988, 65–74). New York functioned primarily as the originating point for aesthetic statements sent down to the provinces—and out to the rest of the world, where many writers found the same professional associations in Paris or Moscow as in Taos, New Mexico.

For New York came into its own as a world city after World War I, the foreign and domestic observers that Bayrd Still surveyed (1956) agreed. Instead of offering just another national city to replace Chicago, New York was "the first capital of the world" (A. Chevrillon, quoted 262). Its skyscrapers were "the great buildings of the world" (R. Brooke, quoted 259), its transportation system and its Fifth Avenue "unsurpassed" (A. Bennett, quoted 283; L. Fulda, quoted 285), its Broadway brighter than "a hundred Eiffel towers" (P. de Rothschild, quoted 260), with "more" orchestral concerts "than Berlin" and theaters "far better... than a dozen Londons" (Mencken, quoted 274). Also displaying "more contrasts than any other city in the world" (V. Vinde, quoted 329), it was "the only city... sufficiently wealthy to be modern" (B. Faÿ, quoted 298), then "more degraded and degrading than anything [in] Britain or Germany" (M. A. Hamilton, quoted 319): "For New York is all the cities" (W. L. George, quoted 293), "the new Cosmopolis" (J. Huneker, quoted 368).

This world city brought into focus issues of ethnic diversity and mass culture incipient in Manhattan's multinational beginnings. It was a Dutch "company town" (Reynolds 1984, 3) "bought" from various tribal nations, a British possession, and the inaugural capital of the United States. Manhattan included the first North American settlements of free blacks and Jews, eighteen languages among its first five hundred inhabitants, Englishmen in its Dutch government, men from "Dutch and other ethnic groups" among its first British-appointed officials, and both Iroquoian trails and Dutch canals under its U.S. streets (Reynolds 1984, 3–10; Lankevich and Furer 1984, 5–31).

Open in all seasons, New York's vast harbor made it a center of exchange for commerce and communications as well as for people. Shipping dominated its commercial activity until after the Civil War, when other media of economic exchange established national then international headquarters there for banking and stocks, printing and publishing, radio and television. Like the old immigration centers at Castle Gardens and on Ellis Island, the 1886 Statue of Liberty and the 1950 United Nations Secretariat symbolize its continuing stature as the multiethnic gateway between the United States and the world. Down to its streets and neighborhoods, New York resembles the Southwest "borderlands" that Gloria Anzaldúa (1987) has recognized as a creative place where all belong but none is uncontested owner.

As a result, a "contentious process of mixing" has informed not only New York's social and economic affairs, but also "the battleground quality of its intellectual life," as historian Thomas Bender puts it (1987, xvi)—particularly when we juxtapose the professional associations dominated by whites (and emphasized by Bender) to the literary life of ethnic neighborhoods. Indeed the parallel development of neighborhood-city images in Harlem and on the Lower East Side gains point from its antithetical relationship to the economic city's megalopolitan transformation by the elite Lost Generation. While many ethnic and working-class novelists continued to use the standard economic city model to protest against crushing nationwide oppression—from James T. Farrell's Chicago (1934) to Mike Gold's New York (1930), Chester Himes's Los Angeles (1946), and Harriette Arnow's Detroit (1954)—and while Harlem Renaissance literature often contrasts the ethnic neighborhood's vitality uptown to the economic artificiality of Anglo dominance downtown, many middle-class white writers dismissed the economic city model for comprehending cities. Caught up in postwar disillusionment, they turned its imagery of alienation and mechanization into the psychological fragmentation and mass conformity of a modernist megalopolis.

New York literature written during the 1920s by white authors as diverse as Hart Crane, Edith Wharton, John Dos Passos, F. Scott Fitzgerald, and Nathanael West dramatize the reach as well as the internal emptiness of megalopolis. Especially wealthy or successful, or sufficiently educated and mobile to expect to become so, they were powerful enough to construe themselves as individuals. Their writing was rootless and abstracted, whether expressed in the expatriate aestheticism of Greenwich Village, in the international revolutionism of *The Masses* and *New Masses*, in the consuming hysteria of the Jazz Age, or in media clichés. It accompanied social "shrinkage and fragmentation" (Bender 1987, 249–55) as well as psychological alienation. The literary megalopolis such writers created fails to tap the life source of civic joinings. It offers no solid, organic ground upon which to sing the sensory "blood-clots of song / From the wounds of humanity," which allowed a white working-class poet like Carl Sandburg to appeal to Harlemite Langston Hughes (1940, 29) as a fellow "lover of life." Neither does it offer any inclusive, communal ground of hope for reaching out to embrace "the cosmic 'I' of all peoples," as Hughes (1945)[1] saw his "brother" Walt Whitman do. So a megalopolitan poem like Hart Crane's "The Bridge" ([1930] 1946) reduces the organic unities of "Meistersinger" Whitman (38) to "fused" abstractions (3), like the geometries of Joseph Stella's postwar painting *Brooklyn Bridge* (1917–20, fig. 10). In contrast to both Whitman and Hughes, Crane envisions nothing like "the whole city... alive" in John Marin's (1977, 105) prewar etchings of the Brooklyn Bridge (1910–13, fig. 5) nor anything like the expressive neighborhood street life in Italian-American Ralph Fasanella's *Sunday Afternoon* (1953, fig. 11).

The Anglo-American poet who tried hardest to carry on Whitman's line, Crane exemplifies the personal alienation that repeatedly marks the biographies of megalopolitan authors and, on a larger scale, "the disruption of the continuity from... past to... present" (Hazo 1963, 98) that they saw all around them. Like Whitman (and Hughes), Crane was an urban vagabond, unmarried, separated from his childhood family, and linked to other outcasts by his homosexuality.[2] But his "smithereened" life (Hazo 1963) lacked the connective tissue that Whitman's political involvements brought him or the community of Hughes's larger racial family. Crane's megalopolitan epic "The Bridge" fragments the organic continuities of Whitman's holistic vision, enforces fusion only in the abstract, and sounds a hollow claim to grandeur. Although reverencing Whitman in its central section, "The Bridge" ([1930] 1946, 38) nonetheless lacks any sense of human interaction, of organic place, of dynamic continuity. It addresses "Recorders ages hence" in impersonal, epic language (32), in contrast to Whitman's personal, intimate appeal to "you... years hence" in "Crossing Brooklyn Ferry" ([1856, 1881] 1965a). Crane's poem reaches through diversity and materiality and space and time to assert a "mystical synthesis" (Crane quoted in Quinn 1963, 71), but does not "love" the changing "appearances" as well as the "soul" of the world (Whitman [1856, 1881] 1965a).[3] Instead of presenting the act of crossing a particular Brooklyn ferry or bridge, Crane reifies Brooklyn bridge into the bridge for all time and space, using its purified form to symbolize a fusion he could not feel. "The Bridge" does indeed capture the "alternate

Figure 10. Joseph Stella, *Brooklyn Bridge* (1917–20), oil on canvas, 84 × 76 in. Courtesy of the Yale University Art Gallery, Collection Société Anonyme.

Figure 11. Ralph Fasanella, *Sunday Afternoon—Stickball Game* (1953), oil on canvas, 36 × 40 in. Courtesy of the artist.

possibilities of ... salvation or damnation" that Alan Trachtenberg (1965, 13) has identified as Brooklyn Bridge's meaning in U.S. culture, but the poem remains trapped within those abstract contradictions. In place of hope, it offers the disembodied "harp and altar, of the fury fused" (Crane [1930] 1946, 3).

More often simply lost in the detritus of cities, these Lost Generation writers also felt disillusioned with the reportorial objectivity and narrative coherence of realist and naturalist writers who depicted the economic city before the war. While the standard Chicago novel's authorial distance, documentation, and narrative dichotomies express the city's resistance to civic control, those literary conventions also assert symbolic comprehension. In novels of megalopolis written after World War I, modernist techniques like collage and the grotesque do no such thing. They present a mental world as much in pieces as the cities they symbolize— like Nathanael West's junk shops ([1933] 1962) or movie lots ([1939] 1962, 97) full of leftovers from old stories. When the city-town and the economic city both ceased to be meaningful and writers lost faith in progressive powers, their patterns of comprehension also ceased to hold.

Discontinuity and the failure of cohering urban patterns, as well as lost hopes, often mark the distance between pre- and postwar New York novels, even those written by the same author. The two best known novels of Edith Wharton, a woman born over thirty years before Crane, provide an exemplary comparison. *The House of Mirth* ([1905] 1964, 72) reveals the city-town's loss of power to the economic city, yet the Anglo-American dream of civic community—of a "republic of the spirit"—is still alive and attractive there. That same dream is only "gruesomely preserved" in *The Age of Innocence* ([1920] 1962, 51), which examines the past with postwar disillusion. Whereas *The House of Mirth* extends the explanatory power of the economic city to the aristocracy of old New York at the turn of the century, *The Age of Innocence* allows no one city paradigm to provide conceptual continuity.

The House of Mirth views in a rather positive light the genteel intimacy that Lily Bart's marriage to her old family friend Lawrence Seldon could offer, as well as the honest partnership that marriage to nouveau riche Simon Rosendale would mean. She pursues neither of these possible dreams, however.[4] Simultaneously she resists dependence on her aunt Mrs. Peniston, and rejects an extramarital liaison with sleazy Gus Trenor, along with the threats of conformity and prostitution that these alternatives entail. Lily Bart is unwilling to give up either wealth for gentility or gentility for wealth.

Wharton is nonetheless firm in presenting the economic city as the defining system within which all these lives—and New York itself—operate. Although bachelor Selden and widow Peniston are remnants of the old city-town, they are childless and their social "influence, in its last analysis, was simply the power of money" (270). Like so many characters in standard Chicago novels, Lily Bart discovers that she is "just a screw or cog in the great machine" (319),[5] her fall counterbalanced by Simon Rosendale's rise. "Highly specialized" from the start (7), Lily Bart "only fits into one hole" in the urban machine, and she kills herself in the end when she is "thrown out into the rubbish heap" (320). In its thorough development of the economic city's logic, *The House of Mirth* offers an integrated image of New York before the Great War. It demonstrates "the power of the marketplace," as critic Wai-Chee Dimock (1985, 783) has argued, "in its ability to assimilate everything else into its domain."[6]

Wharton shared with other turn-of-the-century authors—including the economic city's newcomers and the residential Chicago novelists—social comprehensiveness and a detailed historical perspective. After World War I, however, her personal present and the entire Western world's seemed radically disconnected from the past and its patterns of comprehension. Her intense three-year affair with Morton Fullerton, her expatriation to Paris, and her divorce in 1913 carved a psychological chasm between *The House of Mirth* and *The Age of Innocence* (Wolff 1977, 144–51, 192–202, 220–28, 259–63; Lewis 1975, 205–31, 332–39, 363–89). Beyond the pale of her aristocratic New York upbringing, she also immersed herself in the global disruptions of war. Arranging lodging, feeding, day-care, and employment facilities in Paris for over nine thousand wartime refugees in 1915 alone, she earned the French Legion of Honor for her American Hostels for Refugees. But the war exhausted her dreams and hopefulness, as it did so many others'. In particular she grieved over the Germans' destruction of "the thousand and one bits of the past that give meaning and continuity to the present" (quoted in Wolff 1977, 262).

Written from this postwar global perspective, *The Age of Innocence* is anticontinuous in structure, despite its historical setting in 1870s New York. Its plot dramatizes the transformation of the old city-town into the economic city during the generation before Lily Bart's in *The House of Mirth*. But *The Age of Innocence* nonetheless belongs to the postwar generation after Lily's. In its structural shifts and epochal breaks, Wharton projects the sense of discontinuity that divorce and war raised in her consciousness. She also brings postwar disillusion to bear on old ideals, especially on the old city-town embodiment of community.

Structurally the two-part division of *The Age of Innocence* emphasizes the disjunction between the urban worlds of a declining aristocracy and an upstart plutocracy. Whereas book I centers its action on the private familial scandal of Ellen Olenska's flight from her husband, book II introduces the contrapuntal action of the public financial scandal of Julius Beaufort's banking failure. Whereas the old city-town's family settings— usually the parlors, dining rooms, ballrooms, and libraries of private residences—dominate book I, book II moves into the economic city's public domain. The increasingly illicit meetings of Newland Archer and Ellen Olenska take place in unrestricted settings open to a public on the move in book II—along the sidewalks, on a ferry boat, at a railroad station, and in "the congestion of carriages" where a street lamp abruptly spotlights their embrace (230). These contrasts spell a radical break from the past. An abrupt chronological gap of "nearly twenty-six years" (273) between the penultimate chapter and the novel's epilogue confirms the break between "the old ways" and "the new order" (275-76). That structural gap consigns city-town New York to the remote, irretrievable past, which is the first half of the novel. Structurally, *The Age of Innocence* presents a divided, not an integrated, view of urban experience.

Perhaps because Wharton leaves the city-town in structural control of part I, Louis Auchincloss (1971, 123-39), James Tuttleton (1972) and Cynthia Griffin Wolff (1977) have all found "nostalgia" in *The Age of Innocence*. But disillusionment, not nostalgia, informs Wharton's assessment of Old New York's communalism, its clinging to homogeneous customs and kinship networks. Wharton reaches through the intervening decades to "reconstruct—archeologically, as it were" a lost city, as Tuttleton has argued. But contrary to his interpretation of this "archeological motive," Wharton reconstructs the old urban community as dead and deadening, not "vitalized" at all (cf. Ammons 1980, 131). As the pattern of Wharton's metaphors makes clear, Old New York is a "family vault" or "pyramid" or "necropolis" inscribed with "hieroglyphic" social forms ([1920] 1962, 266, 48, 247, 45). Its family connections find their full expression in "funereal" banquets (77). It is ruled from "mausoleum" mansions (110) by elders who are "gruesomely preserved." Newland Archer's most revered relatives are like "bodies caught in glaciers [that] keep for years a rosy life-in-death" (51), while the matriarch of his wife's family is buttressed by corpulence "like a flood of lava on a doomed city" (32). Led by the living dead, this graveyard of urban community sustains itself by denying life to its own descendants, filling the veins of the unimaginative with "preserving fluid" (154) and "bur[ying] alive" any rebels (43, 117–18) who dream of "other cities beyond New York" (235). Itself a travesty of the dream of community, Wharton's Old New York smothers any other urban dreams in *The Age of Innocence*.

Without viable dreams for the future or even a single, comprehensive structure for what already exists, New York City disintegrates in John Dos Passos's 1925 novel, *Manhattan Transfer*. Echoing earlier economic city novels, it includes elements similar to many in *A Hazard of New Fortunes* and its Chicago successors: the jarring realities of public transportation epitomize the city; its heterogeneous inhabitants lack community; and the poor and the prostituted are the city's most pathetic victims. But it lacks the cohering structure of these earlier novels. Dos Passos's "nightmarishly modern" novel about the years leading to and through World War I discards the linear, mechanical connections of the economic city for the synaptic, electronic energies fueling the communications revolution. Its title "refers to the station exchange in which the old-fashioned steam-cars used to be switched to electric power," as critic Diana Festa-McCormick (1979, 143, 157) has noted. That transit symbolism has, moreover, less to do with an oppressive economic system than with missed connections among human beings. Lack of community is now complete. Not even shared economic interests or narrative continuity bind together the spiritually impoverished and prostituted characters Dos Passos presents in collaged bits and pieces. They are "crushed and jostling like apples fed down a chute into a press" (Dos Passos [1925] 1953, 3), like the refuse and passengers in the post-Whitmanian ferry scene that introduces the first chapter.[7] Like the people in the hotels in which Dos Passos himself was raised as an illegitimate, then adopted, child (Ludington 1980, 1–2), they bump together by superficial coincidence.

Although Dos Passos believed in the power of economic forces, his fictional double Jimmy Herf complains that economic explanations do not suffice for this chaos: "God I wish I could blame it all on capitalism" ([1925] 1953, 265). Similarly, Bud Korpenning, the country migrant whose arrival and suicide mark the beginning and end of the novel's first section, searches in vain for "the center of things" before he ends up on the Bowery, then dead (4, 24, 25). *Manhattan Transfer*'s New York collage allows no systemic vision. Only self-divided, name-changing Ellen Thatcher claims she's found "the center of things" (267), and that center does not hold. *Manhattan Transfer* is a carnival of table-hopping grotesques, not pressed close together as in the cabaret scenes of Harlem Renaissance literature but forever moving apart. It is the "Animal Fair" of the novel's middle chapter (217–36),[8] where people are trivialized as nursery rhymes and song snippets, caught up in private fantasies and ambiguous sexual identities.[9] "Fragmentation," as Dos Passos called it, made New York his symbol for the postwar world. It was simultaneously "marvelous" and "hideous" (quoted in Wagner 1979, 63), as turn-of-the-century Chicago had been, but also incoherent and boundless, megalopolitan.

Dos Passos assumes a hard-boiled attitude toward the present's fragmentation, in the alcoholic irregularity of his personal life as in the rejection of any truth beyond the "animal fair" in his novel. But F. Scott Fitzgerald, even less discreet about the revels that led him and Dos Passos to be caricatured as "'*Enfants Terribles*' of the New York literary world" (Mellow 1984, 162) and "the arch type [*sic*] of what New York wanted" (Fitzgerald [1934] 1945a, 26),[10] mourned the loss of old coherences and hopes. Nostalgia for Old New York did color Fitzgerald's attitudes—toward Wharton, too, whom he admired as "grande dame" of the art world's New York–Paris axis (quoted in Mellow 1984, 204) despite her dismissal of him as simply "awful" when he paid a drunken visit to her Parisian salon in 1925 (Mellow 1984, 253).[11] Just a year younger than Fitzgerald's own mother, Wharton undoubtedly reminded him of the old-family aura of St. Paul, Minnesota, the home base for his otherwise itinerant childhood.[12]

Fitzgerald's fiction presents regional cities of the Midwest and South as private, refined city-towns "where the old families formed a caste" and "everyone was Who's Who to every one else's past" (Fitzgerald 1973, 191; [1920] 1951, 40). He usually presents New York by contrast as a radically new city. Nonetheless the title character of "The Rich Boy" ([1925] 1926, 40) is able to count New York "his city" because "his name had flourished through five generations." When Fitzgerald himself found only a tawdry "Carnival by the Sea" there, he grieved deeply the loss of Old New York (Fitzgerald 1945c, 89–90; cf. Fitzgerald [1918] 1971). He laments the end of this urban dream in his essay "My Lost City" ([1934] 1945a, 25–26), which recounts his youthful infatuation with the city-town's gentility, as well as the economic city's dream of individual success and even the cosmetic glamour of megalopolis. His essay begins with the latter two, which he introduces as the "triumph" symbolized by a ferry-boat approach to the city in 1907 and the "romance" forecast by actresses seen there in 1912. "In time I was to achieve some of both" of these dream "symbols," he writes; "but there was a third symbol that I have lost somewhere, and lost forever." That third dream is the "metropolitan urbanity" for which "the metropolis of 1920" offers "no forum."

The urbane city-town that was symbolized for Fitzgerald by Edmund Wilson's bachelor apartment in 1917, then "lost forever" after the war, involves the same aesthetic refinement and privileged security that Melville's "Paradise of Bachelors" exposes in London's Temple Inns, that Laughlin's *"Just Folks"* rejects in Chicago's Hull-House, that Wharton's *The Age of Innocence* vitiates in Old New York. Unlike these others, however, Fitzgerald offers no critical awareness that the "finer distillation of all that I had come to love at Princeton," the "gentle" music, the "great baracades [sic] of books," and the "safe" fellowship he finds "in Bunny's apartment" (25) are bought at the price of others' poverty and his own removal from familial and civic affairs. He laments its loss with a nostalgia that resists and thus imputes tremendous power to the "hysteria" of megalopolitan disillusion and fragmentation in the late 1920s (32).[13]

In *The Great Gatsby,* it is specifically the period of the war[14] that separates the family-based, orderly city-town of narrator Nick Carroway's Midwestern childhood from megalopolis in New York. Both chronologically and geographically, *The Great Gatsby* consigns the city-town to "the ragged edge of the universe," while the up-to-date, albeit "distorted," excitement of New York swirls at the world's "warm center" (1925, 3, 177–78).[15] The disjunction that matters most in this novel of failed dreams, however, is mythic. In fact, Nick can—and in the end does—return to his Midwestern "city where dwellings are still called through decades by a family's name" (177). But neither he nor Gatsby nor anybody else can relive the "transitory enchanted moment" of discovery "somewhere back in that vast obscurity beyond the city." When the "fresh, green breast of the new world" lay before the Dutch sailors (182), New Amsterdam, Manhattan, and New York all belonged to the "orgiastic future" of timeless potentiality (182). Now they are locked in the "past" that no one can "repeat" (111).

The pastoral vitality, Eden-like belonging, and consequent hope that the Harlem Renaissance found in its neighborhood city all fail New York in *The Great Gatsby*. The novel's symbolic center, "about half way" between suburbs and downtown, even negates the pastoral. Fitzgerald's justly famous wasteland image—a dump stretched out beneath the billboard gaze of Dr. T. J. Eckleburg—represents his controlling, antipastoral metaphor for megalopolis: "This is a valley of ashes—a fantastic farm where ashes grow like wheat into ridges and hills and grotesque gardens; where ashes take the forms of houses and chimneys and rising smoke and, finally, with a transcendent effort, of ash-gray men who move dimly and already crumbling through the powdery air" (Fitzgerald 1925, 23). In the valley of ashes, the city's physical and human refuse disintegrates into the antithesis of the Puritans' organic, communal city on a fruitful hill.

Although Fitzgerald differentiates suburbs from downtown, the disintegration of the valley of ashes rules throughout, in the carelessness of East Egg, the raw vulgarity of downtown, and the hysteria of West Egg. No longer a particular place, the city extends beyond city limits into urbanism as a way of life-in-death. The imagery of urban artificiality derived from the economic city's environment becomes a psychological part of a megalopolis.[16] The despair of the wasteland's "crumbling" people differs little from the cynicism of the wealthy urbanites who attend Gatsby's parties. The list of their names reduces them metaphorically to subhuman plants and animals—Clarence Endive, Ernest Lilly, Newton Orchid, the Leeches, the Fishguards, George Duckweed, Edgar Beaver, the Catlips, Francis Bull—and even dismantled pieces of anatomy and strained gestures—Miss Claudia Hip, S. W. Belcher, the Smirkes, and the Dancies (Fitzgerald 1925, 61–63; cf. Fisher 1928). They are, as has been noted by many critics, grotesques. And socially, they whirl apart in Fitzgerald's boundless "carnival," like the New Yorkers in Dos Passos's "animal fair."[17] Nick Carraway discovers a pervasive uncertainty of relationship at his first New York parties: the Buchanans of East Egg are "old friends whom he scarcely knew at all" (6); in Tom Buchanan and Myrtle Wilson's downtown apartment, nameless people constantly "disappeared, reappeared... lost each other ... [and] found each other a few feet away" (37); and at Jay Gatsby's West Egg mansion, groups "dissolve and form in the same breath" (40). In *The Great Gatsby*, urban society, like the individual psyche and the cityscape, has disintegrated and "cracked-up," as Fitzgerald's own life later did ([1936] 1945b).

Jay Gatsby is an exception to the rule of disintegration, a self-improving descendant of Philadelphia's Ben Franklin and an urban partner to Hopalong Cassidy. But his doomed attempt to "repeat the past" (111) proves that rule's death-dealing power. By titling Gatsby as "great," identifying his "conception of himself" (99) with the Dutch sailors' first view of the New World, and contrasting his "extraordinary gift for hope" (2) to the emptiness of Dr. T. J. Eckleburg's wasteland, Fitzgerald poses his story as an all-out attempt to resurrect the nation's pastoral dream of possibility—the dream whose collapse World War I signaled.[18] Before the war, James Gatz created the idea of Jay Gatsby,[19] then figuratively wedded his self-made manhood to aristocratic Daisy Fay. In postwar New York, the "new world, material without being real" (162), he tries to maintain his dream by erecting an ostentatious mansion to woo his putative bride and denies the intervening years during which Daisy married Tom Buchanan and bore a daughter. Cut off by history from the "fresh green breast of the New World," he sets his sights by the carnival's artificial "green light" on the end of the Buchanans' dock (182). He vainly seeks to realize his transcendent dream with a woman whose voice is "full of money" (120) in a disintegrating world of materialistic consumption. And so he cannot escape the "foul dust that floated in the wake of his dreams" (2). The "ashen, fantastic figure" of George Wilson (162), his lover's husband's lover's husband, the "foul dust" of megalopolis, finally murders him. Whereas Newland Archer loses "the flower of life" when he decides not to act out his love for Ellen Olenska within the rigid caste of Old New York in *The Age of Innocence* (Wharton [1920] 1962, 275), Jay Gatsby loses life itself when he tries to realize his dream in the disintegrating wasteland Fitzgerald paints as New York. In Fitzgerald's view, postwar New York embodies the death of old dreams and kills any new dreamers.

The Great Depression reinforced the changes World War I worked into the urban experience and literature of many privileged white Americans. The depression revealed the Empire City's external *"limits"* (Fitzgerald [1934] 1945a, 32) and the self-destructive power of materialism, making clear that a pervasive mind-set, not external conditions of wealth, sustained megalopolis. Accordingly Nathanael West's New York in *Miss Lonelyhearts* (1933) is, like Crane's, rationally abstracted from sensual experience; like Wharton's, cut off from the past and skeptical—even cynical—about its dreams; like Dos Passos's, cut up into snippets of mass culture; and like Fitzgerald's, a wasteland that kills dreamers as well as dreams. Like these other writers, too, West himself was both genteelly educated and radically alienated. In particular, he was a New Yorker who denied his Jewish birthright. The Semite's capacity to sit "in a cloaca to the eyes" with "brows touch[ing] heaven" (West quoted in Light 1961, 18)—the very capacity of oppressed groups cherished as the root of neighborhood city dreams by writers on the Lower East Side and in Harlem—West rejected.[20] Changing his name from Nathan Weinstein,

West wandered among the literary celebrities of New York, Paris, and Hollywood until he died in a car accident in 1940—just a day after Fitzgerald, the contemporary writer whose work most influenced his own (Martin 1970, 386–88).

For both Fitzgerald and West, cities dominate the physical, social, and psychological character of the United States.[21] Urbanization spans the American continent in their novels, from New York in *The Great Gatsby* and *Miss Lonelyhearts* to Los Angeles in *The Last Tycoon* (1941) and *The Day of the Locust* (1939). Nature perverted by urban artificiality offers no viable physical alternative to the city in either author's fictions. In *The Great Gatsby,* greater New York centers in the valley of ashes, which betrays Gatsby's pastoral dreams. In *Miss Lonelyhearts* ([1933] 1962, 219, 173–74, 212), the remote countryside offers "nothing but death"; a city park is a wasteland of "decay"; and the pastoral myth itself becomes a newspaper cliché, " 'the escape to the soil' bit." Socially and psychologically, too, their fictional characters are trapped and vitiated by artifice. The "ash-gray" nullity and hysteria that negate humanity in *The Great Gatsby* congeal into masses of "dough" "stamped" into conformity in *Miss Lonelyhearts* (169), because West sees the influence of mass media—the newspaper in *Miss Lonelyhearts* and the movies in *The Day of the Locust*—radiating out from the center of megalopolis. By reducing cultural myths to stereotypes that actively pervert any personal dreams and turn them into nightmares, West's urban world comprehends and extends Fitzgerald's. Denied any firm ground in historical or contemporary reality, dreams and all other symbols become arbitrary. In this way West anticipates postmodernism.

Echoing Dos Passos's use of newspaper headlines and layout to epitomize urban fragmentation, *Miss Lonelyhearts* breaks up its structure into short, headlined prose blocks. Its plot is, moreover, a newspaper story. But West's *New York Post-Dispatch* is not a work place[22] so much as a metaphor for profane, one-dimensional meaning. It dramatizes the disintegration of meaningful order, of social communication, of personal identity, and of dreaming itself among its New York readers and writers—and, by extension, throughout the urban United States. As an institution of megalopolis, the *Post-Dispatch* interiorizes the economic city, pursuing "the business of dreams," advertising get-rich-quick schemes, and guaranteeing other forms of self-improvement ([1933] 1962, 198) rather than trading in corn, streetcar lines, or even external consumer goods and entertainments.

The *Post-Dispatch* offers hyped-up headlines and five-column-inch stories as truth. It manipulates readers with stereotypes for human behavior, arbitrarily interpreting a laugh, for instance, as "bitterness" one minute, "sour-grapes," "a broken-heart," or "the devil-may-care," the next (184). It teases rather than satisfies its readers' needs for the guiding, participatory, and multidimensional meanings ascribed to myths by cultural theorists such as Elizabeth Janeway (1971, 7–68). Newsprint formulas move into a vacuum of authority in West's disordered, violent urban world. The desperate public, failed by traditional religion—as well as Anglo-American myths of community, individual success, and technological progress in cities—takes up newspapers in place of Bibles, elevates lonelyhearts columnists into "the priests of twentieth-century America," and prays to the "Miss Lonelyhearts of Miss Lonelyhearts" instead of God. West allows no alternative. When the Miss Lonelyhearts of the *New York Post-Dispatch* "searched the sky for a target" against which to vent his own despair, he found "no angels [or] flaming crosses. . . . Only a newspaper" (173–76).

Miss Lonelyhearts thus constructs a travesty of social communication and self-expression. Letters from readers stereotyped as Sick-of-it-all, Desperate, and Broad Shoulders pass through Miss Lonelyhearts's helpless hands, as do the canned replies that the cynical editor Shrike dictates. There is no dialogue. Miss Lonelyhearts himself, whose newspaper alias masks his gender and personal name,[23] finds it impossible to write what he really wants to say. His correspondents are lost in their clichéd letters, "all of them alike, stamped from the dough of suffering with a heart-shaped cookie knife" (169). Even when people meet face to face, they talk "in headlines" (195). Underlying desperation breaks out only in inchoate violence—finally directed against Miss Lonelyhearts when one of his readers fires off a gun that has been wrapped, appropriately, in newspapers.

The tragedy of Miss Lonelyhearts, however, is not his violent death—presented as a fumbling accident—but his conversion to the newspaper city's blasphemy. Miss Lonelyhearts tries to hold on to his own religious beliefs—and even his nightmares—as dreams that go beyond newspaper stereotypes. He wants to create a meaningful response to the disorder and pain of urban experience. In West's view, as in Fitzgerald's, such dreaming is admirable—more courageous than the bankrupt pastoralism that keeps Miss Lonelyhearts's fiancée ignorant of "city troubles" (228), more hopeful than the cynicism that keeps Shrike in charge of "this unbelieving age" (211). But when Miss Lonelyhearts confronts the neediness of his readers Faye and Peter Doyle in the flesh, he succumbs to the illusion of authority granted him by the newspaper. Once he begins to play the priest that

Shrike has declared him to be, Miss Lonelyhearts forgets the difference between manufactured stereotype imposed from without and personal or communal vision created from within. He identifies himself as the God of his religious dreams and groups Peter Doyle with "Desperate, Harold S., Catholic-mother, Broken-hearted, Broad-shoulders, Sick-of-it-all, Disillusioned-with-tubercular-husband" (246–47). His delusion propels him toward his death.

Before he gives in to delusion, Miss Lonelyhearts reflects, "although dreams were once powerful, they have been made puerile by the movies, radio and newspapers. Among many betrayals, this one is the worst" (221). West's novel dramatizes this "worst" megalopitan betrayal of dreams and dreaming. Not only is Miss Lonelyhearts prevented from enacting his own dreams—entrapped (like Newland Archer in *The Age of Innocence*) in dreams of others' choosing, then killed (like Jay Gatsby) by one of the city's despairing grotesques. Even more devastating, his dreams themselves are perverted by the stereotyped illusions of "this unbelieving age."

Literature's megalopolis offers no escape from despair. "The terrible thing about having New York go stale on you is that there's nowhere else," says a character in *Manhattan Transfer* ([1925] 1953, 220); "it's the top of the world. All we can do is go round and round in a squirrel cage." Dos Passos himself retreated from this despairing view by turning back to the image of the economic city in the 1930s. The economic explanation for despair that Jimmy Herf cannot buy in *Manhattan Transfer* is offered as truth in Dos Passos's *The Big Money* (1936), the final volume in his comprehensive documentary trilogy, *U.S.A.* Even earlier, Wharton retreated to the image of the city-town in her four *Old New York* novelettes (1924), indulging the nostalgia she eschewed in *The Age of Innocence*. Perhaps because they turned their minds away from megalopolis, Dos Passos and Wharton managed to continue to work and live into their seventies. Crane, on the other hand, drowned in a despair that undermined his Whitmanian ambitions, killed himself at age thirty-three. Fitzgerald and West died at forty-four and thirty-seven respectively—convinced that there was no escape from megalopolis for them in life.

But first Fitzgerald and West pursued the megalopitan logic its final miles, to the western edge of the "squirrel cage"—Hollywood. They were not alone. Begun as a temporary "colony" of Anglo and Jewish New Yorkers, Hollywood became the permanent "base" of a national entertainment "industry" in the 1920s. Still "financed by New York" in 1926, the movies became the nation's fifth largest industry, a world famous "carnival" of studios, stars, and scandals (McWilliams 1946, 331–33; Starr 1985, 313–14). White authors who had haunted Thirteenth Street rushed off to "Tinsel Town" during the Great Depression. These were often last-ditch moves. West was "desperate, impoverished, and bewildered.... often sick and alone" during his first year there (Martin 1970, 266). Fitzgerald was at the nadir of his own now sodden career and deeply cynical about the motives of Hollywood's new migrants. "All gold rushes are essentially negative," he wrote in a letter three months before his death (14 Sept. 1940 to Gerald Murphy, quoted in Mellow 1984, 481).

In Fitzgerald's terms and from West's perspective, too, Hollywood aimed not at real success, but at mass illusions of glamour, and its glamour was broadcast to define reality for the nation. As their literary contemporary Leo Rosten (1959, 2142) explained, Hollywood gained such primacy because its "colony of producers, writers, actors, [and] technicians" were "reported to the world in greater detail than any other single group in the world, with the possible exception of Washingtonists." For Fitzgerald and West, Hollywood was the production outpost of megalopolitan illusions, the West Coast sunset land of the national dream, the last stop before death. "Isn't Hollywood a dump—in the human sense of the word?" Fitzgerald asked (29 July 1940 letter to Alice Richardson, quoted in Mellow 1984, 471). "A dream dump," West replied in *The Day of the Locust* ([1939] 1962, 97).

In describing the genre of Hollywood fiction in the 1930s, Walter Wells (1973, 12–13, 104, 111) has listed its defining characteristics as the "overriding... theme of dissolution," the "death of the Great American Dream," and "the persistent confusion between reality and illusion." These are telltale signs of literature's megalopolis, and nowhere are these themes more concentrated than in *The Day of the Locust*. On movie sets and even in remote canyons, "neon" colors paint the "sterile" ground, while reflected city lights make the sky "like a batik parasol" at night (3, 71–72). On movie sets and in Hollywood's residential districts, a "monstrous" extravaganza of building styles from around the world constructs a prototype for postmodern architecture—"Mexican ranch houses, Samoan huts, Mediterranean villas, Egyptian and Japanese temples, Swiss chalets, Tudor cottages, and every possible combination of these styles" (132). Just as artificial, moreover, the people are grotesques in every sense of the word. They include a vaudevillean salesman who puts on acts "like a mechanical toy" gone haywire (44), a five-year-old boy who performs bump-and-grind routines in drag, a movie/drugstore/rodeo/real cowboy, a dwarf who spews obscenities, and a midwestern "automaton" whose "enormous hands" crawl around like untamed animals (31).

All this adds up to a cheat. Hollywood's reduction of human expression to arbitrary forms in West's novel is epitomized by a whore-goddess who tells come-on stories accompanied by "pure" gestures (131). Fay Greener's movements have no illustrative content and bear no relationship to the stories she tells. Nor do her words have any personal content; they are stories from trade papers and fan magazines and legends that she shuffles like "a pack of cards" (60). In "the final dumping ground" of illusory dreams (97), "any dream was better than no dream," as Faye herself says (60). Her illusions command her admirers' desperate attention just as Hollywood's dream-making seduces the nation's sea-to-sea megalopolis and abuses its license. Cinematic images of catastrophe and heroism, violence and passion, make everyday life seem monotonous and thus reduce formerly distinct towns to suburbs of Hollywood's domain. Conversely, they cover up megalopolitans' emptiness with fake inflated dreams, including an impossible promise of some vaguely glamorous tomorrow. The most desperate believers are the "people who come to California to die" (3, 27, 78, 65), without ever finding comfort in dreams whose significance is that they are illusions. Profound spiritual hunger leads to riot as the climax of megalopolis in *The Day of the Locust*.

Art provides no buffer against violence and despair, West insists. His central character, Tod Hackett, is an apocalyptic painter and a film studio hack. His name suggests the death and fakery that he exposes in Hollywood yet becomes a part of. His script-writing contributes to Hollywood's cheat, while his great work-in-progress, *The Burning of Los Angeles,* foreshadows its apocalypse. He himself is injured in the riot at the end of the novel and carried away mimicking an ambulance siren's scream. He is not saved through his understanding that the "people who come to California to die" are only the most obvious victims of mass deception, that they will be only the first Americans to explode in "civil war" against the tyranny of illusion (78). For him, such destruction is the only undeceptive vision megalopolis allows. None of the despairing literature of the Lost Generation offers any hope instead.

6

The Urban Home of the Harlem Renaissance

Physically uprooted, socially rejected, and culturally neglected, the African-American creators of the Harlem Renaissance had a stronger claim to "lost" status than the Lost Generation. They, too, were an extremely mobile crew. Nonetheless, they felt joined, not estranged, by their wanderings, because they were part of the great migration of black people to the urban Northeast around World War I. Collectively, they developed a hopeful vision of an urban home that was at once an organic place, a birthright community, and a cultural aspiration (Bremer 1990; cf. hooks 1990, 46–47). In all three of these dimensions, the vitality of their vision reached out across continents, through oppression. Harlem, New York, their capital city within a city, marked its center. Whether or not they happened to be living there at any particular time, they regarded Harlem as their primary, symbolic home. They tested the strengths and limits of its home spirit in their works as in their lives.

To this end, young Langston Hughes came from Cleveland via Mexico City in 1921 to add his poetry to Harlem's Jazz Age rhythms. That same year, Charles S. Johnson arrived from Chicago to break ground for the Urban League's new magazine, *Opportunity,* and Jamaican Claude McKay returned from a London sojourn to prepare *Harlem Shadows* (1922) proclaiming the locus of a new renaissance in its title. Like most of their colleagues, these three men came to Harlem only after extensive urban experience elsewhere. W. E. B. Du Bois had already arrived from the faculty of Atlanta University, Jessie Fauset from Philadelphia, James Weldon Johnson and Walter White from Jacksonville and Atlanta respectively, all to staff the NAACP and its *Crisis* magazine. After 1921, a steady stream of city-bred young people kept coming. Arna Bontemps from Los Angeles, Nella Larsen from Chicago, Rudolph Fisher from Washington, D.C., Dorothy West and Helene Johnson from Boston. Those who grew up in small towns had lived in other major cities before moving to New York: Idaho's Wallace Thurman worked with Arna Bontemps in the Los Angeles post office; Eatonville, Florida's Zora Neale Hurston came to New York from service as a manicurist in Washington, D.C. In fact, Hurston was the only Harlem Renaissance writer raised in the rural folk traditions that several sought to tap. None came fresh from farms to the big city. Cosmopolitan and on the move, they were urban wanderers in need of a home.

However, the best publicized "New Negro" leaders were more often away than in Harlem during the 1920s.[1] Claude McKay took off in 1922 for a twelve-year vagabondage through major cities of Europe and Africa. Rudolph Fisher did not move to Harlem from the Washington, D.C., annex of the renaissance until four years later. Nella Larsen moved uptown only in 1927 and was off to Europe in 1930. Loyal Langston Hughes eventually made his permanent home in Harlem, but during the 1920s he came only for weekends, vacations, and special occasions, spending most of his time at sea or in college. Even Countee Cullen, the only renaissance leader to list New York (falsely) as his birthplace—he had indeed been raised there (Borders 1975, 4ff.)—was away four of the five years between 1925 and 1930, at Harvard, then in Paris. The young "Niggerati," as Hurston dubbed them, were often off at college, and so many flocked to Paris each summer that Alain Locke once called it a "transplanted Harlem" (2 Sept. 1926 letter to Langston Hughes, Hughes Papers).

Even for the older writers, who were also political organizers, editors, and its most stable residents, Harlem was a cultural mecca for a rather brief time. Charles S. Johnson started the migratory tide turning toward southern colleges in 1928 after only seven years in New York; James Weldon Johnson, Du Bois, Arthur Schomburg, Bontemps, and Larsen followed suit—mostly to Fisk University in Nashville. Nearly all, young and old alike, had moved on by 1932, as the depression stripped away Jazz Age excess to expose Harlem's underlying poverty (Osofsky 1966).

Physical distance seems to have had little impact on their sense of Harlem as home, however. James Weldon Johnson considered himself a

New Yorker by a "blood tie" because his "father and mother first met in this city" and because he first "learned to walk and began to talk" on a visit there, he explained in a 1931 farewell speech (2). In residence at Fisk thereafter until his death, he still was enough a part of Harlem to be president of the League of Negro Writers that Claude McKay, Gwendolyn Bennett, and others who had been "in the thick of the Harlem Renaissance" organized there in the mid-1930s (McKay 8 Aug. 1935 letter to Johnson, in Johnson Papers). A writer's sense of Harlem as a home to recall or go to or aspire toward could even grow with distance. McKay published his superb 1928 novel, *Home to Harlem,* from abroad, then wrote Hughes in 1930, "I am thinking of coming home next fall or winter.... [although] I am really a poet without a country" (30 August, Hughes Papers).

Generally, the writers' wanderlust reinforced their identification with Harlem as the hub of a dynamic world. Their historical works describe settlement of that neighborhood-city by African Americans as a mass movement through the city streets: after "the first apartment house [was] rented to colored tenants ... in 134th Street near Fifth Avenue," "the Aframericans pushed forward from Fifth towards Seventh Avenue." Like the proud black soldiers of the 369th Infantry regiment who marched through New York in 1919, Harlem's new residents were "an army" that eventually pressed "across the Lenox Avenue dead-line" at the end of World War I, "sweeping up" from 145th Street to 164th and down from 125th Street to 110th by the end of the depression, as James Weldon Johnson's *Black Manhattan* ([1930] 1958, 145–49) and McKay's derivative *Harlem: Negro Metropolis* (1940, 17–22) together tell the story.

Harlem was indeed the goal of many African-American migrants in the 1910s and 1920s. By 1930, its two square miles had collected nearly 225,000 residents—over two-thirds of New York's African-American population—having nearly quadrupled itself since 1910 (Wirtz 1988, 14). Because Manhattan's economy was trade and service oriented (C. S. Johnson 1925, 279), moreover, it did not draw the predominantly rural, unskilled African Americans who migrated to other northern cities for industrial jobs. The new Harlemites came from southeastern seaboard cities more than from the rural South and were often cosmopolitan indeed. One-fourth came from the Caribbean, like McKay, Eric Walrond, and Arthur Schomburg (J. W. Johnson [1930] 1958, 14–53; C. S. Johnson 1925, 279).

Harlem's streets and dynamic movement made it a busy center for human association, institutional continuity, and cultural power for the renaissance writers. They spoke of themselves as the "*Negro* Renaissance," and their careers were profoundly connected with the people of Harlem despite their wanderings. In particular, the Harlem Renaissance grew out of two forms of collective urban activity requiring large numbers of people: politics and theater. During the decade leading to war in 1917, the NAACP and the Urban League both organized and headquartered themselves in New York, and in 1921, an international convention of Marcus Garvey's Universal Negro Improvement Association drew attention to Harlem's political ground. In that watershed year, Florence Mills and *Shuffle Along* celebrated black theater's hard-won arrival on Broadway—theater by and for African Americans having moved uptown to Harlem during the previous decade (Johnson [1930] 1958, 126-44, 170-81). Thus the renaissance grounded itself in the root meanings of cities (Steiner 1973, 3) and dramatized Harlem's special power to gather African Americans and broadcast their achievements to the nation. The theater and politics of Harlem constituted the Jazz Age image that drew the younger writers, led by Langston Hughes.[2]

Socially, literary life in Harlem was an intensely collective affair, inextricably mixed with politics and entertainment. The "younger generation" was first gathered and labeled as such at a 1924 dinner hosted by *Opportunity* magazine's Charles S. Johnson. The Civic Club dinner was attended by race and welfare leaders and established literary critics—both black and white (Van Doren 1924)—to honor the young Harlem Writers' Guild and its first New York novel, Jessie Fauset's *There Is Confusion* (1924). It spurred the famous special issue of the *Survey Graphic* that became *The New Negro* (1925), which epitomized the Harlem Renaissance as "a communal project," as critic Houston Baker (1987, 77) confirms the point. Countee Cullen recognized the young people's communal debt to the older generation by reciting "The Fledgling to the Eagle" at a Du Bois dinner a month after the *Opportunity* affair. Whether or not one was physically present, being named at one of the *Opportunity* or *Crisis* dinners held annually to award literary prizes—and to consolidate political ground—effectively defined membership in the Harlem Renaissance.[3]

The young and old, black and white, guest lists for such affairs also exemplified the double patronage system that embedded Harlem's literary life (like that of the Chicago women) in social dependencies and constraints. Within the black community, the small group of organizational gatekeepers who spoke for "our people"—often enough for the younger blacks to mimic the phrase—also controlled the few established channels for communication among educated blacks and their white supporters in New York City and nationwide. These "race leaders" were genuinely helpful in promoting the works and maintaining the social ties—even publishing the gossip—of the young renaissance writers on the move. But their competing enterprises and beliefs also represented political constraints, against which Hughes, Hurston, Thurman, and Douglas rebelled in 1926 by putting out their own magazine, *Fire!!,* explicitly dedicated to artistic inspiration unlimited by politics.[4]

These four were also deeply beholden to Harlem's more infamous white patrons. Specifically, all were the financial "godchildren" of Caroline (Mrs. R. Osgood) Mason, who was, in turn, advised by Alain Locke, the black academic founder of *The New Negro* and Washington, D.C.'s self-proclaimed "midwife" to the renaissance.[5] Similarly, the NAACP's Walter White led Hughes to white writer Carl Van Vechten; and it was Van Vechten, not White, who successfully recommended Hughes's *The Weary Blues* to their mutual publisher, Alfred Knopf. Van Vechten secured Knopf's publication of other work by African Americans, too, including two of the best renaissance novels set in New York, Rudolph Fisher's *The Walls of Jericho* (1928) and Nella Larsen's *Quicksand* (1928), as well as the 1927 reissue of James Weldon Johnson's foundational work, *The Autobiography of an Ex-Coloured Man* (1912). Although Van Vechten took pains to make clear that the originality of their talent was the cause, not the result, of his interest, he was indeed "an open sesame" for the numerous Harlem Renaissance writers he favored (Fauset n.d. letter to Hughes, Hughes Papers).

Nathan Huggins (1971, 85) has most forcefully articulated the common perception that Harlem's literature "might have been more honest" without its white patrons. The distinction between personal honesty and social communication is, however, not so simple, since self-expression and social interaction feed each other. Besides, the younger renaissance writers probably felt no less constrained by the leaders of their own race, to whom they were inextricably bound, than by their white patrons. They expressed their feelings toward both in filial metaphors with highly mixed emotions. Most white patrons, moreover, offered support on more general, less personally intimate and importunate ground—underwriting organizational activities, for example. Nonetheless, all white support—and its receipt—was likely crosscut by ambivalence. Especially poignant was the older race leaders' dependence on whites to buttress their own patronage powers. For the renaissance was, like Harlem itself, ultimately dependent on white financing and, for a place in the national scene, on white contacts.

Such contacts inevitably linked Harlem literary life with entertainment. Van Vechten, the best known white guest and host of parties dedicated to interracial celebrity, promoted Harlem's cabaret industry by sharing his passport to Harlem low life with other white visitors—often expecting the company of his black friends on excursions into slumming and sensationalism. The wealthiest black Harlemites who supported the writers were also associated with the entertainment scene: a numbers king financed the *Opportunity* contests; the head of a beauty shop empire named her famous Harlem salon after Countee Cullen's "Dark Tower" column in *Opportunity*; and a cabaret owner named his club for Gwendolyn Bennett's "Ebony Flute" column and decorated it with Aaron Douglas murals.

Although James Weldon Johnson thanked Carl Van Vechten for a "cabaret jaunt" (24 May 1926 letter, Van Vechten Correspondence) and joked that he should have Van Vechten introduce him to Harlem some day (19 June 1930 letter, Van Vechten Correspondence), ignorance of the Prohibition cabarets such as Johnson implied was hardly possible with NAACP balls at the Savoy and an NAACP party at the Club Ebony. Although young Countee Cullen apparently managed to write his *Poetry* prize-winning cabaret poem "Threnody" (1925) without ever visiting a cabaret, his closest friends finally supplied his lack with a graduation excursion led by librarian Regina Anderson (Andrews) and *Opportunity* secretary Ethel Ray (Nance). These roommates and other Harlem Renaissance women were best known as hostesses of parties at their own apartments (Hull 1987, 5–6, 11–12). As women, they were limited in their enjoyment of the cabarets by vulnerability to the virulent stereotype of black female promiscuity, which Paula Giddings (1985, esp. 35, 85–89) has analyzed so well. Nonetheless, attending *Opportunity* banquets took them to the cabaret spots, and many of the people they met at Fauset's literary salons also showed up at Thurman's raucous rent parties—in the same apartment that housed *Fire!!* No wonder many Harlem Renaissance writers complained about the "hectic" city life (e.g., Wallace Thurman 17 May 1928 letter to Harold Jackman, Thurman Collection).

Harlem's endless mix of work and play, of high culture and low life, points to another way in which the renaissance writers were deeply involved with the people of Harlem at large. There were, after all, only so many places for African Americans to congregate at work, play, or rest during Jim Crow rule, even in the North. And no African American, no matter how educated, was ever far beyond the menial labor and poverty of Harlem's vast working class. True, among the established leaders, James Weldon Johnson had become a United States diplomat and Du Bois had gained eminence as a scholar. And true, the younger writers had access to privately funded college stipends, professional work in publishing, librarianships, and teaching—all part of the intelligentsia's bookish world. But Claude McKay worked as a railroad steward while he wrote the clarion poem for the New Negro, "If We Must Die" (1919); Hughes was waiting on tables—having just returned from one of his several stints as a messboy at sea—when *The Weary Blues* (1925) was going to press; Cullen met the genteel Yolande Du Bois while he was a busboy at a resort she visited; and Hurston was a maid as well as a manicurist in Washington, D.C., then a popular novelist's secretary and chauffeur in New York. Whether menial or professional, whether "in service" downtown or "entertaining" uptown, most of Harlem's jobs depended on the discretionary spending habits of the wealthy. Although writers were near the center of Harlem's new black bourgeoisie, their status was deeply confused by their close identification with both servants and playmates of the wealthy and the white.[6]

Like its physical dynamism, Harlem's social life was the result of its unique cultural status as the "Negro Capital" or "Mecca" or "Promised Land." More than any other city, it symbolized black cultural aspirations, and its writers contributed to this meaning. Their poetry, in particular, was cited to prove that contemporary African Americans could achieve the highest forms of civilization. Probably for that reason, poetry was and still is considered the literary core of the Harlem Renaissance. But that neglects a significant body of Harlem fiction grappling with its ghettoized complexities; histories and memoirs reflecting the writers' self-consciousness about their culture-making;[7] dramas playing to local theatrical strengths; and journalistic pieces reaching a mass audience.[8] For the Harlem Renaissance was a civic as well as an aesthetic moment, "inscrib[ing] Afro-American modernity in mass, urban, national, and international terms" (Baker 1987, 83).[9] Indeed its aesthetic achievements have specifically civic strengths and limitations.

Because Harlem was self-conscious about its status as the "Negro Capital"—as both the acme and unofficial government of African-American civilization—whatever literature African Americans published was subjected to heated debate there on its political as well as aesthetic merits. Writers involved in Harlem's social circles were especially aware of the terms of such debate, which inevitably turned on the question of whether or not a work represented "The Race" in two senses (cf. Carby 1987, 164): Could it stand as a respectable representative expressing "the best that has been known and said" by African Americans, in terms likely to win white support? And could it put forth a compelling representation of the common core of black experience, its vitality as well as its harsh and unjust circumstances?

Culturally, then, Harlem imposed exceptionally difficult demands on its writers, and these expectations were contradictory at base. Insofar as Hughes's jazz poems, for example, represented the pinnacle of aesthetic innovation, their lowlife subject matter and form earned him dismissal as "the poet low-rate of Harlem" (1927 *Chicago Whip*, quoted in Hughes 1940, 266). Insofar as his poems effectively represented the vitality of black folk culture during the 1920s, they deflected attention from the structural inequities on which it did its riffs (cf. Baker 1984, 130). Harlem's dual patronage system reinforced the contradictory cultural expectations; black patron-leaders of the renaissance insisted on respectability in the literature they wrote and promoted while their white counterparts often called for the primitive. Only protest fiction was suspect on both fronts, and perhaps as a result, its unequivocal directness is only occasionally voiced in Harlem Renaissance writing.

The aesthetic recognition of the Harlem writers depended in large part, moreover, on their ability to display to Americans at large the "fresh, unused material" that white Carl Van Vechten's *Nigger Heaven* (1926, 222) so explicitly promoted—including new as well as long ignored and previously stereotyped features of African-American culture. Because they could not assume even an elementary level of black cultural literacy on the part of their nonblack audience, they had to explain what they sought to invoke. Often they did so in advance, Hughes prefacing *Fine Clothes to the Jew* (1929, xiii) with "A Note on Blues," for example. Thurman and his white collaborator, William Jourdain Rapp, likewise included a glossary of "Harlemese" on the playbills for their 1929 *Harlem,* which they promoted as an accurate representation of the "Real Harlem" (e.g., 3 Mar. 1929 *New York World* clipping, Thurman Collection). Appended glossaries became commonplace in both black and white novels about Harlem (e.g., Fisher 1928, 295–307; Van Vechten 1926, 285–86; Bodenheim 1930, 279–80). It was risky, however, to insert explanatory asides and referential portraits. In novels designed to express communal life, such documentation tends toward self-conscious awkwardness and superficiality, as in Thurman's *Infants of Spring* (1932). The "Niggerati" even objected that Fisher's *The Walls of Jericho* (1928) was "too much surface" (Hughes 13 Sept. 1928 letter to McKay, McKay Papers), although the novel's sly portraits and witty glossary effectively contribute to its focus on masquerade. Hurston successfully transforms code-switching into aesthetic play in her delightfully slangy, outrageously Biblical "Book of Harlem" (1925–27),[10] but it remains unpublished.

In any event, and even when absent physically, the Harlem Renaissance writers were on the spot to represent the race in the "Negro Capital" of the country. They had good reason, then, to understand Harlem experience—their own and their fictional characters'—as symbolic, resonant, typifying. Hughes's 1940 autobiography presents as a mythic moment his own arrival in Harlem from Latin America at age nineteen:

> At every [subway] station I kept watching for the sign: 135TH STREET. When I saw it, I held my breath. I came out onto the platform with two heavy bags and looked around. It was still early morning and people were going to work. Hundreds of colored people! I wanted to shake hands with them, speak to them. I hadn't seen any colored people for so long—that is, any Negro colored people.
>
> I went up the steps and out into the bright September sunlight. Harlem! I stood there, dropped my bags, took a deep breath and felt happy again. (81)

As a new home place—signified by 135th Street and already known to his imagination—Harlem represented the vitalizing *raison d'être* of Hughes's travels. He viewed it as his birthright community—embodied in "Hundreds of colored people!" Hughes expected Harlem to welcome him, as its leaders already had by publishing "The Negro Speaks of Rivers" earlier that year, as proof that a "younger generation" of poets had arrived to assure the people's future (Bontemps 1972, 2–3ff.). Thus Harlem, with its Jazz Age promises of fame, stood as a powerful symbol for his and the people's cultural aspirations.

The mythic terms of Hughes's 1940 retrospective derive from a pattern established in Harlem Renaissance fiction and poetry during the 1920s. It is epitomized by the opening paragraphs of Rudolph Fisher's "City of Refuge," which was first published to the nation in *Atlantic Monthly* in 1925 then immediately reprinted in *The New Negro* as yet more proof of black America's achievement:

> Confronted suddenly by daylight, King Solomon Gillis stood dazed and blinking. The railroad station, the long, white-walled corridor, the impassible slot-machine, the terrifying subway train—he felt as if he had been caught up in the jaws of a steam-shovel, jammed together with other helpless lumps of dirt, swept blindly along for a time, and at last abruptly dumped.... Jonah emerging from the whale.
> Clean air, blue sky, bright sunlight.
> Gillis set down his tan-cardboard extension-case and wiped his black, shining brow. Then slowly, spreadingly, he grinned at what he saw: Negroes at every turn; up and down Lenox Avenue, up and down One Hundred and Thirty-fifth Street.... There was assuredly no doubt of his whereabouts. This was Negro Harlem. (57–58)

Reminiscent of the railroad entry scenes of standard Chicago novels, the mythic Harlem arrival is nonetheless different in almost every way. It marks the black person's deliverance from the "white-walled" subway world's Anglo and technological domination into what Fisher himself called blacks' "promised land" (letter to Carl Van Vechten, Van Vechten Correspondence). Harlem's physical reality is life giving: "Clean air, blue sky, bright sunlight." Dynamic, it opens out along its streets—"up and down Lenox Avenue, up and down One Hundred and Thirty-fifth Street"—offering a social "refuge" to which the African-American newcomer belongs by birth: "Negroes at every turn." Although its social familiarity can prove dangerous—as it does in this case in the person of a trickster from King Solomon Gillis's southern hometown—it also provokes growing awareness and assertive self-expression. For despite all its limits, this symbolizes the height of African-American experience: "This was Negro Harlem."

Hughes's autobiographical and Fisher's fictional accounts of arrival both bear the earmarks of renaissance Harlem's self-portrait: physical vitality in city streets, social belonging despite danger, and cultural promise. These elements recur over and over in Harlem Renaissance literature. Harlem writers used them within a framework of urban life that incorporates pastoral values, to create their composite structure for Harlem as home.

Within that framework, Fisher's King Solomon Gillis is unusual in fitting the stereotype of the rural southerner lost in the city. Most of the newcomers in Harlem Renaissance fiction move through a world of cities, and the subway that often delivers them—like Gillis—to Harlem is only the last leg of a long journey. In Wallace Thurman's *The Blacker the Berry* (1929), lonely Emma Lou Morgan's journey to Harlem traces her author's own journey—from Boise, Idaho, via Los Angeles, to New York. No less than the novels of men, those of Harlem Renaissance women portray mobile urbanites—like themselves in this regard and in contrast to the residential lives and novels of turn-of-the-century white women in Chicago. Philadelphia-bred Jessie Fauset's fictional families come to New York from Richmond and Philadelphia in *There Is Confusion* (1924) and *Plum Bun* (1929). Both the protagonist and antagonist in Nella Larsen's *Passing* (1929) come from Chicago, the birthplace of their author, as does her fictional counterpart, Helga Crane, in *Quicksand* (1928).

Harlem is continuous with other cities, although fictional characters often think it represents a break from the past. In *Flight* (1926, 209), for example, Walter White's heroine thinks of her string of urban residences—in New Orleans, Atlanta, Philadelphia, New York's Washington Square, then Harlem—as "one of those Harlem apartments... with no hall and with each room opening into the next one. Railroad flats, she had heard them called. She felt that she was always... opening and closing behind her, never to be reopened, the door of the next cubicle." But despite Mimi Daquin's attempts at "flight," her Atlanta past catches up to her in New York. In novels by Fauset and Larsen, intimates from other times and places crop up on New York's buses, at railroad stations, in front of department stores, even at private parties. James Weldon Johnson's anonymous narrator in *The Autobiography of an Ex-Coloured Man* ([1912] 1927, 3, 199) was only the first of many black characters to find that trying to forge a new life in New York—especially trying to pass as white—is "playing with fire," a "serious" gamble (3, 199), and "dangerous," according to *Passing*'s Irene Redfield (Larsen 1929, 117–18), especially at the center of black America where one constantly risks being discovered. Because black "social circles are connected throughout the country," as Johnson's ex-colored man demonstrates (82), it is hard to escape one's past but easy to establish a valued sense of belonging in a new city, since "a person in good standing in one city is readily accepted in another."

Not only communal ties but common racist restrictions limit social mobility and maintain the urban network underlying geographical mobility in Harlem Renaissance literature. "Brass Spitoons" (1929, 28–29), the poem Hughes wished he had used for the title of his second book, *Fine*

Clothes to the Jew (1940, 264), opens with a traveler's itinerary of various cities, held together by a repeated command:

> Clean the spitoons, boy.
>   Detroit,
>   Chicago,
>   Atlantic City,
>   Palm Beach.
> Clean the spitoons.

Whether in Detroit, Chicago, Atlantic City, Palm Beach—or New York—"boy" will find the same commands, even the same dirt, of beck-and-call service:

> The steam in hotel kitchens,
> And the smoke in hotel lobbies,
> And the slime in hotel spitoons:
> Part of my life.

Wherever he is his social "place" remains the same, and his material success depends on his response to the command that punctuates the rest of the poem: "Hey, boy!... / Hey, boy!... / Hey, boy!... / Hey, boy!... / Com' mere, boy!"[11]

Nevertheless, the black network of social ties is a source of expansive strength in numbers, centered in the congestion of Harlem but also linked to other cities. Like the continuities in residential novels based in Chicago, it is not limited to cities. It even expands beyond the United States. African-American writers come to envision Third World oppression as connective, linking Harlem, for example, to the ambiguously fertile "garbage dump" of a Caribbean *favella* in James Baldwin's *If Beale Street Could Talk* (1974, 200). Hughes's wartime "Broadcast to the West Indies" (in 23 July 1943 letter to McKay, McKay Papers) beams greetings from "Radio Station: Harlem" to Jamaica, Haiti, Cuba, Panama, St. Kitts, and the Bahamas, then to "All you islands and all you lands":

> I, Harlem,
> Speak to you!
>
> I, Harlem,
> Island, too
>   In the great sea of this day's turmoil.

>...........................
> Island within an island, but not alone.

Hughes's poem lists what these places share: imposed "Suffering," "Domination," and "Segregation" but also the organic vitality of "your people, your fruit, / Your sunrise and your song." Oppression from without and vitality from within knit these supposed islands together—Harlem at their expressive center.

During the renaissance years, it was the Jamaica-born poet Claude McKay to whom Hughes sent his later "Broadcast," who most fully realized the simultaneously cosmopolitan and pastoral dimensions of this vision. His best-selling novel, *Home to Harlem* (1928), achieved the profound union toward which the Harlem Renaissance labored: the embrace of folkish, organic, even rural culture in a city-centered cosmopolitanism. But McKay's work and life show just how difficult this ambitious, often inchoate, project could be. The novel flew in the face of pastoral tradition, which intertwined with personal memory for McKay more than for any other Harlem author and dominated his first renaissance poems. Having been born in the Jamaican hills and raised there until his mother's death, McKay repeatedly equates Jamaica with tropical nature and maternal home in his early poems (e.g., "Flame Heart," 1920, 30; 1922, 9). Having come to the United States as an "alien guest" and having worked out of New York in the segregated ranks of railroad stewards ("The City's Love," 1922, 16), he equates the United States with urban technology and political exclusion. The very titles of his first books of poetry clearly implicate Harlem in this rural/urban split: *Spring in New Hampshire* (1920) and *Harlem Shadows* (1922).

"When Dawn Comes to the City" (1922, 16) could even stand as a lesson book example of the pastoral. It typifies the conventional content of McKay's many pastoral poems, although it is much freer in its rhythms than most. Its close-cropped lines on "grumbling ... rumbling" city traffic and the "cold ... dark" urbanites who "shuffle" to work at "dawn in New York" contrast unappealingly with the entrancing repetitions of the lush, nostalgic lines recalling his home on "the island of the sea / In the heart of the island of the sea," where

> ... the shaggy Nannie goat is calling, calling, calling
> From her little trampled corner of the long wide lea
> That stretches to the waters of the hill-stream falling
> Sheer upon the flat rocks joyously!

>   There, oh there! on the island of the sea,
>   There I would be at dawn.

In a few of his early poems, McKay breaks out of such pastoral contrasts and points toward images of organic urban vitality. In "The Tropics in New York," published in both *Spring in New Hampshire* (1920, 26) and *Harlem Shadows* (1922, 8), for example, McKay finds a tropical home *within* the city,[12] in a street-side fruit display:

>   Bananas ripe and green, and ginger-root,
>   Cocoa in pods and alligator pears,
>   And tangerines and mangoes and grape fruit,
>   Fit for the highest prize at parish fairs,
>
>   Set in the window, bringing memories. . . .

Spilling over into the second stanza, this city harvest gathers together the most exotic fruits of country life. Its mouth-watering catalogue is far more compelling, even more fertile, than the "nun-like hills" where the fruits were raised and toward which the poet assumes a conventional posture of pastoral loss in the end: "I turned aside and bowed my head and wept." When McKay frees New York from direct contrast to rural settings in his early protest poems, the poet gains energy from the city—albeit energy of a decidedly negative sort. "The White City" (1922, 23) is typical; it attributes to the nation's urban power the "dark Passion" of an organic, hate-filled sexuality. Arousing the poet's sexualized hatred in turn, it transforms him from a "skeleton" into a "vital" being.[13]

Clearly, however, the pastoral convention of urban alienation stands at the center of McKay's early city poems. Even in the black domain of uptown Harlem, the poet, like the prostitutes in "Harlem Shadows," goes "wandering from street to street" (1920, 32; cf. 1922, 22).[14] When a cabaret performer's graceful body recalls "a proudly-swaying palm" in his widely anthologized poem "Harlem Dancer" (1920, 33; 1922, 42), McKay is quick to insist that her "self was not in that strange place." It is a major shift when his best-selling novel, *Home to Harlem* (1928), realizes a sense of communal belonging, as well as natural vitality, in Harlem.

What made it possible for this novel to heal the powerful pastoral split between McKay's urban surroundings and his rural longings there? In part, the answer lies in the novel's title and the nostalgic sense of belonging with which renaissance writers generally viewed Harlem from afar as home. During his years abroad, McKay learned to distinguish his relationship to Harlem from his relationship to New York and to see Harlem, no less than rural Jamaica, as his home. He did so by identifying white New York, but not black Harlem, with European cities (to which many U.S. authors before the Civil War also attributed negative images of urbanization). Meeting the face of "an iceberg" in the "cold white city" of London during his earliest experiences abroad in 1919–20, McKay longed for the "refuge" of a U.S. city's black belt (1937, 304). Even the Russian and African cities he visited seemed lifeless to him and unable to arouse passion in those they oppressed, or in McKay himself, during his next twelve years abroad. So the group of twenty-one urban poems that he collected from his travels under the heading "Cities" (1922–34?)[15] depicts the Old World's colonial cities as splendid but dead. Like "mighty... fortressed" New York, Cadiz was a "jeweled sceptor" and Berlin a "granite pile," but the oppressed colonials there and in other cities offered their conquerors only the dead "tribute" of "broken" and "fettered" "ruins" ("The White City," "Cadiz," "Berlin," "Tetuan," "Tanger," "Marrakesh" in 1922–34?). McKay learned emotional distance from them. Despite his claim in the title poem of his "Cities" cycle to "love all cities," he wrote Hughes in 1929 (14 May, Hughes Papers) that he "could never love" a city like Marseilles "as Harlem." Thus he explained the difference between his European urban novel *Banjo* (1929) and *Home to Harlem:* "Briefly, 'Banjo' is objective, 'Home to Harlem' subjective."

Insofar as McKay identified New York, but not Harlem, with the foreign cities he toured, he was able to divest himself emotionally from New York as dead while intensifying his emotional bond to Harlem as alive. By the same token, imperial, alien, "objective" New York also defined the limits of "subjective" Harlem as home for him, particularly as the one surrounds the other. McKay, however, like most other Harlem Renaissance writers, emphasized the center more than the boundaries of Harlem's home strength. His old feeling of alienation from white-dominated cities is present in *Home to Harlem* but distanced from Harlem itself, focused on Pittsburgh's white-controlled railroad yards. It is an alienation felt most by the writer-artist Ray, one of McKay's alter egos in this novel. The other, Jake, is a heavy laborer, a man of the streets and the people, who countermands Ray's urban alienation by expressing McKay's new feeling about Harlem. Parts I and III open and close the novel with a sustained emphasis on the sexual ripeness and violent energies of Harlem as experienced by Jake. *Home to Harlem* thus brings powerful feelings of origin and belonging to bear on black America's capital city. Jake and Ray together represent McKay's ambivalent attitudes toward Harlem and New York, which Günter Lenz (1988, 313-16)[16] analyzes as an internal tension between "nature" and "technology" within greater New York, but it is Jake's Harlem—specifically its internal, organic vitality—that rules *Home to Harlem*.

It was no easy feat to infuse folkish pastoral vitalities into Harlem's cosmopolitan world. Moving beyond the residential scope of the Chicago women's novels, Harlem Renaissance literature overturns pastoral conventions on a large scale. The difficulty of its achievement cannot be overestimated, even though McKay was the only major renaissance writer with roots to shake loose from the pastoral soil. In contrast to McKay's Jamaican hills, the rural South held few positive associations for stateside African Americans. The darker aspects of plantation slavery and debt-bound tenant farming were historical familiars. Postwar protests, like the NAACP's antilynching campaigns, and reports from "down home" kept wounds fresh. Since most Harlem Renaissance writers had grown up in cities, moreover, no childhood nostalgia mitigated their generally negative rural associations. Perhaps it should not be surprising, then, that they joined white small town cynics like Sherwood Anderson and Sinclair Lewis in challenging the American cultural habit of rural nostalgia.

But it is nonetheless surprising that African Americans brought the pastoral values of organic energy and Edenic belonging to bear on the urban setting of Harlem. That meant setting aside common assumptions about urban artificiality and alienation that went well beyond pastoral conventions and were undoubtedly consistent with much of their own experience, personally and historically, as black Americans. Such assumptions are strongly expressed in Jean Toomer's *Cane* (1923), for instance. Although *Cane* rejects the pastoral cliché of rural fertility, it reinforces the cliché of urban artifice with its theme of sterile sexuality.[17] The novel is set in Washington, D.C., however, not in Harlem; and even as a New Yorker in the 1920s, Toomer disavowed any place in the Harlem of the renaissance (N. McKay 1984).

Most Renaissance writers refused to apply such conventions of urban sterility to Harlem. Even an author who feared that natural forces were dangerous to human ambitions affirmed their powerful presence in the city. Like Willa Cather (1915, 200), Nella Larsen identified urban nature with dangerous sexual storms. Confronting the stereotype of black women's sexuality in the process, moreover, Larsen created "the first truly sexual black female protagonist in Afro-American fiction," as Hazel Carby argues

(1987, 174). In Larsen's *Quicksand* (1928), Helga Crane finally gives in to the undertow of sexualized nature in Harlem. She collapses from the weight of social contradictions, the constant strain between alienation and belonging that derives from her white and black, Danish-African-American identity. With powerful compression of theme and imagery, Helga Crane's tragedy is played out in a world that overturns pastoral contrasts between country and city. Instead of assigning to these places the polar oppositions of fertility and sterility, Larsen finally locates their contradictions within Helga Crane herself—and therefore in all places.

Specifically, Helga Crane searches for a social environment where she can express her complex humanity, especially her aesthetic fusion of passion with curiosity in an exotic, "intensely personal taste" (1). In the beginning, her aesthetic ambitions are repressed by the "machinery" of the rural college at which she teaches and by the "easy unhuman loveliness" of its natural surroundings (34). Thus contradicting pastoral convention, the country setting is initially alienating and humanly sterile to her. Later she has contrary responses to a socially respectable and potentially fertile union with the college's new president, but she violently rejects that part of herself. She flees north to Chicago, responding positively there, again in contrast to pastoral conventions, to a "home" in the natural "eddies" of people to which she feels "drawn by an uncontrollable desire to mingle" (65). Later, the dark crowds of "teeming black Harlem" make the same bodily, life-sustaining appeal to her as Chicago's "moving multi-colored crowd" and evoke in her the same "magic sense of having come home" (95). But she is disowned in Chicago by her white uncle, and her sense of belonging to the Harlem crowds becomes a prison that "yoked [her] to these despised black folk" (125). Finally, she is unwilling to relinquish all community with African Americans to live in Copenhagen, although it offers wealth to express her exotic taste. Back and forth Helga Crane swings among always partial and contradictory possibilities. She finds no place that offers her both passionate belonging and social respectability, both fertile intercourse and aesthetic pleasure.

Because Helga Crane initially understands herself in aesthetic terms, she looks forward to finding chaotic natural forces "held prisoners" within the city's "maze of human beings" (34). But she must acknowledge her sexual passion, too. In the end she learns that nature concentrated *within* urban society has no less power than it does constraining rural Naxos society from without. Rejected by the college president when she finally seeks an illicit liaison with him in Harlem, she despairs and plunges into a storm in the city streets, where she is nearly drowned in sudden "rivers" of rain and wind (245-46). She seeks shelter in a storefront church, but finds another storm there, where she finally releases the passionate nature within herself to others in orgasmic "rites" that "appeal for... her soul" with the "contact of bodies" and the "concerted convulsion" of the urban congregation (251-53). It is the triumph of her own nature within the city, then, that consigns her exhausted self to the arms of the Reverend Mr. Pleasant Green. And the quicksand, the "quagmire" (236) of passion reveals itself as enslaving when he carries her off to a debilitating lifetime of "natural" child-bearing in the stereotypical backwardness of rural Southern poverty.

Part of an urban network that extends even across the Atlantic, Larsen's Harlem nonetheless harbors the forces of nature—its link to the rural South—in its heart, in the hearts of its people. The natural core of this urban world bodes both life and death. Bringing organic imagery to bear on Harlem life also means flirting with particularly damaging racist stereotypes, as *Quicksand* makes clear when the storefront congregation simultaneously mistakes and exposes Helga Crane as "a scarlet 'oman" (251). The stereotype of black women as sexually loose and of all blacks as primitive—at best Edenic, more often uncivilized and backward, all too often savage and even inhuman—has a long and infamous history as rationalization for rape, enslavement, lynching, and other forms of oppression. It was not rooted out during the renaissance years, but its negative evaluation was directly challenged.

In the effort to overturn that stereotype, Harlem Renaissance writers were involved with and supported by two intellectual movements. On the one hand, a cult of African primitivism and black exoticism gave aesthetic value to organicism, especially to the rhythmic chants and body imagery of Harlem Renaissance poetry. Black scholars like Howard University philosopher Alain Locke and Philadelphia art collector Albert Barnes helped articulate a positive evaluation of the primitive in convincing terms. On the other hand, black folk culture studies gave academic value to the textures of daily life among black people. Du Bois's own study of *The Souls of Black Folks* (1903) deserves credit for this development, to which Zora Neale Hurston and Philadelphia's Arthur Fauset contributed significantly. White New York anthropologists like Hurston's Columbia mentor Franz Boas also provided disciplinary clout. Both movements attached positive value to blacks as natural primitives, despite fear of stereotyped and natural dangers (expressed by women like Nella Larsen) and the continuing desire for conventional respectability reinforced by Harlem's organizational gatekeepers.[18]

Like *Quicksand,* both movements identified as the source of organic vitality not a particular setting but the people themselves. According to the Africanists, African Americans carried a *racial* heredity of primitivism "in their blood"—even though they had been so violently torn from Africa that Cullen's best-known poem "Heritage" (1925, 36–41) can only puzzle, "What is Africa to me?" According to the folklorists, African Americans were historically linked to their *ethnic* heritage by songs and dances and stories—even though they had left the rural settings of the South behind them. Both movements spawned research into distant cultures—African arts and rural southern folkways—but collected those materials in the city. They urged black urban artists to tap primitive instincts and folk forms as inherent well-springs of creativity, carried within them wherever they might live.

Consequently, the black city of Harlem Renaissance literature, like residential Chicago in turn-of-the-century white women's novels, is not denatured or cut off from rural life. Like Chicago's women, Harlem Renaissance writers accepted the city as given—a complex world of life and death, promise, fulfillment, and disappointment. They did not view it as negating, an artificial encrustation on some nonurban reality, nor measure it against such an external standard. When Harlem falls short in renaissance literature, it falls short of its own complex standards as a black city within a white city. At the end of Wallace Thurman's hit play *Harlem* (1929), for instance, a rural southern migrant condemns Harlem for failing to live up to its claim—recorded in Fisher's story of that title—to be a "city of refuge." "City of refuge? City of refuse!" she harrumphs. In her family's experience, the concentration of African Americans in Harlem spawns licentiousness instead of affording protection. Nonetheless, the problem is not that Harlem is, by definition as a city, inherently artificial but that it has failed to be the home it promised to be.

Indeed, Harlem Renaissance literature offers organicism as the first noteworthy strength of Harlem as home and depicts Harlem's physical vitality specifically in its street life. For although the spatial structure of Harlem in literature is far more thoroughly urban than rural-environed Chicago in turn-of-the-century residential novels, its streets, like those, are open roads to the country and arteries for the rural/urban exchange. Streets epitomize Harlem as the physical homeplace of the African-American world. They gather up its energies in a rich social network of intersections and transformations. They express those energies in elements of color, texture, sound, and taste, which always recall Harlem elsewhere. All the more starkly, therefore, do the mechanistic oppressions of greater New York's street and subway system contrast with the vitality of Harlem's streets. The subway entrances and el exits to their realm provide an important and ultimately tragic example of white novelist Marge Piercy's contention (1981, 209) that our cities are "grids of Them-and-Us experiences."

Streets regularly stand out as the locus of life in Harlem Renaissance literature. The histories use street names not only to track the settlement of Harlem but also to delineate its most distinctive physical feature, the colors of its people—the "sudden change" in complexion at 110th Street on the northwest corner of Central Park and the emergence of its densest color "nearing One Hundred and Thirty-fifth Street" (Johnson [1930] 1958, 145). Named streets focus the breath-taking, breath-giving enormity of Harlem's concentrated blackness in Hughes's and Fisher's mythic entrance scenes: "135TH STREET.... Hundreds of colored people!" (Hughes 1940, 81) and "Negroes at every turn; up and down Lenox Avenue, up and down One Hundred and Thirty-fifth Street" (Fisher 1925, 58). By naming them, Harlem authors invoke the familiarity of New York's streets to confirm Harlem's status as the "Negro Capital."[19]

Similarly, when Jake Brown longs back to Harlem from abroad in *Home to Harlem* (McKay 1928, 5), he longs most for its street life: "Fifth Avenue, Lenox Avenue, and One Hundred and Thirty-fifth Street, with their chocolate-brown and walnut-brown girls, were calling him." While McKay's masculinist enjoyment of women as food offers a troubling glimpse into the sexual politics of the Harlem Renaissance, a similarly intense sensory response to Harlem's streets also characterizes the novels of his female compatriots. Larsen's *Quicksand,* for example, identifies Helga Crane's "magic sense of having come home" in Harlem specifically with its street life (1928, 95) and associates the home feeling with her earlier experience in Chicago's streets: "As she stepped out into the moving multi-colored crowd, there came to her a queer feeling of enthusiasm, as if she were tasting some agreeable, exotic food—sweetbreads, smothered with truffles and mushrooms—perhaps. And, oddly enough, she felt, too, that she had come home. She, Helga Crane, who had no home" (Larsen [1928] 1969, 65). Like McKay's Jake, Larson's Helga experiences the "magic" of street crowds as "exotic food"—simultaneously tantalizing her appetites and strengthening her with a sense of nurturance. Basic enough to be found anywhere and portable enough to go anywhere, such transforming sensory experience is concentrated most vividly in Harlem's streets in Renaissance literature. The streets equal sex and food and breath—a life-giving home.

Nearly every Harlem Renaissance novel offers a Seventh Avenue parade—only less formal and more lively than the political *Parade on Seventh Avenue* that James Van Der Zee photographed in the 1920s (n.d., fig. 12). Literature's Seventh Avenue parades embody an exuberance of high hopes based in organic vitality and the expressiveness of human fashion, gesture, even song. The sensory life force of Seventh Avenue is even strong enough to transform time and weather. In Rudolph Fisher's belated Renaissance work, *The Conjure-Man Dies!* ([1932] 1971), for example, Seventh Avenue is exempted from the daytime cold of winter as "the sun grinned down ... beaming just a little more brightly and warmly" on the "parade" of Sunday people in their "rainbow" skin colors and costumes there (86–87). The opening paragraph of this first black mystery novel explicitly contrasts the remarkable vitality of Harlem's Seventh Avenue to the lifeless white streets downtown: "Encountering the bright-lighted gaiety of Harlem's Seventh Avenue, the frigid midwinter night seemed to relent a little. She had given Battery Park a chill stare and she would undoubtedly freeze the Bronx. But here in this midrealm of rhythm and laughter she seemed to grow warmer and friendlier, observing, perhaps, that those who dwelt here were mysteriously dark like herself" (3).

Such uptown/downtown contrasts are common. Always to Harlem's advantage, the streets of New York are monstrously unnatural, like Chicago's streets in its standard novels. Fauset's *Plum Bun* (1929, 87) provides a typical description: "Fifth Avenue is a canyon; its towering buildings dwarf ... the people hurrying through its narrow confines." And although the "river ... of life itself" in bohemian Fourteenth Street resembles Harlem's "stream of life" in that novel, Fauset insists that the current of vitality is "thicker," "fuller, richer," "deeper, more mightily moving" on Lenox Avenue and Seventh Avenue at 137th and 135th Streets (87, 96–97). The vitality of Harlem's street life is even frightening to Fauset's "passing" heroine, "combining," as it does, "the customs of the small town with ... cosmopolitanism" and threatening her with exposure. So she leaves "home" and moves downtown, "To market, to market / To buy a Plum Bun." Perversely "glad" to leave the life of Harlem's streets, "she strained for last glimpses" from "the lurching 'L' train" (96–98), which here again "kill[s] the streets" (Howells [1890] 1965, 54) and epitomizes the life-destroying capacities of the economic city.[20]

Figure 12. James Van Der Zee, *Parade on Seventh Avenue* (ca. 1924), photograph. Courtesy of the Studio Museum in Harlem Archives, James Van Der Zee Collection, and the Donna Van Der Zee Collection.

Thus powerfully contrasted to such inhuman mechanization, Harlem's streets *are* its people. The streets themselves even have human personalities in *The Walls of Jericho* by Rudolph Fisher. Fifth Avenue is a "fallen" aristocrat "moving uncertainly" in the "backwoods" above 125th Street (Fisher 1928, 3-4); Seventh Avenue is a collective "promenade" of "triumphant" Sunday church-goers in all their "satisfied self-righteousness" (44-45). In all their variety, the streets are both home to Harlem residents and Harlem residents themselves. "Such skillful humanization of inanimate objects" (Singh 1976, 86) breaks down the distinction between human beings and their urban environment, enveloping people in an organic vitality that is compatible, even conterminous with human life.

Above all, the crowds in Harlem streets represent African Americans' general belonging to each other and their hopes of generative connections with each other. This is the second major strength that the renaissance writers locate and test in Harlem as home: its power as a birthright community. So the "hopes" of Thurman's Emma Lou Morgan are always "high" when she walks among Seventh Avenue's "heterogeneous ensemble of mellow colors" and looks for a lover among the "Black men. Yellow men. Brown men" there in *The Blacker the Berry* ([1929] 1969, 94, 106). That such hopes may be disappointed is also clear in Thurman's novel, where dark Emma Lou discovers an unexpected midday emptiness on 135th Street when she first arrives, then feels the exclusionary impact of color prejudice at Harlem's unemployment agencies as well as its parties.

At best, however, Harlem's streets are a synergistic meeting place in literature, offering possibilities beyond the limits of racist hostility. Filled with children as well as adults, women as well as men, the streets create a neighborhood extension of family life and generation,[21] like the open-ended, future-oriented city-towns of pre–Civil War white literature. Harlem streets are not always happy—any more than families are always happy. "Life for me ain't been no crystal stair," a mother tells her son at the end of Hughes's *The Weary Blues* ("Mother to Son," [1925] 1935, 107). Nonetheless, passing the torch from parent to child does open up the chance to reach new heights:

> So boy, don't you turn back.
> Don't you set down on the steps
> 'Cause you finds it's kinder hard.
> Don't you fall now—
> For I'se still goin', honey,
> I's still climbin',
> And life for me ain't been no crystal stair.

Particularly, children embody creativity for the future. Unlike the adults imitating white ways in Harlem dives in Wallace Thurman's "Terpsichore in Harlem" (n.d., 5), for instance, "the many groups of little yellow, brown and black boys who occasionally gather on the sidewalks" need no ready-made props to "amuse themselves and passersby with their dance antics.... without the aid of music except such as is provided by their whistling, humming and clapping of hands." Unfettered "out in the middle of the street," the energies of children can even transform adults. In Fauset's first novel, *There Is Confusion* (1924, 47), narrowly ambitious artist Joanna Marshall becomes generous and loving when she joins "a band of colored children... dancing and acting a game" in the streets. There she finds her inspiration to create a unifying "Dance of the Nations," which allows her to crash a color barrier to embody "America" at a Greenwich Village benefit (232). In this moment of triumph, Harlem street life crowds inside—even downtown—without losing its generative fullness.[22]

Langston Hughes especially realizes an inside/outside synergy between Harlem's streets and cabarets in the interlocking opening section of his first book of poetry, *The Weary Blues* ([1925] 1935, 21–40). "The Weary Blues" opens the book "on Lenox Avenue" (23–24), while "Lenox Avenue: Midnight" closes it, playing "the weary, weary heart of pain" in "a jazz rhythm" (39–40). With the streets and cabarets alluding back and forth to each other, Hughes brings the social life of blues on the outside fully to bear on the jazz inside. "The Weary Blues" itself, for example, makes the cabaret a part of the street, the street a source of the music, and the audience one with the performer:

> Droning a drowsy syncopated tune,
> Rocking back and forth to a mellow croon,
>   I heard a Negro play.
> Down on Lenox Avenue the other night
> By the pale dull pallor of an old gas light
>   He did a lazy sway....
>   He did a lazy sway....
> To the tune o' those Weary Blues.
> With his ebony hands on each ivory key
> He made that poor piano moan with melody.
>   O Blues!

This is a permeable world in which even death becomes the occasion for life—for a street prostitute in "To a Little Lover-Lass Dead" (31) as also for the dancers and musicians inside in "Harlem Night Club" (32):

> Jazz-boys, jazz-boys,—
> Play, plAY, PLAY!
> Tomorrow.... is darkness.
> Joy today.

All derive today's joy from tomorrow's darkness, laughter from tears, the very "rhythm of life" from the "jazz rhythm" of a *danse macabre* in "Lenox Avenue: Midnight." Thus connected, Harlem's streets and cabarets transform the very stuff of minority oppression into human universality in this stellar example of what Houston Baker (1984, 13) calls "the blues matrix at work," "negotiat[ing] an obdurate 'economics of slavery' and achiev[ing] a resonant, improvisational, expressive dignity."

Usually, however, confining the communal life of the streets threatens violence, even death, in Harlem Renaissance literature. Without the streets' openness toward the world and the future, cabarets become ghettos in microcosm. They compress Harlem's social variety dangerously and thus oppose, rather than extend, its street life—as even a curious white guest like Carl Van Vechten could see. His *Nigger Heaven* (1926) poses such an ominous contrast between expansive liveliness outdoors and compressed deadliness indoors, personified in "Anatole Longfellow, alias the Scarlet Creeper" (3). At the beginning of the novel, on Seventh Avenue, 'Toly is a wondrous figure, admired by all, sure of his power, heading toward his liaison with flashy Ruby Silver, and merely "irked" by his rival, the "pompous" Bolito King. But in the cabaret scene that ends the novel, the Creeper attacks his rival and kills him. The barroom violence realizes the explosive potential of the "kaleidoscope" of dancing "black bodies, brown bodies, high yellows" that "crowded about each other, all the incongruities, the savage inconsistencies, the peculiar discrepancies, of this cruel, segregated life" (14, 215).

The variety of skin colors that graces the life-giving parades on Harlem's streets emphasizes a dizzying, disorienting claustrophobia when crowded into a cabaret. Nauseated by the swirl of "sooty black, shiny black, taupe, mahogany, bronze, copper, gold, orange, yellow, peach, ivory, pinky white, pastry white" in a cabaret, *Quicksand*'s Helga Crane is overcome by a painful awareness of her entrapment in Harlem (Larsen [1928] 1969, 130). Practically every book of Harlem Renaissance literature includes a cabaret scene; its more formal counterpart, the charity ball; or its less formal counterpart, the rent party. Whether slumming or do-gooding, spending money or raising it, in the presence of whites or not, Harlemites usually experience danger at such affairs. Their "inherent variety"—of "personal station ... age ... [and] occupation," as well as color—collides in fighting at a charity ball in *The Walls of Jericho* (Fisher 1928, 70–71). The always dizzying effect is intensified when drunkenness and sexual desire add to the "whirl" at a rent party in *The Blacker the Berry* (Thurman [1929] 1969, 171): "Leering faces and lewd bodies. Anxious faces and angular bodies. Sad faces and obese bodies. All mixed up together." Sickened by the close press of hysteria, Thurman's Emma

Lou Morgan "began to wonder how such a small room could hold so many people."

With a sociological explicitness that the "Niggerati" themselves generally avoided, Carl Van Vechten answered the question. The double meaning of his novel's title, *Nigger Heaven,* meant that the "heavenly" coming together of African Americans in Harlem was the flip-side of a "cruel" crowding. Ruby Silver interprets Van Vechten's title with naïve enthusiasm on the night she meets the Scarlet Creeper: "Dis place, where Ah met you—Harlem. Ah calls et, specherly tonight, Ah calls et Nigger Heaven!" (15). But Van Vechten's hero, would-be writer Byron Kasson, later reveals that "Nigger Heaven" is also slang for the segregated balcony for blacks at the theater: "Nigger Heaven! That's what Harlem is," he breaks out to his fiancée, as they retreat back to Harlem from a downtown date spoiled by white racists. "We sit in our places in the gallery of this New York theatre and watch the white world sitting down below in the good seats in the orchestra. Occasionally they turn their faces up towards us, their hard, cruel faces, to laugh or sneer, but they never beckon. It never seems to occur to them that Nigger Heaven is crowded, that there isn't another seat, that something has to be done" (149). A ghetto's enforced crowding: that was the prison in which the Harlem Renaissance danced, the source of tears in its laughter.

Van Vechten's black friends objected that he was giving away "family secrets" (Charles S. Johnson 10 Aug. 1926 letter, Van Vechten Correspondence-*Opportunity*), and so he was. The Harlem Renaissance writers walked a delicate line. While emphasizing the fertile dirt in which their dreams grew, they also recognized the extent to which ghettoized crowding limited the power of Harlem's vitality and community, even turning these forces back upon themselves. Thus the dense diversity of Harlem is both positively rich and horribly disorienting in renaissance literature. It is full of dangers as well as dreams. Its tensions and deceptions press beyond logic toward a truth that embraces make-believe, too.

Harlem's third home strength is its consequently ambivalent fulfillment of cultural aspirations, which Zora Neale Hurston (1934) put in specifically urban terms: the Harlem Renaissance sought the "fabulous cities of artistic concepts... within the mind and language of some humble Negro." But as Harlem's sensory life and community were both expressive and ghettoized, so also was its "fabulous city of artistic concepts" deceptive in its power. It threw into question the relationship of art to truth: Is the artist a con man or a prophet? Is a con man's game true or false when he fakes a heavenly conversion to win money and sympathy—and wins a convert to God in the process? Is it "the prophet's power" or "the actor's" pleasure that motivates the preacher himself? These questions troubled genteel poet Countee Cullen, himself a Harlem minister's adopted son, in his only rough-edged work, a novel called *One Way to Heaven* (1932, 16).

For the most part, however, the renaissance writers were not moralistic, accepting the ambiguities of make-believe as part of Harlem's creative power. Rather than aspire to some unvarnished truth, they offered Harlem's own self-dramatization in place of racist stereotypes imposed from without. As Henry Louis Gates (1988) has argued of African-American tradition generally and particularly of Zora Neale Hurston (along with Ishmael Reed and Alice Walker), the Harlem Renaissance artists considered the "double-voiced" make-believe of the "signifying monkey" an essential part of Harlem's power to generate art and symbolize aspiration. It seems both wonderful and awful that Thurman's heroine in *The Blacker the Berry* could not "tell whether the cast was before or behind the proscenium arch" in the Lafayette Theater, what with all "the spontaneous monkey shines" of the audience and "stereotyped antics of the hired performers" (Thurman [1929] 1969, 202–3). So *Quicksand* (Larsen [1928] 1969, 253, 128–30) does not condemn the "concerted convulsions" that "possessed" Helga Crane in the "rites" of a storefront church any more or less than the "jungle" rhythms that "drugged" her earlier in the "hell" of a subterranean cabaret. Most Renaissance novels explicitly embrace all such fusions of truth and pretense, even of paradise and damnation. The rhyming, rhythmic, double-voiced "truths" of jazz and blues, of jive and sermons, all become the stuff of literary art for Johnson, Hughes, Hurston, Fisher, and others. Fisher's work especially shows that Harlem life is, at base, a masquerade, a mystery story. In *The Conjure-Man Dies* (Fisher [1932] 1971, 209, 226), the mystery can only be solved by a doctor—like Fisher himself—who is also a "detective" and a conjurer, reading the "past, present, and future" beneath a person's face.

Fisher probes the segregated underpinnings of this insight in *The Walls of Jericho*. Published in the same year as McKay's *Home to Harlem* and Larsen's *Quicksand* (arguably the fictional high point of the Harlem Renaissance), *The Walls of Jericho* weaves into a particularly rich design the characteristic renaissance tropes for the dreams and dangers of ghetto life. Streets embody sensory vitality; indoor dances work as dizzying concentrations of Harlem's variety; street "dozens" and church services are ritual maskings and unmaskings. Mapped out by street names and crowned by the inevitable parade of Seventh Avenue, Fisher's Harlem is, like the old city-town, expressive of its human inhabitants, animistic even, down to the "malicious" piano that the hero wrestles with the help of his "companion" truck Bess (23, 46). From working-class "rats" to "dicty" blacks and patronizing whites, Fisher's Harlem displays its tensions in housing fights, sexual rivalries, and an extended take-off on the NAACP's annual charity ball.23 Organized into a rhythmic sequence of chapters capped by a tongue-in-cheek "Introduction to Contemporary Harlemese" (295–307), the novel itself embodies the tension and exuberance of Harlem's street jive (e.g., 201–3), social call and response (e.g., 101, 132), and preacherly "good show" (178–80). *The Walls of Jericho* fuses sensory, communal, and aesthetic playfulness with a profound critique of Harlem's deceptive culture.

The novel's "surface" is nonetheless energetic—even "too much" (Hughes 13 Sept. 1929 letter to C. McKay, McKay Papers). Its several plots strain in various directions. "Dicty" Fred Merrit dares to pass in a borderline white neighborhood where he is unwanted and eventually burned out; within the apparently genial society of a rough Harlem pool hall, the black owner stands revealed as arsonist and rapist; and through it all, working-class Joshua Jones—Merrit's piano mover and a regular at Patmore's Poolhall—struggles to extricate his middle-class girlfriend Linda Young from Patmore's power and himself from his own hard shell. The elaborate surface of the novel's linguistic play builds up layer on layer of clichéd verbal gestures to cover these "smoldering" subjects and whatever "itches" one would "prefer not to be seen scratching" (63, 109). It also counterpoints sermon and jive, when the words of the church's "leading man" are roughly translated (178–80) by Joshua Jones, brashly yet stereotypically nicknamed Shine. Such energy of elaboration betrays the underlying pain and suspicion of their world. Fred Merrit's attempt to pass no less than Shine's (and Fisher's) linguistic play eventually stands revealed as a masquerade for the tragedy of a divided city.

In Fisher's Harlem, jive is the stuff of which the dreams and nightmares of Harlem's streets and balls and pool halls and theaters and churches are made. It symbolizes Harlem's community—and its secrets. Shine's closest pool hall buddies, Bubber Brown and Jinx Jenkins, repeatedly "do the dozens" and finally egg each other on to a fight, out of "deep affection" (10–11). As do their nicknames, jive hides their full humanity from each other and from themselves. Fisher's glossary is integral because his whole novel is an exercise in meaning and its "perversion." "Beneath the jests, the avowed fear, the merriment, was a characteristic irony, a markedly racial tendency to make light of what actually was grave" (Fisher 1928, 29). And what is deadly grave is the separation of blacks from whites, of Harlem from the rest of New York, of a part of humanity from the whole.

The walled city is Fisher's synthesizing metaphor. Far more developed here than in Elia Peattie's *The Precipice* (1914, 89), it stands for both the divided city of Harlem, New York, and the "double-voiced," divided self. *The Walls of Jericho* thus links social segregation to psychological and cultural pretense. Shine describes the Biblical outlines of the story:

> Well, this Joshua thought he was the owl's bowels, till one day he run up against a town named Jericho. Town—This place was a flock o' towns. It was the same thing to that part o' the country that New York is to this....
>
> But try and get in. This burg has walls around it so thick that the gals could have their jazz-houses on top.... And here this red hot papa, Joshua, who's never had his damper turned down yet—here he is up against that much wall—and the damn thing don't budge. (181–82)

He continues his namesake's story until the walls tumble down, but he doesn't report to his pool hall buddies the still deeper lesson the minister had drawn in church: "You, my friend, are Joshua. You have advanced through a life of battle.... And then you find yourself face to face with a solid blank wall—a wall beyond which lies the only goal that matters—the land of promise. Do you know what that goal is? It is the knowledge of man's own self" (186–87). Wrapped up in Harlem's jive, Joshua has been walled off from himself. The segregation of one part of humanity from another is not just an external division, then; it divides each part internally. Not only is Harlem divided from greater New York, Fisher reveals; Harlem is self-divided as well. So, by implication, is the rest of New York.

Few of Fisher's compatriots were willing to look at this psychological tragedy—a canker at the root of black urban folkways. It explains the mythic power they all found in Harlem and the danger they recognized at its borders. Over and over their works present Harlem and New York as a dual city. Occasionally this amounts to "two visages" of a single city (Fauset 1929, 241), to a contrast between its privileged and oppressed classes that echoes the economic city imagery of standard Chicago novels. But usually the division runs so deep that it implies two distinctive yet interpenetrating cities, or "a Negro city within a city" (White 1926, 187).

Again and again, African-American literature articulates the physical, social, and mental transformations that occur at the borders. It dramatizes the risks involved in crossing: the schizophrenia of playing different roles downtown and uptown; the self-deception of masking anger in deference and tears in laughter; the blinding danger in trying to pass for white or wishing the border away.

"Novels of passing" figure prominently in Harlem Renaissance literature. Passing is the ultimate masquerade but hardly the only one in this urban world. Indeed, in some sense, any art is a masquerade—the more deceptive the more profound, as Vladimir Nabokov argues (e.g., *Pale Fire* 1962). Insofar as renaissance literature recognizes and even celebrates the mix of sex and soul, of jazz and blues, of promise and limitation, of truth and deception in the heart of Harlem, it offers an image of home that accepts the ambiguities of human life. Insofar as Harlem Renaissance writers recognize that they are both a divided and a connected people—and ritualize that tragicomedy in their art—they are closer to the truth of modern life than are those who think of home as undivided and pure, like some pastoral myth.

Harlem's truth needed its special place in the human community. As cultural aspirations gave meaning to Harlem as sensory place and birthright community, so the place and community legitimized Harlem's home in art. And unfortunately, Harlem as place, community, and aspiration was finally limited by greater New York, as Claude McKay's early poems and others' works suggest. While the Harlem Renaissance realized both the strengths and limitations of home in Harlem, white America did not. The literature of the Harlem Renaissance was often denied status in greater New York in the name of art itself—even by friends.

Such civic denial is evidenced in the story of the monument to James Weldon Johnson proposed after his death. Johnson, author of the first black New York novel, *The Autobiography of an Ex-Coloured Man,* also co-authored black America's "national anthem," "Lift Every Voice," and served as United States consul to Venezuela and Nicaragua. When he moved to New York to become its "citizen" in 1914, he already regarded the city as "home" (Johnson 1931, 2). There he assumed leadership of the NAACP—as its first black executive secretary—in time to help act out his "cherished belief" that African-American art could "destroy race prejudice" by presenting "the Negro as a creator and a contributor to American civilization" ([6 Mar. 1927] letter to Carl Van Vechten, Van Vechten Correspondence).

When Johnson died in 1938, Carl Van Vechten, his literary executor, formed the James Weldon Johnson Memorial Committee, including Johnson's honorary pallbearers and luminaries Mayor La Guardia, W. E. B. Du Bois, Eleanor Roosevelt, Langston Hughes, Duke Ellington, and Marian Anderson (15 Dec. 1938 list, Van Vechten Correspondence). They adopted an idea proposed by Harlem sculptor Augusta Savage that a statue be erected at Seventh Avenue and 110th Street—at the corner of Central Park "where Harlem meets the rest of Manhattan" (Hughes 1941).

From the start, Johnson's widow, Grace Nail Johnson, was particularly emphatic about the "large N.Y. idea" (19 Dec. 1938 letter, Van Vechten Correspondence). A public statue in the location Van Vechten had mentioned would be "to the credit of all, as befits the man, the location, the city," she wrote (20 Nov. 1938 letter, Van Vechten Correspondence). By way of confirming her understanding of the project as a "civic expression" (4 Jan. 1939 letter, Van Vechten Correspondence), she proposed that the monument be inscribed with a poem that Johnson had sent Van Vechten back in 1925 (28 Feb. 1939 letter, Van Vechten Correspondence). Johnson had "wondered" then if he and his dear friend "love[d] the city in about the same way." "My City," his widow now wrote, was the poem in which Johnson had "declared" New York his "home." "My City" (1935, 37) is typical of the Harlem Renaissance in locating home in an urban, rather than a rural, setting. It is unusual in extending that imagery beyond Harlem to embrace all Manhattan:

> When I come down to sleep death's endless night,
> The threshold of the unknown dark to cross,
> What to me then will be the keenest loss,
> When this bright world blurs on my fading sight?
> Will it be that no more I shall see the trees
> Or smell the flowers or hear the singing birds
> Or watch the flashing streams or patient herds?
> No. I am sure it will be none of these.
>
> But, ah! Manhattan's sights and sounds, her smells,
> Her crowds, her throbbing force, the thrill that comes
> From being of her a part, her subtle spells,
> Her shining towers, her avenues, her slums—
> O God! the stark, unutterable pity,
> To be dead, and never again behold my city!

Van Vechten proposed instead that the monument be inscribed with Johnson's sonnet to African-American artists, "O Black and Unknown Bards," thus obscuring the civic emphasis Johnson's widow supported. The Committee for a James Weldon Johnson Memorial adopted Van Vechten's idea at a meeting attended by only six members, all male (12 December 1939 minutes, Van Vechten Correspondence). The same meeting endorsed the location proposed by Augusta Savage, but chose Richmond Barthé to sculpt an allegorical statue quite different from the representational death mask of Johnson that Savage had already completed.[24] These decisions limited the civic dimensions of the project and turned it toward more abstract aesthetic ends. It is quite possible that the men who made the decisions lacked some more profound respect for embodiment—in place and in human form—that Grace Johnson and Augusta Savage shared as women, the "strong sense of place" that Toni Morrison has also described herself as "rooted in" (1976, 167–68).

In any case, New York City's powerful park commissioner, Robert Moses, jammed the entire project. In 1941, he rejected the proposal to site Barthé's allegorical nude at Seventh Avenue and 110th Street because, he proclaimed, the statue would be a bad influence on the children of Harlem (n.d. letter to Walter White, enclosed in White 2 Apr. 1942 letter to Van Vechten, Van Vechten Correspondence). In 1942, Moses suggested placing the Johnson statue inside Central Park, near a Puerto Rican and black area where "no white man or dicty Negro has ever set foot," Van Vechten complained (9 May 1942 letter to Walter White, Van Vechten Correspondence). Then Moses suggested saving the statue for a proposed postwar housing project deep in Harlem, since World War II had made metal for statues impossible to obtain (4 Dec. 1942 minutes, Van Vechten Correspondence). By the time Moses finally agreed to the original proposal in late 1945, the costs of casting had increased far beyond the funds that had been raised before the war (Walter White 25 Oct. 1945 and 5 Feb. 1947 letters to Johnson Memorial Committee, Van Vechten Correspondence), sounding the death knell for what would have been the first public monument to an African American in the city of New York.

But in 1941, Van Vechten had taken up another, related cause. He discovered that his alma mater, Yale University, "in the thickest part of the collegiate world," did not have "any Negro books at all" (14 Aug. 1941 letter, Van Vechten Correspondence). When Van Vechten later decided that a statue was "rather a waste of time" (Van Vechten 1960, 18), he chose to endow a literary archive at Yale instead, thus separating what became the James Weldon Johnson Memorial Collection from its Harlem home. Ironically, Van Vechten determined that while Yale needed "help," the Schomburg Collection at the Harlem branch of the New York Public Library was "already ... outstanding" and not in need. He found Yale's commitment to archival preservation for perpetuating "the fame of the Negro" among scholars preferable to the Schomburg Center's commitment to "dissemination and widespread use" of black literature among "the black masses" (Hutson 1978, 17; Arthur Schomburg, 16 Feb. 1933 letter to Langston Hughes, Schomburg Papers).

The decisions of white Americans Robert Moses and Carl Van Vechten, then, finally denied Johnson's public citizenship in greater New York. His statue remained unbuilt, and he was memorialized in an academic library away from the city he claimed as his home.[25] Similarly, the Harlem Renaissance itself has often been treated as solely an aesthetic moment rather than also a civic enterprise, and its image of home has consequently been ignored. Properly attended to, Harlem's vision of home demonstrates that "sense of race" per se "isn't foreign, see, it's opposite, a sense of home," as Jewish-American author Meyer Levin wrote (1933, 271). But if that sense of race is not affirmed by those beyond its bounds, it can be home only in a limited way. Cut off from the surrounding island of New York, Harlem could only be an imperfect home to African Americans, and no home at all to others. Segregated from greater New York, the sensory place, the birthright community, and the cultural aspirations of Harlem could not fully be joined. When New York lost the statue of James Weldon Johnson, it lost a complex symbol of Harlem's uniqueness and its connection to New York. Today, too, when we treat Harlem's art apart from its place and community—when we separate art from civics, as Angela Davis (1987, 21) has argued Anglo-Americans continue to do—we obscure the power and poignancy of the renaissance vision of Harlem as home.

7

Neighborhood-City Dreams

When Carl Van Vechten abstracted art from Harlem's civic legacy and assigned it to the academic world, he reinforced the ascendancy of megalopolis.[1] In greater New York during the Harlem Renaissance, the macrocosmic reach of megalopolitan images denied the microcosmic rootedness of the neighborhood city in almost every way. While the neighborhood city affirmed natural continuities and based itself in sensory street life, megalopolis was all abstraction, disjunction, and fragmented artificiality. While the neighborhood city found strengths as well as limits in racial community, megalopolis defined alienation. While the neighborhood city symbolized dreams and cultural aspirations, megalopolis bred despair. Megalopolis, moreover, asserted Euro-American hegemony on a continental, potentially global, scale.

Given all this, how did the Harlem Renaissance writers find creativity in the ghetto? How did they resist the all-consuming logic of the postwar megalopolis, affirm art even in masquerade, and create the alternative imagery of the neighborhood city? First, concerned with matters of food and survival rather than the "bourgeois" questions of value that occupied Euro-American modernists (Baker 1987, 7), they placed their imaginative worlds in organic context instead of abstracting it. Second, they turned external racist pressures toward affirming internal communal connections and resisting alienation. Third, they envisioned dreams in the natural context of their lives and identified dreaming with their communal traditions. Finally, the dreams of their art came out of a worldview based in continuities between the material and the ideal, between self and community, between past and present and on to future.

Connections between their dreams of belonging and other urban visions indicate the depth of their power. Indeed, Harlem continued the dream of the pre–Civil War city-town's orientation toward the future and the expansiveness of turn-of-the-century Chicago's residential novels. Of course, pre–Civil War African-American writers like Harriet Jacobs and Frederick Douglass were aware of the limitations within which Harlem Renaissance literature would work to affirm dreams.[2] Perhaps Chicago's disfranchised white women were too. Exploring similarities over time between the perspectives of African Americans and white women, Patricia Hill Collins has argued persuasively that "the material conditions of oppression can vary dramatically and yet generate some uniformity in the epistemologies of subordinate groups" (1989, 756–57). Shared poverty, voluntary group cohesion, and cultural difference also seem to have encouraged neighborhood-city imagery among many white ethnic and working-class writers throughout the twentieth century. Jewish-American Alfred Kazin's childhood memoir, *A Walker in the City* (1951), makes use of the street to delineate urban experience much as do *The Street* (1946) by African-American Ann Petry and *Down These Mean Streets* (1967) by Puerto Rican Piri Thomas. So, too, in the visual arts, Italian-American Ralph Fasanella's *Sunday Afternoon* (1953, fig. 11) shows colorful people pressing out of buildings and making the street over to games and conversations. Examples go on and on through different historical epochs, racial and ethnic experiences, and media of expression.

But the full force of street life vitality and community, of immanent and expressive dreams, emerges most powerfully from those who have wrested it from racial oppression in barrios and Chinatowns and ghettos. Such a vision is broadly shared among artists of color, despite vast differences among aesthetic traditions and ethnic urban histories. They are joined by Jews who experienced not only immigrant poverty but also a racialized ethnic identity, a history of life-threatening persecution, and no "presumably secure Americanism" at least up until the middle of the twentieth century (Chametzky 1986, 61).[3] Especially for Jewish-American immigrants from Eastern Europe early in the century, New York's Lower East Side was a capital city much like Harlem. Over time, it developed similar supports for its writers, which may well suggest some necessary preconditions for any countercultural movement in art. In turn, leading writers among its ranks developed various postures toward their community and articulated its literary contours in ways that also parallel and help to further clarify what sustained the Harlem Renaissance as a neighborhood-city home in the midst of megalopolis.

The intense literary productivity of New York Jews into the 1930s was grounded, like the Harlem Renaissance, in a large and concentrated urban ethnic population. Just before Harlem's rise, New York City's Jewish Americans also increased their numbers dramatically in a short period of time and a very constricted area. Infused by huge migrations of Eastern Europeans, including whole families and refugees from the pogroms of 1881–82, 1891, 1899, and 1903, the Jewish population of New York grew from 80,000 in 1880 to 1,100,000 in 1910 (Howe 1976, xix). Eastern European Jews made up a full 25 percent of the city's population in 1910, mainly packed into its most densely populated area, the Lower East Side (Bremer 1965, 66). Even in 1890, before its population peaked, Jacob Riis ([1890] 1970, 71) figured the neighborhood's density at 330,000 people per square mile, nearly twice that of Old London at its worst. Like Harlem's new African Americans, the Lower East Side's newest citizens were well acquainted with cities. Although often misinterpreted as a rural people—premodern, caste-bound, and nonindustrial—their *shtetls* in Eastern Europe were not villages (Howe 1976, 10) but rather like city-towns, and their immigrant journeys often included stays in major European cities.

Jewish literary activism, like that of Harlem Renaissance writers, expressed a powerful yet frustrated and critical commitment to participate in U.S. culture at large. Like African Americans from the South, Jews from Eastern Europe saw New York as a "promised land," or at least its gateway. As such it resonated deeply in their religious traditions and symbolized their commitment to the national dream of freedom. During Passover celebrations in the midst of anti-Semitic pogroms, for instance, Eastern European Jews did not pray " 'May we be next year in Jerusalem,' but 'Next year—in America' " as immigrant Mary Antin remembered in her autobiography *The Promised Land* (1912, 141; cf. African-American Claude Browne's 1965 autobiography *Manchild in a Promised Land*). The symbolism of the Promised Land identified Jews and African Americans as "chosen people" who must endure worldly suffering and exile for a greater glory and home. In effect they shared the symbolic situation of the New England Puritans three hundred years earlier on their "errand into the wilderness" toward the "city upon a hill" (cf. Yezierska 1932, 55).[4] Whether escaping European pogroms or Southern lynchings, their arrival in New York symbolically reenacted both Anglo America's Puritan founding and the Biblical prophesies of the newcomers' own religious traditions. When New York's hostility frustrated migratory hopes it doubled their mythic legitimation and gave both groups a powerfully critical perspective on U.S. culture.[5]

Additionally, their literature could draw on their own developed urban institutions and cultural resources. The heavily populated Lower East Side, like Harlem, had sufficient cultural capital to figure—echoing the Puritans again—as an exemplary "city upon a hill." Each neighborhood became a "city within a city," and each was described in these words by major writers (Cahan 1896, 51; Ellison 1952, 142). Each had its own places of worship, schools, newspapers, clubs, cafes, and theaters. The garment industry gave the Lower East Side a strong economic base, and even Harlem had a sizeable middle-class contingent during the 1920s. Both ethnic communities became headquarters for national, multi-ethnic political organizations committed to their needs—Jewish-led unions, the NAACP, and the Urban League. They also had distinctive cultural riches of language, folkways, and ritual aesthetic forms. The Yiddish language and Eastern European folktales, theatrical and Talmudic traditions, and Judaic religious ritual provided a thick cultural ground for art—as did "Harlemese," Southern and African folklore, spirituals, blues, and jazz. Moreover, Jewish- and African-American writers lived crowded together with the ethnic working class; they had a common self-consciousness about "our people" and the know-how to use their cultural resources well. They worked simultaneously, if paradoxically, to strengthen their collective cultures and to open doors to their acceptance in the outside world. The Lower East Side was a staging ground for upward mobility to Williamsburg and Brownsville, the Upper West Side, and beyond (Howe 1976, 555). Harlem was a "city of refuge" from the life-and-death forms of racial prejudice in the South.

On this basis—concentrated population, critical commitment, and rich cultural resources—talented writers sought to establish the Jewish- and African-American people each as "a creator and contributor to American civilization" (J. W. Johnson letter to Carl Van Vechten, n.d., in Van Vechten Correspondence). They did so over three generations in both Harlem and the Lower East Side, and in Williamsburg and Brownsville, too. Out of each generation emerges a characteristic style of cultural leadership, along with a distinctive imagistic phase in the literary articulation of ethnic dreams in neighborhood cities.

In their first generations (that of the Lower East Side only longer in the making than Harlem's) each marginalized community had a widely recognized "founding father" with an engaged style of literary activism. Abraham Cahan arrived on the Lower East Side in the early years of its Jewish formation, in 1882 with the first wave of Eastern European refugees; James Weldon Johnson came to Harlem in 1913 just as World War I industry began to draw African Americans north in great numbers.[6] Their voices called their people to participate in political associations. Cahan initiated the use of Yiddish in newspapers in 1882, and Johnson coauthored a "national anthem" for African Americans even before he moved to New York. Cahan, founding editor of the largest Yiddish newspaper in the United States, the *Jewish Daily Forward,* and Johnson, an early organizer and first African-American head of the NAACP, were both kingpins in the networks of their neighborhoods' intelligentsia as well as gatekeepers for literary publication. Just as the younger generation of Harlem Renaissance writers valued Johnson's patronage yet chaffed at his "dicty" taste, so writers on the Lower East Side were both proud and resentful of Cahan's power to, in effect, "edit all the Jewish papers" (Leon Crystal 6 July 1942 letter to Cahan, Cahan Papers).

Out of their life experiences, each of these organizational leaders published a prototypical ethnic New York novel. Cahan's and Johnson's novels dramatize for an uninformed Anglo-American readership the urban history of their respective ethnic groups and the loss of ethnic dreams as the price of assimilation. *The Rise of David Levinsky* (1917) moves well beyond Cahan's earlier novel *Yekl* (1897), in which the title character is Americanized as Jake simply by putting on the clothing and slang of New York's Anglo dance halls and newspapers. Like Johnson's *Autobiography of an Ex-Coloured Man* (1912), *The Rise of David Levinsky* reveals deeper transformations and deeper betrayals of ethnic heritage as the title character tries to achieve social dignity in New York. Although Cahan's novel is flawed by flat diction and Johnson's by a disjointed structure, both establish an economic city context for their characters' lives. Simultaneously, they point beyond the economic city to communal alternatives, which successive generations would elaborate into countercultural dreams.

As fictional autobiographies, *The Rise of David Levinsky* and *The Autobiography of an Ex-Coloured Man* belong to the self-conscious ethnic tradition of persons enlightening strangers about their group histories. Mary Antin (1912, xiii) introduces her autobiography with a personal disclaimer and a representative claim:

> I have not accomplished anything, I have not discovered anything, not even by accident, as Columbus discovered America. My life has been unusual, but by no means unique. And this is the very core of the matter. It is because I understand my history, in its larger outlines, to be typical of many, that I consider it worth recording. My life is a concrete illustration of a multitude of statistical facts.... it is illustrative of scores of unwritten lives.

Although more self-assertive, Cahan's and Johnson's fictional autobiographies likewise present the truth of an individual story as less important than its illustrative power. They take pains to document their groups' collective experiences. Johnson's novel explores the class dynamics of Atlanta's black community and New York's gambling district as well as illicit miscegenation and patronage. *Chedars* and *shuls,* the 1881-82 pogroms, and the Eastern European immigrants' ascendancy in the New York garment industry color Cahan's story. The novels cover broad chronological and geographical ground to establish a sort of pseudostatistical significance for their ethnic everymen. Simultaneously, they make ironic use of the Anglo-American tradition of exemplary autobiography—or "how to make good"—when their everymen become antiheroes by trading valuable ethnic dreams for the alien, addictive "white man's success," money (Johnson [1912] 1935, 193).[7]

With additional irony that points to a central double bind for any marginalized group, each of these New York ethnic everymen betrays his heritage in order to revenge an insult against it. David Levinsky scuttles his old dream of going to college, a dream deeply rooted in the intellectual passions of a Russian youth spent reading Talmud under his mother's care. He does so specifically to beat his old boss in the cloak-making industry, to avenge his Russian-Jewish heritage against that German-Jew's derision (Cahan [1917] 1966, 188). Similarly, Johnson's title character puts aside his dream of bringing to the classical concert stage the black ragtime that "the people like," a dream conceived on a visit to his mother's birthplace in the South. He tries to become an "ex-colored" man out of a "diabolical" desire to get the secret best of whites after he hears about the burning of a black man in the South (Johnson [1912] 1935, 100, 3). Both David Levinsky and the ex-colored man seek success on others' terms, not as expressions of self but as reactions against the rejection of their groups—in the ex-colored man's words, out of "shame that I belonged to a race that could be so dealt with" (188-89). In doing so each loses an identifying ethnic dream closely linked with his mother, her birthland, and its distinctive culture of religious ritual or secular song.

Disavowing their own familial and ethnic dreams, they enter into their business ventures explicitly as "games" (Cahan [1917] 1966, 189; Johnson [1912] 1935, 195). Each is a gambler enchanted by, then addicted to, New York City. New York hooks the ex-colored man with its glittering excitement, which "becomes as binding and necessary as opium is to one addicted to the habit" (90). He feels its "air of enchantment" before he ever sets foot in its streets. Approaching the city by ship from Cuba, he finds the city's "fatally fascinating" welcome to those who dream of a new life there enchanting and deceptive. New York "sits like a great witch at the gate of the country, showing her alluring white face and hiding her crooked hands and feet under the folds of her wide garments—constantly enticing thousands from far within, and tempting those who come from across the sea to go no farther" (Johnson [1912] 1935, 89–90; cf. "The White City" in McKay 1922, 23). Having also "succumbed to the spreading fever" of America, young David Levinsky confronts the "new world" with the innocence of "a new born babe," awed by the same brilliant sea and land, the same display of technological prosperity. Each newcomer believes he has found "an enchanted spot" (Johnson [1912] 1935, 89), "something enchanted" (Cahan [1917] 1966, 87). But like the ex-colored man, it is David himself who is "in a trance" as a result of a "magic" that is essentially "hostile" to him (Cahan [1917] 1966, 87).

The ex-colored man literally becomes a gambler, escaping the "spell" of club life only when he "contract[s] the money fever" for more conventional forms of "a white man's success" (113, 195, 193). Initially "a sort of practical joke" or a con man's slight of hand, his passing for white escalates like obsessive gambling until he is "playing with fire" (3), the very fire of racial prejudice that horrified him in the South. If anything, David Levinsky's "intoxication" is even more twisted. It, too, is based in New York's "mystery" and the "magic wad" of its money (283, 61). But the city becomes addictive for David Levinsky because its intellectual culture taps Old World "magic" (204). An old Talmudic "spell" echoes in the "magic" of the City College "temple," then in the "intellectual intoxication" of social Darwinism, which Levinsky uses to rationalize his ruthless business practices (59, 139, 168–69, 283). His memory of a love story heard in the Old Country is the "drug" that puts him under the "spell" of an immigrant poet's Americanized daughter, then gets him mixed up in a real estate "gamble" she encourages (434, 452, 464). Like the ex-colored man "playing with fire," Levinsky is "moth-like... drawn to the flame" (452).

Although the journalistic realism of *The Rise of David Levinsky* resembles that of many standard Chicago novels[8] and the compressed lyricism of *The Autobiography of an Ex-Coloured Man* resembles modernist style, both present alternatives to the materialism of the economic city and megalopolis, even in the "mystery" they attribute to New York. Most importantly, they distinguish from materialism's alien and deluding mysteries the expressive ethnic dreams that later neighborhood literature would embrace. The antiheroic stories of David Levinsky and the ex-colored man point toward the true promised land that they themselves refuse to enter: an urban home continuous with the birthplace of their mothers, where the ritual, communal voices of Talmud and ragtime sing.[9] What makes *The Rise of David Levinsky* the fountainhead of Jewish-American neighborhood literature is its early elaboration of the family religion of Talmud, which David later gives up. Similarly, *The Autobiography of an Ex-Coloured Man* is "the first [fiction] to sense the musical possibilities of ragtime" (Van Vechten 23 March 1925 letter to Johnson, Johnson Papers) and other evolving forms of black culture, whose spiritual roots Du Bois (1903) traced to the "soul of black folks." It was up to the next generation of New York's Jewish- and African-American writers to affirm these dreams in the city's promised land.

Some Jewish writers—especially German-Americans—felt less confined within the ghetto, established close associations with non-Jewish leftists, and continued to use the model of the economic city to analyze and target capitalistic injustices.[10] Many others, however—particularly among Eastern European immigrants—remained closely tied to ghetto communities and developed images of vital street life, powerful community bonds, and emergent dreams that closely resemble the composite renaissance portrait of Harlem. For example, Sholom Asch's *The Mother* (1937), originally published in Yiddish, fills in the very "odor" of cooking onions and "noise of the street" that make the Lower East Side "home" for its immigrants (85–86). It shows family women becoming "well acquainted with [their] neighbors" (156; cf. Stansell 1986, e.g., 41–42) and artist groups singing folk music "as though they belonged to the same family" (251). It dramatizes as a "Jewish triumph" the artist who recognizes his people simultaneously "in the mirror of [his] mind" and in his "living model" of a pregnant woman, "mother and child all in one.... Beginning and end united, like a circle" of generation (275, 188–89).[11] In *Aaron*

Traum (1930, 143–46, 365–66), Hyman and Lester Cohen create an artist for whom "nought but the dirt of the sidewalks," "all the places where he had slaved and starved," "the street...singing her disordered song," and all the "stories [he has] heard" are "*his* New York"—wondering, "How had he emerged from it all?"

Most persistently and richly, the fictions of Anzia Yezierska articulate the dreams of the Lower East Side. She dramatized the second-generational vitality of its literature much as Langston Hughes did for Harlem. Both led as representatives, not organizers, of their New York communities. As young Hughes's first publication in *The Crisis* marked the arrival of the "New Negro," Yezierska's work, immediately successful when she began writing in her thirties, was seen to embody the voice of Jewish immigrant culture. She "was Poland. She was the whole turgid stream of European immigration pouring into our home country," proclaimed a columnist (Frank Crane, clipping in Yezierska Papers) reviewing her first collection of short stories, *Hungry Hearts* (1920). Yet her life, in contrast to Hughes's as the "poet low-rate" of Harlem, exemplified Jewish Americans' more certain access to mainstream culture: she was honored by a celebrity dinner at the Waldorf Astoria on the occasion of her first novel, *Bread Givers* (1925); she was declared by Gertrude Atherton (1923) to be "the most remarkable case of sheer genius...imposing itself upon an unsympathetic world"; and headlined as a "Sweatshop Cinderella" (Yezierska 1950, 40), she was whisked off to Hollywood to join Metro-Goldwin Meyer's stable of famous writers.

As her trek to Hollywood and Hughes's continual travels suggest, both these authors lived somewhat apart from the ethnic groups and communities they represented. Neither had strong family ties. They both felt their fathers had rejected them; Hughes's mother nearly always lived at a distance, and Yezierska's was dead; Hughes had only a stepbrother, and Yezierska's sisters seem to have played no important part in her life; Hughes was unmarried and childless, and Yezierska was twice divorced, her only child left in her second husband's custody. Both were loners in their daily habits. They maintained little daily intimacy or organizational involvement in Harlem or on the Lower East Side, despite close association with important groups and projects in their communities.

The masculine ethic of independence may have helped Hughes to remain consistently productive in his position just to the side of his community's center. But Yezierska continually felt caught between worlds. She felt smothered when living and working on the Lower East Side[12] and cut off from the source of her art during her years in Hollywood and on Fifth Avenue.[13] Like the heroine of her title story in *Children of Loneliness* (1923a, 110), she felt trapped "either among those who drag me down or in the awful isolation of a hall bedroom"—either staying at "home burning for life" or self-exiled in a "loneliness that's death" (cf. Gerstenberg 1912, 119). Paradoxically, however, Yezierska's sense of being caught between smothering Jewish poverty and arid gentile success made her representative of other second-generation "children of loneliness, wandering between worlds that are at once too old and too new to live in" (1923a, 123), just as Hughes's wanderings made him representative of those other mobile urbanites who found a symbolic home in Harlem.

Hughes's poetry and Yezierska's fiction express voices that are more communal than personal. Unlike Johnson's and Cahan's fictional autobiographies, their art constructs autobiographical fictions. Hughes adapts Whitman's "cosmic I" to the perspective of the "darker brother" singing America in Harlem and beyond. He speaks as "I" whose "old man's a white old man / and my old mother's black"; as "I" who "am a Negro" and have "been a slave"; as "I" who have "known rivers" and "bathed in the Euphrates when dawns were young"; as "I" who "was a red man one time," too ([1925] 1935, 109, 52, 19, 51, 100). The numerous anthologies Hughes edited, of African literature and African-American poems, stories, folklore, humor, jazz, also made public other voices of this "cosmic I" that knows its dark side.

Yezierska, on the other hand, stuck to her own fiction and fictionalized autobiography. The details of plot and character seem much more personal in her work, which shifts disconcertingly between first- and third-person and includes barely disguised counterparts for her family members, scholarly lover, and writer self.[14] Her narrative voice often offends, as it challenges, the standards of distance and invention that dominate Western aesthetics as well as U.S. urban traditions. "She writes about life, not as a reporter, social student, slummer or reformer, but as one who has lived it," explained an early advocate of her lack of conventional "literary style" (William Lyon Phelps quoted in Yezierska 1950, 125). Yezierska herself used an autobiographical story, "An Immigrant among the Editors" (1923a, 56), to explain: "With me my thoughts were not up in my head. They were in my hands and feet, in the thinnest nerves of my hair, in the flesh and blood of my whole body.... [Thinking was] like tearing myself out inch by inch from the roots of the earth." In another such story, "My Own People" ([1920b] 1975, 240, 249), she identifies this organic, rooted voice as communal. Yezierska's fictional counterpart Sophie Sapinsky comes to see "her own life" in that of her gossipy landlady, Hannah Breineh, and behind their two lives she sees "the massed ghosts of thousands upon thousands" of struggling, unheard immigrants. Only then can she write living words. " 'Ach! At last it writes itself in me!' she whispered triumphantly. 'It's not me—it's their cries—my own people—crying in me!' " Yezierska's people speak in her fictionalized self-portraits as in her other characters. What often sounds overblown to Anglo ears is not a self-indulgence, but a communal expression of immigrant dreams and Yiddish flourish.

The sounds of the people dominate Hughes's Harlem literature. In his collection of poems *The Weary Blues* ([1925] 1935, 107, 66, 23, 36, 37, 32, 105, 27) a mother reminisces and instructs her son: "Life for me ain't been no crystal stair. / . . . / So boy, don't you turn back." A church congregation exclaims, "Come with a blast of trumpets, / Jesus! / . . . / Sweet silver trumpets, / Jesus!" in "When Sue Wears Red." And a variety of voices sing lines of song:

> I got the Weary Blues
> And I can't be satisfied.
>
> Shake you brown feet, honey,
> Shake 'em swift and wil'—
>
> My man's done left me,
> Chile, he's gone away.

The audience responds, "Sing 'em, sister!" and "Play, plAY, PLAY!" while "The low beating of the tom-toms, / The slow beating of the tom-toms" echoes voices of African ancestors. Spoken words and song intertwine in "The Cat and the Saxophone (2 A.M.)":

> . . . You like
> liquor,
> don't you, honey?
> BUT MY BABY
> Sure. Kiss me,
> DON'T LOVE NOBODY
> daddy.
> BUT ME.

The many voices of the ghetto also intertwine in Yezierska's fiction, "one minute" in the rough dialect of "an East Side yenteh—the next minute [in] the rhythm of the Bible" (1923b, 43). Indeed, the whole Lower East Side seems to grow out of the resonance of her characters' very names, recurring in infinite variations. Hanneh Hayyeh and Moses Rifkin in *Hungry Hearts* (1920a) (named from immigrant Mary Antin's famous autobiography)[15] transform into Hannah Breineh and Morris Lipkin in other works ([1920c] 1975; 1923b; 1925). A hunchbacked fish peddlar from Yezierska's childhood, Zalmon Shlomoh,[16] is called by his full name in *Children of Loneliness* (1923a, 18) then divided into Zalmon and Shlomoh in other stories (1925; 1927). Yezierska's family members are named and nicknamed repeatedly. The result of all this is a sense of continuing reality, linking various novels and stories together into an envisioned Lower East Side rather like William Faulkner's Yoknapatawpha County.[17]

For Hughes and Yezierska both, the sounds of the people are vitalizing and pressing, invoking oral tradition in print. In keeping with Walter Ong's discussion of "orality" (1977), they emphasize the community's participation over time in the dreams, art, and stories of the urban present, giving them reality well beyond individual imaginings. Hughes's poetry repeats the old religious experiences of spirituals, the jazz forms spun out of jam sessions, and the folk tales that every Aunt Sue (Hughes [1925] 1935, 57) told her children. In precise parallel, Yezierska's fiction embraces the faith of the Torah and Psalms in communal readings (despite her personal hatred of her father's Talmudic misogyny), elaborates the rhythms of Yiddish and Hebrew, and tells the folk tales of her immigrant history, the "one story [she has] to tell" (1923a, 18).

The sounds of the people press toward a truth beyond logic while also placing dreams in sensory reality. Hughes reveals laughter in the tears of blues, spirit in the sensual exhibitions of jazz, just as Yezierska hears "hollering noise" in the music of her people, "beautiful song" in the discord of the streets, until "it began singing in my heart, the music of the whole of Hester Street" (1925, 22).[18] Generally, spirit is not split off from body, music from noise in their works. Not to be rescued *from* poverty, the spirit of the people lives *in* poverty. Dreams emerge in the reality of people's lives, as they do in the shotgun shacks made into altars and the Jim Crow birds mingled with doves of peace in John Biggers's 1987 painting of Houston's African-American Third Ward, *Shotguns* (fig. 13). In his famous poem also anthologized as "Harlem," Hughes eventually found the people's "Dream Deferred" ([1967] 1968) in the festered sores, stinking meats, crusted sweets, sagging loads, and ever-threatening explosions of their lives. In the 1920s, he and Yezierska found their peoples' dreams in the dirt of their ghetto lives, especially in the streets they made famous: Lenox Avenue, Seventh Avenue, Hester Street. As black Harlem's streets transform ghetto death into neighborhood masquerade in renaissance literature, so the streets in New York's Jewish ghettoes could also be "our sweet, lawless, personal, high-colored life," as Yezierska's contemporary Samuel Ornitz put it (1923, 31).

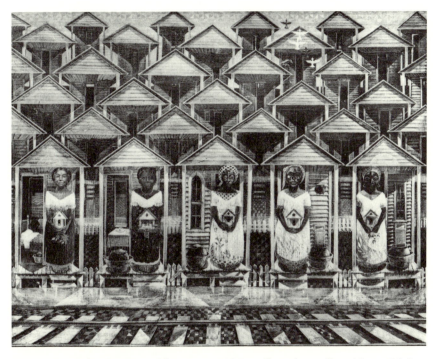

Figure 13. John Biggers, *Shotguns* (1987), oil and acrylic, 40 × 56 in., photograph by Earlie Hudnall. Courtesy of the artist.

For Yezierska, as also for Hughes more than any other renaissance author, the vitality of ethnic neighborhoods can gather inside into intimacy. While the family flat is always too intimate in her work—stifling, deafening in its closeness—more loosely related domestic gatherings offer positive images of home on Hester Street—in a basement boarding house feast in "My Own People" for instance ([1920b] 1975). *Arrogant Beggar* (1927, 238, 226) culminates in the creation of a coffee shop as an "artists' corner" in the "tenements where everything is so ugly and alike." In this venture into communal homemaking, Adele Lindner is inspired by a washerwoman who evokes "a long-forgotten picture of my own mother" (168)—as a grandmother's memory inspires the creation of a working girls' club in one of Chicago's minor residential novels (Laughlin 1912, 100). Yezierska's Muhmenkeh, first named in *The Bread Givers,* develops a generous character in *Arrogant Beggar* and creates "a sense of peace, of homecoming" for Adele, a stranger in her basement apartment (173). A feast of sugar-water wine and butterless cake to which she invites neighborhood children epitomizes Muhmenkeh's ability to realize the "home feeling in the heart," the "plenty" of dreams out of poverty's "nothing" (213, 224-26). Even after Muhmenkeh's death, Adele feels Muhmenkeh "alive" inside of her as she works for "my people" (235), haggles with them for food, reminds them of old homes in Paris or Poland (230, 252), and joins them in "the music for which I was starving" (241) in Muhmenkeh's Coffee Shop.

Always mediated by the textures of "my people's" songs and speech, and at best guided by a maternal presence, the neighborhood city's memories and possibilities come together beneath the streets in Hughes's cabaret blues and Yezierska's basement feasts. These are centering elements, too, in two third-generation novels that follow the ghetto streets out toward multicultural dreams, *Call It Sleep* (1934) by Henry Roth and *Invisible Man* (1952) by Ralph Ellison. They affirm the symbolic vitality of the Lower East Side and Harlem as urban homes even for those who have moved on and who present themselves as individual and universal, rather than ethnic, artists.

Roth and Ellison both have distanced themselves personally from the representative ethnic experiences portrayed in their novels. Ellison insists that his "book is not autobiographical" (Ellison 1963, 320), and Roth that his "violates the truth" of his own life (Roth 1969, 267). Generally, the two men have presented themselves as loners,[19] and their fictional characters have been consequently misunderstood as alienated, too. More specifically, neither has identified himself primarily as an African- or Jewish-American writer. Each has named three Anglo writers—including modernists Joyce and Eliot in both cases—as literary forebears (Ellison 1963, 326; Roth 1969, 270-72). Both have interpreted their novels as "ethnic" or "minority" works only in the sense that they use African- or Jewish-American materials, because "the individual is a minority" whose "specific circumstance"—including its racial dimensions—realizes the "universal" (Ellison 1963, 322), or just "because that's the life I knew best" (Roth 1975, 152).[20] Especially have both rejected any reading of their novels as "social commentary" or "protest" (Roth quoted in Lyons 1976, 160; Ellison 1963, 321-22). They have thus separated their work from economic city ethnic novels by their compatriots Mike Gold and Richard Wright, to which leftist critics with strong ethnic identifications have compared them unfavorably.

Nonetheless, Roth's and Ellison's own life journeys—and their novels—intersect with the patterns of ethnic neighborhood experience that the Lower East Side and Harlem developed in literature. Born in Eastern Europe, Roth was two years old when his family immigrated to New York in 1908. He lived first in Brownsville—New York's second best-known Jewish neighborhood—then from 1910 to 1914 on the Lower East Side, and finally in a mixed Irish-Jewish-Italian part of Harlem. Significantly, Roth modified the autobiographical beginnings of *Call It Sleep* ([1934] 1960, 9-11; cf. Roth 1969, 265-66) so that his fictional counterpart, two-year-old David Schearl, fits the Jewish immigrant archetype still more closely. David enters "the Golden Land" not in 1908 but in "1907, the year that was destined to bring the greatest number of immigrants to the shores of the United States." And thereafter, David's story takes place entirely within the neighborhoods of Brownsville and the Lower East Side, except for a comic excursion uptown to the Metropolitan Museum. Although complicated at its edges by the ethnic diversity and "hostility" that Roth himself experienced in Harlem, *Call It Sleep* centers in the "homogeneous" Jewish community of family and *chedar* with which Roth "completely identified" on the Lower East Side (Roth 1969, 265-66).

Similarly, the careers of Ellison and his invisible man follow the pattern common to Harlem's literature after World War I. Although Ellison did not come to Harlem until its postrenaissance years of depression, he arrived there as a Tuskeegee graduate from Oklahoma City in his early twenties, much like the collegiate Harlem Renaissance generation from southern cities before him. Like the earlier youths, he held a variety of jobs—from newsboy to receptionist to wartime sailor to college lecturer—and became involved in a network of artists, intellectuals, and social activists as a musician, a photographer, and a writer of radical commentary for *The New Masses* (Ellison 1963, 317; Reilly 1970, 2). With New York as a home base even after his peripatetic career led him elsewhere, Ellison's experience prepared him well for the *Invisible Man*'s invocation of the city as a "symbolic" home and promised land: "That's not a place, it's a dream" (1952, 136). Its hero enters Harlem in proper mythic style—after being breathlessly "crushed" and mechanically propelled on the subway—perhaps at 125th Street, where Ellison himself is pictured on the back cover of his novel's 1952 paperback edition. Just like Fisher's King Solomon Gillis, the invisible man is exhilarated by "so many black people," by their uninhibited crowding and talk, and especially by "the shock of seeing a black policeman directing traffic" (140–43).

Although *Call It Sleep* and *Invisible Man* both dramatize individual quests for identity by characters who often feel isolated, the child David and the young invisible man are ethnic everymen who find—and enlarge—themselves through communal, ethnic forces. In particular, rural-based black folkways claimed in the city hold the key to the invisible man's identity. He uses folk tales to find himself apart from the stereotypic "figments of the imagination" (3) ready-made to define him like the megalopolitan newspaper clichés in *Miss Lonelyhearts*. Ellison's hero names himself after Bre'r Bear: "Call me Jack-the-Bear" (9). He identifies himself with Buckeye the Rabbit, too (211), affirming these tricksters as his own close relatives. His most exhilarating experience of self-affirmation comes when he puts aside shame about his home-boy heritage to eat a yam on the open street—using soul food to claim an identity that even extends beyond black culture to both Jehovah and Popeye: "I yam what I yam!" (231). The invisible man finds the answer to "who I was" (3) in the communal "unrecorded history" that African Americans tell "on the [street] corner" (407), not in the nation's common stereotypes nor even in its dominant myth of freedom as independence. He rejects the free-floating identity of a confidence man as no less false and empty than any of the other externally imposed identities he assumes—only more chaotic, "without boundaries" (431–32). Instead, he finds an identity within and looks for a "socially responsible role to play" by affirming his black "invisibility" and submerging himself in daydreams, even reefer dreams, of African-American folk history and stories and music in his underground "hibernation," the "end [that] is the beginning" (9, 503).

Similarly, David Schearl must wrest an identity out of communal forces. He appeals to family history and religious tradition to distinguish himself and his dreams within the dark forces of sexuality and death. Not quite six years old, in Brownsville he finds escape only in his mother's arms from "The Cellar" of book I. A period of "too pure" transcendence—first "alone" (296) then companioned by an older Catholic boy—offers respite on the roof of his Lower East Side tenement home a few years later. But Roth, like Ellison, rejects both self-negation and transcendence as solutions to the problem of identity. Eventually betrayed by his rooftop comrade's anti-Semitism, David ventures into the street to affirm that "he had always been one of" a gang of Jewish boys from which he'd stayed aloof before (359). Once he establishes that communal street base, he begins to understand who he is and who he might become. He does so, as the novel climaxes, by creating his own versions of the Old World family history symbolized by "The Picture" in book II and the Biblical story of Isaiah's transformation by "The Coal" in book III. The social contexts of his self-creative achievement are confirmed when the rabbi declares him "a true Yiddish child" (365) and his father finally embraces him as "My sawn. Mine. Yes" (437).

The path to that final affirmation in *Call It Sleep* precisely parallels the final movement of *Invisible Man* through heavily peopled neighborhood streets, down into the technological power sources that lie beneath them, toward a visionary revelation that presses beyond ethnic boundaries. David, longing for his mother but unable to go to her, runs instead through streets that are "Humanity. On feet, on crutches, in carts and cars.... Human voices, motion, seething, throbbing, bawling, honking horns and whistling" (407) to a spur of streetcar track where a neighborhood gang had once challenged him to thrust a shaft of metal into the third rail. There he seeks to find the light and power of Isaiah's revelation by tapping the buried electricity with a milk dipper like his milkman father's. When he joins himself to that "titanic.... barbaric.... Power" (419)—with an electric flash and a scream—the neighborhood's myriad voices also come together:

"W'at?

    W'ut?

                  Va-at?

Gaw blimey! W'atsa da ma'?" (419)

They reach out to him as he plunges to where the awful light narrows to "nothing," then beyond to "Nothingness beautified." And out of his vision of a foundational, unifying beatitude, he gives back his own child's voice—"WHISTLE!"—into the multi-ethnic crowd (428–31).

So, too, the invisible man runs through neighborhood streets, affirming his complicity with Harlem's people in the violent race riot that gathers them into a powerful "crowd," "a dark mass in motion" (475). As David longs for his mother, so the invisible man wants to go back to the "stable familiar face" of an older Harlem woman who had comforted him. Instead he runs to a break in the surface of the streets. Echoing David's experience, he plunges through an open utility hole, down onto the coal heaps that fire the city's furnaces, and into a visionary "state neither of dreaming nor of waking, but somewhere in between." There "the darkness" of a castration dream turns to the "light" of revelation, and he awakens "whole," with his own voice, to "laugh" (493–94). "Hibernating" then as "Jack-the-Bear," "in a border area" of Harlem, he wonders if "even an invisible man might have a socially responsible role to play," if "on the lower frequencies, I speak for you" (503).

Both David's and the invisible man's ultimate dreams are prophetic. Their fusions of dream and reality, of street life and technology, move well beyond what is "objectively" knowable. They envision inchoate possibilities for communal roles that they do not effect in mature social actions. David's vision is a child's dream in that elusive realm we "might as well call . . . sleep" (431), which many critics have even equated with death. And the invisible man enjoys his light only in secret underground, his vision only "between . . . dreaming and waking." Nonetheless the dreams are powerful and compelling—and so much alike in promoting an urban dialogue of self and other—because they are dug up from beneath the surfaces of urban street life. Simultaneously symbolic and sensuous, they achieve the "spiritually earthy" quality of "mediating between dung and God" that artist Aaron Douglas proclaimed the goal of the Harlem Renaissance ([21 Dec. 1925] letter to Hughes, Hughes Papers). It is the same quality that Leslie Fiedler, following Nathanael West (Fiedler 1960, 105; cf. West quoted in Light 1961, 18), has identified as the definitive mark of "Jewish character." Indeed, "by using this same mythic touchstone," another critic (Alter 1973, 65) has objected, "one might justifiably conclude that the most remarkable American Jewish novel is neither *Call It Sleep* nor [Saul Bellow's later] *Herzog* but Ralph Ellison's *Invisible Man.*"

The profound similarities between Roth's and Ellison's novels—and their authors' social postures—culminate the sequence of parallels between the Lower East Side and Harlem in literature. Conforming to three "phases" in ethnic literary development that several other critics have also identified (e.g., Chametzky 1986, 50–56; Bruce-Novoa 1987, 244–46),[21] these parallels dramatize the importance of community as a base for countercultural literature. Thus the beginnings of a period of strong ethnic literary activity are deeply rooted in activist authorial protest against the alienating powers of the dominant culture—as in the work of Cahan and Johnson. The period's midpoint is stretched between immersion in and separation from ethnic culture, as much a pressure for Yezierska and Hughes as the dominant culture. Only then can universalist writers like Roth and Ellison assume the legitimacy of ethnic perspectives and materials, moving toward a future of pluralism or assimilation, which their mixed reviews consider uncertain.[22]

Urban dreams figure centrally in this developmental sequence. The protagonists of *The Autobiography of an Ex-Coloured Man* and *The Rise of David Levinsky* play New York's addictive and ultimately "hostile" "games" of individual success at the price of deeper ethnic dreams. Hughes's and Yezierska's personae affirm those ethnic dreams, mostly within the neighborhoods centered on Lenox Avenue and Hester Street. David Schearl and the invisible man call for breakthroughs and dialectical syntheses that bring the buried potential of ethnic neighborhood dreams out to the borderland of the divided city, asserting their legitimacy in direct confrontation with the larger, Anglo-dominated city.

Dreams, importantly, signal the difference between neighborhood-city and megalopolitan images, as between urban hope and urban despair. The literature of the lost generation shows that internalizing the economic city's materialism means locking the uprooted urban psyche in artifice and fragmentation, which poisons the sources of urban aspiration, the hope of any future home in the city. Ironically, those who continued to dream had least reason to expect fulfillment.

Their dreams were paraded in the streets of Harlem and the Lower East Side, in continuity with the colors, tastes, and sounds of neighborhood life. They were not private affairs—like Newland Archer and Ellen Olenska's or Jay Gatsby's or Miss Lonelyhearts's—to be smothered or killed or perverted by a society caught in illusions. Nor were they prefabricated illusions. They developed from within as expressive aspirations of the human spirit, like art itself. Perhaps, as Roth and Ellison both suggest and call into question, these dreams can be realized more broadly, but only if they keep their vital ground in particularity, historical continuity, and community.[23]

8

Regional Perspectives and Situated Insights

Despite the strong sense of place in literature's neighborhood city, placelessness has characterized many generalizations about U.S. literary culture, as a former student who grew up in a gardening family with her hands in the dirt has helped me to understand. As conceived during the nationalistic 1920s, the "classic" literary canon set aside our regional "literature of place," along with—indeed largely including—works by women and people of color that new scholarship has recently been recovering and recentering. In contrast to the "rooted" sense of "being 'in *place*' " in the life of African-American Toni Morrison, for instance, the standard version of "American literature ... defines the universal as the literature of time and *space*," in which an alienated hero "conquers space by traveling over it and forms ... his own history" (Morrison 1976, 167–68; May 1986, 1; italics added). The nationalism in our literary canon has abstracted art from the grass roots history of our regions. The economic city and the modern megalopolis epitomize that antiregional abstraction. From world's fair Chicago to the New York-Hollywood axis, our hegemonic literature has presented cities from a nationalistic perspective that expands toward global imperialism and reduces regions to rural backwaters.

I want to challenge, but not to censor the national perspective on urban experience. The economic city and megalopolis have shaped aesthetically powerful works and insightful models for many aspects of urban experience.

Despite their specific origins in the turn-of-the-century mobility of middle-class white men and the rootlessness of the lost generation, they have proved compelling for authors from many backgrounds. Both the tragic and comic dimensions of Sinclair Lewis's *Babbitt* (1922) come from squeezing the economic city's tycoonery and megalopolitan advertising into an Anglo-midwestern Main Street. James T. Farrell's Studs Lonigan trilogy (1934) exposes the barrenness of an Irish-American life overruled by class struggle and mass images of pop-tune romance in Chicago. In *Native Son* ([1940] 1966), Richard Wright shows how economic divisions and megalopolitan stereotypes shape the experience of blacks and whites who might otherwise share feelings of love, fear, and hope in Chicago. In *The Dollmaker* (1954) by Harriette Arnow, the economic city's dichotomy between urban and rural experience emphasizes the severe dislocation of an Appalachian white woman moving to Detroit during World War II. In Bernard Malamud's *A New Life* (1961), megalopolitan alienation structures a Jewish professor's experience in an Oregon college town that he has expected to be a culturally expressive, communal city-town. In Euro-American Joan Didion's Hollywood, the "nothing" of compulsive freeway driving and unseen TV movies anesthetizes the deadly "point" of an abortion in *Play It As It Lays* (1970, 216). Repressed by the "extraordinary popular delusions" of happy homes, megalopolitan violence erupts even in suburbia in Joyce Carol Oates's hard-hitting collection of short stories, *Marriages and Infidelities* (1972, 129–46). And megalopolis reveals its imperialistic reach by invading the rural West Indies when an alienated New York model brings her inability to honor family there in Toni Morrison's *Tar Baby* (1981a). Clearly, women and ethnic writers do not always construct their urban experience in familial and neighborhood terms, although historically they have been situated to do so much more frequently than Anglo-American men.

Such works do not just project skyscraper images onto ethnic neighborhoods, medium-sized low-rise cities, and suburbs either. The national perspective is strong enough to co-opt specifically regional materials. In a strict sense, for instance, *The Day of the Locust* is a regional novel: it uses the features, activities, and concerns of a distinctive region not just as backdrop, inspiration, or detailing but to define its aesthetic structure and themes (Wells 1973, 5–7). West was not among those short-term prospectors in the picture business that one of his characters berates for "go[ing] back East and tell[ing] dialect stories about producers they've never met" ([1933] 1962, 15). But his portrait of a Hollywood that commandeers icons from distant cultures—taking them out of their originating, meaningful contexts—denies the rootedness of culture itself and the significance of regional differences. His Hollywood fakes the Mexican ranch houses to which it has some historically rooted, regional claim no less than the Samoan huts and Tudor cottages to which it has none. Paradoxically, this regional novel dramatizes the antiregional implications of mass culture and the nationalistic bias that has dominated not only our urban understandings but our literary canon.

The problem with the economic city and megalopolis, then, is not that they highlight such aspects of urban experience but that they have overshadowed our regional literature. Especially during the past hundred years of urbanization, the economic systems of *cities* have been identified with the *nation* and its imperialistic reach. By contrast, *regional* city-towns and neighborhoods have been associated with *rural* nostalgia (e.g., White and White 1962, 154). Our urban-identified nation and rural-identified regions have become mutually exclusive territories of the mind, with the former all too often pushing the latter aside. Our national understandings have obscured the interactions between urban and rural America, as well as the regional diversity of U.S. urban experience and literature. Perhaps a renewed regionalism can help open our minds both to the continuities of rural/urban interaction and to the realities of diversity—in concert with the visions of many women and ethnic writers. Such concerted dialogue might well act as an antidote to mass megalopolitan despair.

But first we must learn to recognize as urban some literary works that we commonly understand as regional. For the most part, we label as "city novels" only those of the national economic city and world megalopolis. Though clearly set in a city, a regional city-town novel like Kate Chopin's *The Awakening* ([1899] 1976), set in New Orleans, falls outside the category of urban literature.

In general, the South's regional literature challenges our national urban understandings most profoundly. It is likely to surprise us, however, that southern literature has had anything at all to say about cities until very recently. Set apart from the rest of the nation during the Civil War, the South long epitomized regionalism in the United States. And for just as long, it was viewed as rural and backward, epitomizing the common equation of regional with rural. While it is true that the South has maintained the lowest ratio of urban to rural population in the nation, that does not account for our view of the South as rural. We had trouble recognizing the South's "urban dimension" even when its largest cities were expanding faster than those in the Northeast and Midwest throughout the first four decades of the twentieth century (Brownell and Goldfield 1977, 5; Brownell 1977, 124–25). Similarly, we stereotyped as rural home boys the African Americans who came to Harlem from the South during the early half of that period, despite their cosmopolitan (and partly female) leadership. "South" and "city" remain such antithetical terms in U.S. culture that we have coined the term "sun belt"—echoing farm belt, black belt, and Bible belt—to talk about the recent ascendancy of southern urban power.

In any event, southern literature has often been set in regional cities. George Washington Cable of New Orleans was a contemporary of Joel Chandler Harris from rural Georgia, and Cable's historical novels of the French Quarter are just as deeply rooted in the South's regional culture as Harris's Uncle Remus stories. New Orleans figured as the largest city in the South, the major transportation outlet and financial link to New York and Chicago until Houston, Dallas, and Atlanta eclipsed it in 1950. In southern literature, the "city slicker" often comes from New Orleans, which appears more often than any other large regional city in southern novels. Most fictive southern cities are presented as medium or small, however, without significant industrial machinery, railroads, or skyscrapers, and deeply embedded in the broader region. In the South, most urban growth occurred in cities under 100,000 before World War II, manufacturing lagged until the postindustrial age, and agricultural dependence has remained a rule (Brownell 1977, 128; Brownell and Goldfield 1977, 14). It is precisely the lack of industrial dominance in southern literature that challenges our skyscraper assumptions, lack of industry making southern cities no less cities.

Even during the periods of dramatic urban growth, the South's major writers have seldom focused on cities in their fiction or poetry, though cities have always been part of their fictive worlds. William Faulkner, Zora Neale Hurston, Katherine Anne Porter, John Crowe Ransom, and Richard Wright all wrote about smaller towns and rural settings in the "shadow of the plantation" (Johnson 1934) during the 1920s and 1930s, when southern literature established its claim to regional greatness. Typically in southern literature, rural or small town characters go to "the city" for occasions, especially for breaks from everyday habits and morals: to spend a night in a hotel in Augusta where even the city's mills are "all right to fool around in" in Caldwell's *Tobacco Road* (1932, 239); to elope to

Orlando in Hurston's *Their Eyes Were Watching God* ([1937] 1978); to visit Miss Reba's whorehouse in Memphis in Faulkner's *Sanctuary* ([1931] 1932), *The Mansion* (1959), and *The Reivers* ([1962] 1966); "to see everything there is to see in a city [in Atlanta] so that [a young boy] would be content to stay home for the rest of his life" in "The Artificial Nigger" by Flannery O'Connor ([1955] 1972, 251).

Even when the characters live in a city, southern fictions often arrange to start and finish in the country or in a small town. That is so for the Baton Rouge story of Jack Burden and his political boss, Willie Stark, in *All The King's Men* ([1946] 1968) by Robert Penn Warren. Warren's fictionalized account of Huey Long's life starts with a trip "out of the city" (1) to visit both Burden's Landing and the small town where Willie started his career, then ends with a return to both hometowns after Stark's assassination in the city. Katherine Anne Porter arranges a country-city-country triptych for her story of a young girl's coming to terms with sexual expectations in "Old Mortality" ([1939] 1962). And Ellen Glasgow's novel on a similar theme, *The Sheltered Life* ([1932] 1979, 5), begins by explaining that Queenborough's leading citizens came from the country and often "retired to modest Virginia farms."

This ordering of fictional experience represents a striking regional deviation from the "pastoral design" that Leo Marx (1969, 252–54) has identified in U.S. literature. The city-country-city pattern that Marx finds so "distinctively American" involves "the retreat" to nature "from a relatively complex, organized community"; "the exploration of nature," usually in a wilderness setting; and "the return" to that "relatively complex" society, now acknowledged as "inescapable." *The Jungle* and *Miss Lonelyhearts* exemplify Marx's "pastoral design" with abrupt shifts to country excursions just before the nadir of their heroes' urban careers.[1] Marx uses the "pastoral design" to argue that Americans—presumably all Americans—need the simplicities of distinctively natural settings to provide temporary getaways from urban reality. The South's contrapuntal pattern suggests instead that the organic continuities of wilderness, farm, and community constitute the general rule of life within which the big city offers an occasional holiday, and that we need such Mardi Gras occasions to keep "the old order" and ourselves flexible.

In southern literature, the city both relaxes and clarifies the rule of continuity. It does so in tragic form in *The Awakening* ([1899] 1976). Kate Chopin's novel dramatizes a young matron's awakening to her own disruptive, "sensuous" powers in "the voice of the sea" at a gulfside resort. It is at Grande Isle, not in the city, that New Orleans vacationers form a community close enough to infringe constantly on her "soul" (15, 113). The city itself offers some room for Edna Pontellier to explore alternatives to conventional domestic life—from racetrack indulgences to artistic self-discipline. But community and conventions are only relatively diluted by New Orleans's greater anonymity and labyrinthine privacies in comparison to Grande Isle's connected family bungalows. Mrs. Pontellier finally must realize that an unconventional life "alone" in the city would jeopardize her children's lives; so she goes to the sea to die "alone" (113). Her choice among different kinds of "aloneness" clearly represents a personal tragedy within the continuities of southern literature, although her death invokes the ambiguities that contemporary Chicago women also found in self-expressive breaks from communal continuities: "Alone, yes; but free!" (Gerstenberg 1912, 119).

As also in Harlem Renaissance literature, the continuities of family and community, of past, present, and future, of life and death, expand and limit human possibilities in southern literature. Structurally, they contain occasional urban flings within the environing region. Narratively, they embrace the city in communal conversation—such as the choral "we" who are both family and town in Faulkner's *The Town* (1957, 3). Metaphorically, they include the city in their cyclical symbolism: the wheels of community in Wright's "Long Black Song" ([1938] 1940, 213), the pools of time in Faulkner's *Absalom, Absalom!* (1936, 261), and the spider web world in Warren's *All the King's Men* ([1946] 1968, 188). These circles encompass both town and city in the last two parts of Faulkner's Snopes trilogy. In *The Town* (1957, 315–16), the city of Memphis is "a convergence like the spokes of a gigantic dark wheel lying on its hub." Similarly, in *The Mansion* (1959, 283), the town of Jefferson is "the center" of a wheel, Yoknapatawpha County "enclosing it . . . tied by the diverging roads to that center as is the rim to the hub by its spokes" like "the ripples on living water above the dreamless slumber of your past," and "the web" of humanity's "passions" of "rapacity" and "dreams." Literature's southern city belongs to continuous cycles, its spokes part of a world wheel that includes all humanity, time, and nature.

Within this unity, urban grotesqueries and divisions do not differ in kind from other violations of life's continuities elsewhere in the South. Idiots and freaks, tragic perverts and comic caricatures have long populated all its settings. In contrast to Nathanael West's newspaper readers and F. Scott Fitzgerald's party goers, southern grotesques express deep human obsessions (Beck 1960, 288), not perversions of mass urban forces. Mass culture, in fact, figures little in southern literature. Old genteel conventions and continuing folk ways weave through the entire region instead. The South's genteel culture is as much rural as urban in *The Awakening* and Faulkner's *Sanctuary* ([1931] 1932), while its folk culture is as much urban as rural in *Their Eyes Were Watching God* ([1937] 1978) and Toni Morrison's *Song of Solomon* (1977). The social divisions that these distinctive cultural traditions express are matters of caste, not class. Even in cities, they are not created by the workings of economic machinery but by social responses to the vagaries of sex and race. Whether in rural or urban settings, it is bodily marked divisions such as these that tear most painfully at the web of humanity in southern literature.

Distinguishing the "urban" South seems as ambiguous as defining the concept of city in the United States generally before the Civil War. Southern literature tends to miniaturize cities as "small" and "towns." What is called the "small place" of Queenborough in Ellen Glasgow's fiction (e.g., [1932] 1979, 5), for instance, looks like her native city of Richmond, Virginia. Recent urban historians are similarly undependable in their labeling of southern cities, especially if those cities fail to fit the North's economic city model. Augusta and Montgomery are "market *towns*" that were "displaced" by other "*cities* tied to expanding economic activities [and] transportation networks" in one historical account (Brownell 1977, 143, 127; italics added). Another characterizes nineteenth-century Greensboro as both "the little town" and "the city" (Rabinowitz 1977, 103). Small cities, historical cities, market cities that depend heavily on regional agriculture—most Southern cities until very recently—can easily escape the "city" label we insist on for the large, skyscraping, industrial cities of the North.

But the uncertain differentiation of cities from other settings in southern literature is also a matter of relative salience. Within the national schema of cultural power, being southern has overshadowed differences between country and city, as has being female or black. When minority status—whether of region or gender or race—makes group identity a dominant feature of one's experience, it does so whether one lives on a farm, in a small town, or in a big city; one is still southern, woman, black. This suggests that the rural/urban dichotomy in our generalizations about cities since the standard Chicago novel and the sociological "urbanism" of Louis Wirth (1938) has been mostly the privilege of northern white, middle-class males. Like our other cultural generalizations, it must be contextualized by region, ethnicity, class, and gender. Besides reminding us that urban experience is not monolithic and can be continuous with rural experience, southern literature thus points to nonurban dimensions of our social situations that can shape our literary constructions of cities.

Similarly, the machinery so common in economic city and megalopolitan literature may reflect less an alienation inherent in cities than feelings of alienation from sources that pay no attention to city limits. Anti-*northern* sentiment spawned a powerful strain of anti*urbanism* in the South during the 1920s and 1930s. "The city," then modeled as mechanical in the newly canonized national literature, proved a handy bludgeon for the fugitive poets and agrarian social critics who hammered against the Leviathan northern state in *I'll Take My Stand* (Twelve Southerners 1930). So Allen Tate's poem "The Subway" ([1927] 1977) sounds technological notes similar to the ones that Hart Crane would fuse into "salvation and damnation" in "The Bridge" (1930 [1946]), but tips the balance firmly toward damnation. "Hurled religiously" through "arch on arch" of "musical steel," the subway's "worship" is an "angry" submersion in Tate's poem, in contrast to the sublime elevation of Brooklyn Bridge in Crane's. The abstracted "geometries" that the subway rider internalizes amount to "the cold revery of an idiot," not an epic. But the urban machinery in this poem derives from feelings of alienation, not vice versa. Cities generally—including Tate's own Nashville and other southern cities—have little to do with it. The northern subway imagery implicitly defends the region's own city-towns by contrast, much as did New England literature's images of European "sodoms" in the mid-nineteenth century.

Another regional literature includes other instances in which the city figures only selectively in mechanical images. Frank Norris's San Francisco novels use machinery to encode feelings of alienation from sources other than the city itself. Having moved to San Francisco in his early teens, Norris generally assumed a residential attitude toward it in his novels, in contrast to confronting the national economic city as a traveler to Chicago in *The Pit* (1903). Theodore Dreiser considered *McTeague: A Story of San Francisco* Norris's best book because its realism was "indigenous" not just "to America," but specifically to "California, and San Francisco" (Norris [1899] 1967, ix–x). Edith Wyatt considered his posthumous *Vandover and the Brute* ([1914] 1967) "in its evocation of a city atmosphere . . . far better than 'The Pit'. . . . You seem to be walking its pleasant cosmopolitan-peopled streets, so warm in the sun, so cool in the shade" (Wyatt 1914c).

Indeed, Norris's San Francisco shares in the organic imagery of residential Chicago, the Harlem Renaissance, and the Lower East Side. *McTeague* even sounds a lot like *The Walls of Jericho* (Fisher 1928, 3–4, 44–45, 188–89) when Norris describes a day in "the little world of Polk Street," as if the street were a person: Polk Street "woke.... The street breakfasted.... The street was busiest.... Then all at once the street fell quiet.... The street was asleep" (156, 5–7).

At critical points in their character development, however, both *McTeague* and *Vandover and the Brute* shift into machine imagery. The main characters enjoy an organic sense of street life only as long as their personal lives have promise. Once McTeague sinks into his gross lethargy, his wife into her miserly compulsions, and Vandover into his vices, machinery begins to dominate their perceptions of the streets.² When Vandover gives up all work on behalf of others and art, his San Francisco seems just like Chicago in *The Pit* (1903): "some infinitely great monster" that expresses "Life" as "some enormous engine, resistless, relentless, an engine that sped ... no one knew whither" ([1914] 1967, 202). When McTeague is reduced to alcoholic brutality against his greedy wife, he assaults Trina with fists as "swift as the leap of the piston from its cylinder," and leaves her to die "like a piece of clockwork running down" ([1899] 1967, 317, 312, 318, 320). The pattern in both novels supports the possibility that cities seem organically, humanly familiar or mechanically alien according to how their inhabitants feel—hopeful and connected or despairing and isolated, for whatever reasons. Norris was able to imagine San Francisco as either an organic community or an alien machine, much as the Harlem Renaissance writers would later construct a divided New York as organic uptown and mechanical downtown, in keeping with the racial "twoness" (Du Bois 1903) of their experience there.

That the striking alternation between organic and mechanistic images occurs in Norris's San Francisco novels, not in his Chicago novel, also expresses particular aspects of San Francisco itself as a frontier city. Chartered in 1851, fourteen years after Chicago, in the Gold Rush boom and on the western edge of the continent, San Francisco still seemed an outpost at the turn of the century. Although it was "seventh largest" among the nation's cities by 1890, it was still "a ramshackle, incomplete city," the character of its inhabitants and community still up for grabs (Starr 1985, 180). Besides Norris's, two other important turn-of-the-century novels by Bay Area natives portray San Francisco engaged in a Manichean struggle between "the best" and "the brute" (Norris [1914]

1967, 68, 85–86). Like *McTeague* and *Vandover and the Brute, The Californians* by Gertrude Atherton and Jack London's *Martin Eden* avoid the standard Anglo frontier mythology that locates savagery in the Indian of the "Wilderness" and civilization in the white woman of the "Clearing" (Fiedler 1968; Armitage 1980, 5). In these urban frontier novels, each hero's savage "senses" and civilized "spirit" (Atherton [1898] 1968, e.g. 226) are both identified with women in the city.

Norris works out this schema fairly conventionally in *Vandover and the Brute* ([1914] 1967, 85–86), where the "best" woman and the "brute" woman come from different classes, the former from "one of the best [families] in the city," the latter from the vice district, which Norris's characters view as the city's inner heart. Jack London's *Martin Eden* ([1909] 1973, 2, 31) starts with a woman of the familied "bourgeoisie" who promises to "better" the working-class hero made "beastly" by sexual commerce with lone women of the street. But it goes on to discover the "brute" in the "herd-creatures" of any class or gender and to show the "machine" of materialistic brutishness and the spiritual "life of art" both centered in the city (241, 109, 184, 288).[3] Gertrude Atherton brings these alternatives even closer together in *The Californians* ([1898] 1968, 189, 149, 47), where a Hispanic literary woman of the "spirit" and a reckless Anglo woman of the "senses" are best friends, both engaged in turn to the same man, both wealthy, and both explicitly described as personifications of the region. Together Magdalena Yorba and Helena Belmont represent opposite yet conjoint possibilities that inhere in the frontier-urban society to which easterner Jack Trennahan comes seeking "regeneration" (176). In all these novels, the frontier city itself ever teeters between the moral alternatives the women represent. Like literature's earlier city-towns, regional San Francisco is expressive of its inhabitants' choices.

These choices are complicated, however, by the wealth of possibility that belongs historically and naturally to California's urban frontier. Whereas later Hollywood novels show make-believe possibilities that amount to empty gestures, turn-of-the-century San Francisco novels show meaningful choices rooted in the natural beauty and historical bounty of the region. "Greed" (the title of the 1924 film version of *McTeague;* cf. Atherton [1898] 1968, 170) is fed by the Gold Rush promise of sudden wealth and the pioneer precedent of fame—embodied in both *Vandover and the Brute* and *The Californians* by minor characters with historical family names. In *Martin Eden,* obsession with the lucky strike rules the poor. And for the wealthy in *The Californians,* as ninety years later in Bienvenido Santos's *What the Hell For You Left Your Heart in San Francisco* (1987, 1, 111, 177-79, 191-92), the city offers hilltop, seaward views that reinforce a psychology of possibility—and escape: "One can always live on a hill, and then you don't see the ugly things below," Helen Belmont declares (Atherton [1898] 1968, 5). Geographical escape is an immediate possibility; Eden, Vandover, and Trennahan all ship to sea, while McTeague heads for the gold hills (although such pastoral retreat into wilderness solitude is dangerous here, of benefit only to Trennahan).

Literature's San Francisco frontier offers too many, not too few, choices. It is an urban world without serious external limitations, so its critical problem is not poverty but vice. Alcoholism surfaces as a significant issue, and red-light districts figure importantly. As in earlier city-town literature, vice manifests itself in human choices, not economic systems. But unlike earlier fictions, these San Francisco novels reject cloistered withdrawal as no less isolating and "deadly" (Norris ([1914] 1967, 283) than geographical escape. After a foray into the Tenderloin vice district, Magdalena Yorba is imprisoned in the "deserted...haunted" house of her dying Spanish father (Atherton [1898] 1968, 317, 294), not in any sociable "paradise of bachelors," as in Melville's 1855 short story. Already facing our responsibility for degrading America's Eden, as Wallace Stegner characterizes the lush San Francisco Bay Area in *All the Little Live Things* (1967), the regional novels of Norris, Atherton, and London implicitly argue that hope and health lie in social choices that recognize both moral implications and regional wealth.

Western and southern literature offer samples of the regional diversity in U.S. urban experience. They show how literature combines our models for urban experience—the city-town, the economic city, and their variants—with or against one another, always within a multifaceted context. Regional distance from Chicago and New York can reinforce city/country continuities in one model, displace mechanical imagery in the other. Regional location thus joins gender and ethnicity as formative intersecting dimensions out of which literary artists create. Our regional literature demonstrates once again that diversity is the one sure outcome of this interactive process.

The works of women and ethnic writers may even be said themselves to comprise regional literatures of a sort. They often focus attention on "neighborhoods [that form] a kind of region," as Irving Howe notes of the Jewish immigrant writers whose literature he labels "regional" in *World of*

Our Fathers (1976, 585). Their "regions" are established not by geographical boundaries but by social structures joining "marked" people from many different places—whose achievements have often been set aside, moreover, in terms like those used to diminish regional literature: minor, special, provincial, parochial, peripheral, as critic Emily Toth (1977) has helped us see.[4] Such terms misconstrue their common thrust. As much regional literature constructs place holistically as experienced from within, so the language of much women's literature works out an "impulse toward wholeness" (Stanley and Wolfe 1979).[5] As a regional perspective envisions the nation's literature growing out of a variety of situational dynamics, so authors of different colors contribute "different parts" of the nation's "one immense story" from "a multitude of different perspectives," as Alice Walker puts it (1976; quoted in Hoffman 1982, 4). This brings us back to the point that all knowledge constructed by human beings (like human beings themselves) is situated—in gender and ethnicity, in time and place.

I have written *Urban Intersections* on the simple but ramifying premise that works of literature, as well as the urban lives with which they intersect, need to be situated in historical context. Literature is a part of our cities, created out of the interrelationships and institutional structures that constitute cities as literary centers, and it is published as an act of urban culture making. We can best understand how urban literature works by realizing that it is thus creatively situated in intersections with urban life. And we can best realize that by attending to its diversity.

But cities are also elements in literature. By figuring urban expectations, experiences, and possibilities within their aesthetic structures, literary works interpret what has been and posit what might be. At the civic intersection of life and literature, I believe we can make the fullest use of our literature if we claim it not only as a source of aesthetic pleasure, but also as a resource for interpreting and shaping urban experience. Because urban literature is historically situated, its models are configured in reality and fitted to inform our urban understandings and projects. They are both models of the past and models for what we might seek to reinforce or change in the future.

Literature has tremendous power to increase our knowledge. Because its method is "presentational" rather than "discursive," in philosopher Susanne Langer's terms (1960, 79–102), it emphasizes the conditioned situation and subjectivity of human experience. It imagines the experiences of particular people in particular conditions. Literary presentations of the economic city and megalopolis can thus help us understand the particular attractions and effects of materialism, individualism, and mass culture. Just as particularly, literary presentations of the city-town and its variants can help us understand the "intimately experienced neighborhood" dynamics that have eluded social scientific research (Tuan 1974, 61–66). They take us beyond sentimental idealizations into the mixed experience of community ties, beyond deterministic formulations of oppression into the dynamics of creativity under severe limitations.

Indeed, the old city-town tradition may take fuller advantage of literature's presentational edge than the rather recently established tradition of the economic city and megalopolis. City-town literature constructs a Husserlian "life-world... in which we are immersed," and this is particularly valuable as a "counter-formulation" (Gadamer 1975, 218) to "what we have seen and been sold and what has become familiar" in canons of art as in life. "Familiarity with [established] images breeds acceptance," art critic Judith Goldman (1981, 8) reminds us, and "shortcomings go unnoticed." Expanding the range of urban literature beyond our skyscraper canon, therefore, means fully entertaining literature's presentational power to challenge our assumptions about urban alienation.

Literature also offers valuable prescriptive models for what urban life could become. As anthropologist Clifford Geertz (1973, 126–27) has pointed out, a world view tends to spawn its own fitting ethos, despite logical distinctions between descriptive is's and prescriptive ought's. Thus our established cultural paradigm of the city as an alien phenomenon has, in effect, urged us to develop ever more objectifying means for dealing with urban problems. These may be effective for severing the hold of antagonist forces on our psyches but are as ill-suited for promoting social welfare as scissors are for sewing seams. They encourage us to divide, not to unite our reality. Alternatively, the organic images of the city-town, the civic family, and the neighborhood city encourage us to engage our urban affairs.

The persistence over time of our two traditions and the coherence of the models that structure their infinite varieties, moreover, suggest common patterns in our responses to urban experience that we would be foolish to ignore. Working from the standard U.S. "classics," on the one hand, and from novels by modern British feminists, on the other, Leo Marx (1969, 266–69)[6] and Christine Sizemore (1989, 23)[7] have broken this ground by arguing that "city planners as well as literary critics" should "trace the mundane... implications of" literary structures. Among the great civic gifts of literature—insofar as we remember its varieties—are the public metaphors and compelling stories that support the various projects toward which they might point us. I would like to highlight four such projects.

First, the open-ended structures of the city-town in literature have both temporal and spatial implications. Temporally, its various embodiments, as well as the long-lived city-town tradition itself, demonstrate the importance of emphasizing historical continuity from past toward future in our urban affairs. Entrapment in a past cut off from the future is deadening in Davis's *Waiting for the Verdict* and James's *The Bostonians;* and standard Chicago novels like Dreiser's *Sister Carrie* remind us of the vulnerability that comes from confronting a city as a radically new world. Conversely, a sense of past history provides grounding in Wyatt's *True Love* and inspiration for the future in Hughes's "Mother to Son" ([1925] 1935, 107; cf. Morrison 1981b): "Don't you fall now—/ For I'se still goin', honey." Thus our literature supports recent interests in historical preservation. Boston's Faneuil Hall and San Francisco's cable cars are two examples of functional renovations for continuing use. Our regional literature can suggest particular symbols that simultaneously highlight the past and point toward the future. The echoes of the Gold Rush frontier still sound from the Golden Gate Bridge.

Diverse literary works also demonstrate that open-ended spatial arrangements support feelings of hopefulness—from the panoramas above Chicago and San Francisco streets, down Whitman's "Open Road" ([1856, 1881] 1965b), to the streets themselves in Harlem. Above all, city-town and neighborhood-city structures from Cooper's Templeton to Roth's Lower East Side call for city building that invites easy movement in and out, with plenty of walking room. The "mundane implications" for architecture include discouraging fortress-like walls and fully enclosed malls and encouraging windows and doorways that open to allow interior activities to spill out—like the cabaret music in Hughes's poems. On a larger scale of planning, the dialectic breakthroughs of *Call It Sleep* and *Invisible Man* urge a pluralism of exchange among phases of our common existence—between uptown and downtown, as well as inside and outside. In early city-towns, civic and cultural buildings—for expressive arts, education, and politics—are always nearby, suggesting a multi-use zoning to break down separations among commercial and cultural, public and residential, sectors. Access to parks, natural vistas, and the countryside would further enrich the variety of cityscape. Openness does not mean emptiness—as

The Blithedale Romance, "Crossing Brooklyn Ferry," and the colorful Seventh Avenue parades in Harlem literature remind us. Twists in streets and alcoves in parks provide treasured variations and chances for retreat in *The Awakening* and *The Bostonians,* while grids only reinforce a sense of antinatural mechanization and unrelenting publicity in *The Cliff-Dwellers.*

Second, the alienation central to literature's economic city and megalopolis only emphasizes the importance of urban community. Allowing the noise and messiness of neighborhood gathering places in homey settings, like Muhmenkeh's Coffee Shop in Yezierska's *Arrogant Beggar,* seems necessary in preference to predictable and sanitized francise establishments. At least neighborhoods, and perhaps whole cities, need to negotiate their conflicts as well as their continuities directly, as families necessarily do and as Richard Sennett (1970) and Jane Jacobs (1961) have urged small-scale urban institutions to do too. That means testing ideals rather than sentimentalizing them.

Harlem Renaissance literature reminds us that it also means listening to the voices of strangers. Alienation, not the city itself, is the problem here, as the regional works of Allen Tate and Frank Norris help us realize. We must address sources of alienating inequality and disfranchisement beyond city limits, too. Nonetheless, our cities can challenge the repressive, deadening, and ultimately violent stereotypes that megalopolitan literature dramatizes. Cultural and civic institutions can extend "hospitality to the stranger" (Ogletree 1985), allowing otherwise marginalized ethnic groups to express their stories and rituals. The bloodline memories that Jews call "Yizkov" can support communal identities for people who have felt powerless, and such identities can be shared by maintaining occasions like the San Gennaro Festival in New York's Little Italy, by preserving the freeway murals on Chicago's black South Side or in Los Angeles's barrio, even by creating multiethnic festivals like Milwaukee's Summerfest. For the most part, however, encouraging communal self-expression means setting aside Anglo-American control and exercising sensitivity to the difference between vandalism and folk art. It means engaging the difficulties of pluralism, as in the literature of Chicago's civic family and New York's neighborhoods, rather than pursuing the nationalistic economics and mass culture that dam up expressive community in the standard Chicago novels and New York's later megalopolitan extensions.

Third, our literature's repeated association of alienated feelings with the antinatural city and urban community with earthy organicism calls us to strengthen nature's hand in our urban surroundings. This confirms the ecological mandate that Anne Whiston Spirn has translated into specific planning strategies in *The Granite Garden* (1984). "Acknowledged and harnessed, [natural forces] represent a powerful resource for shaping a beneficial urban habitat," she argues; "ignored or subverted, they magnify problems that have plagued cities for centuries, such as floods and landslides, poisoned air and water" (xi), and, as our literature demonstrates, social and psychic alienation. Revitalizing urban waterfronts and gardens and plantings and skyscapes is a cultural imperative for our well-being. The dominance of mechanical urban imagery in our literary mainstream may well explain why it has been so hard for us to maintain a "recognition of the city as part of nature" despite the greater visibility and concentration of environmental problems there (Spirn 1984, 275). We need to follow the lead of the city-town tradition and connect city and country in public places and events. Besides parks, farmers' markets can nurture our sense of nature's presence, of regional culture, and of the permeable urban/rural boundaries that point toward choice.

Fourth, all such efforts to open up our cities, to encourage expressivity and community, to loosen externally imposed controls, can best be supported by entertaining visionary mystery and playfulness, as Harlem Renaissance and Lower East Side literature calls us to do especially. In *The Walls of Jericho*, the streets *are* living personalities, not just *like* people. Even malevolent pianos and companionable trucks have personal spirits as part of the magical world that feeds Joshua Jones's exuberant jive. In *Invisible Man*, it is a reefer jazz dream that allows the hero to treasure the contradictions of African-American history and of his "social responsibility." Similarly, to cite a more recent example of a nameless neighborhood city in fiction, the destruction of a ghetto's deadly wall in Gloria Naylor's *The Women of Brewster Place* (1983) is accomplished within a dream, which involves hope beyond all probability and is nonetheless real within the fictional world of the novel.[8] For the sake of cultural wholeness, we need the room that these novels create for mystery and play in our cities—as city planners Jane Jacobs (1961, 29–111) and Lawrence Halprin (1972, 7–13) have also urged for various aesthetic and social ends. The mystic strain of dreaming most strongly marks the neighborhood city's countercultural challenge to megalopolitan nightmares. Our neighborhood literature associates it with feminine nurturing—of intimacy by David Schaerl's mother, of community pride by the invisible man's Mary Rambo, of barrier-breaking energy by Brewster Place's Mattie Michael. *"Just Folks"* and other residential novels also mandate reinstating the feminine ethic of care in our urban structures and processes (cf. Sardello 1982; Lauter 1985).

Literature itself is dreams, and cities need its visionary perspectives. Literature articulates some of the urban aspirations that, set in the context of place and community, can make our cities home to us and help us feel responsible to them. For this to happen, we need to recognize the situatedness of our literature and our lives. Various authors' distinctive cultural situations—in time and place, in gender and ethnicity—imply a rich variety of inevitably biased perspectives on urban experience. Whether we stand near the center of our nation's social fabric or at its edges, it is our aesthetic pleasure and our civic responsibility to entertain them all.

Notes

Introduction: Locating Urban Texts and Contexts in United States Literature

1. The Whites' and Marx's "classic" studies—themselves old standards in American studies and based on a narrow range of canonized "classics"—are among those that identify the city with the machine. They set it at the opposite extreme of nature and the untrammeled wilderness, along a spectrum of physical arrangements that finds its positive center in a nonurban "middle landscape" made famous by Marx (cf. Nash 1973, 6). They also identify its social arrangements with conformity as opposed to the antisocial extreme of radical individualism on a spectrum of interpersonal arrangements centered in the communal small town, in keeping with the formulae of social scientists like Maurice Stein (1960). Lined up to reinforce each other, these conceptual schematics provide a neat package and a powerful temptation. They tempt us to limit our understandings of American urban literature to the works that seem to fit the mythologic best—and even to limit our understandings of those works. Indeed, when literary cities are constructed as centers of art or community within this conventional framework, the mythologic declares them too old or too small to be cities and even redefines them as rural (e.g., White and White 1962, 154).

2. When colonists sought land grants for new towns, the Puritan magistrates required that the area be small enough to be both fully cultivated and fully settled by a group of citizens large enough to maintain a church—the essential germ of a city (Carroll 1969, 181–97).

3. As summarized in, e.g., Phillips and LeGates, *City Lights: An Introduction to Urban Studies* (1981, 81–105), which also offers the three political terms polis,

metropolis, and megalopolis to characterize urban development in Western civilization generally. Weber and Lloyd, in *The American City* (1975), use "walking city" and "streetcar city" for the major divisions in their history, along with the "automobile city" to complete the transportation sequence.

4. These three stages are often repeated in discussions of U.S. urban history, presenting it as a compression of a similar three-stage evolution in Western city building from an emphasis on *"cultural factors"* beginning in the Middle Ages and on *"economic considerations"* in the eighteenth and nineteenth centuries to an emphasis on *"political and social institutions"* from the late nineteenth century on (Konvitz 1985, xvi).

Chapter 1: Pre–Civil War City-Towns

1. Doubleday (1972, 227–28) details the story's historical references that mark the "metropolis" as Boston.

2. In "The Romantic Dilemma in American Nationalism and the Concept of Nature," Miller (1990) notes the paradoxes that Romanticism's antiurban thrust had a strong urban base and that the metaphor of "Nature's Nation" justified expansionism. His essay includes an analysis of *The Course of Empire*. Literary critic Albert Gelpi (Stanford University lecture, Spring 1969) has expanded on Miller's ideas by proposing that if America's manifest destiny to settle the continent was confirmed by the New World's uniquely direct access to truth in nature, then nature in effect authorized its own destruction. Not only did the Romantics provide a new "official faith" for American expansionism when they rejected elaborated civilization for untrammeled wilderness, as Miller articulates the irony, but they also left nature doomed, according to Gelpi's emphasis. Cf. Rosenthal (1981, esp. 35–36), which argues that there was no Romantic dilemma because the romantics and the nationalists all saw the city as an ordering fulfillment, not an antithesis, of nature. Other scholars like Sacvan Bercovitch (1975, 89, 107) and Stanley Cavell (1981, 10–11, 79) have also stressed the "Puritan origins" of Romantic nationalism and the Romantics' intention to "settle" the Puritans' founding vision.

Chapter 2: Toward a National Economic City

1. Cf. the characterization of the primates of high society as dead in Edith Wharton's later novel, *The Age of Innocence* (1920), discussed in chapter 5.

2. Washington's pull as literary subject even seemed momentarily strong enough to overcome authorial reticences. *The Gilded Age* was Twain's only foray into

America's urban territory, and Adams, the son and grandson of presidents, published *Democracy* only pseudonymously.

3. Quoted in Cady, "Introduction" in Howells, *Silas Lapham,* vi (cf. Lynn 1971, 282).

4. More intimately than most, these three characters dramatize Howells's changing orientation toward the urban world. Like Howells, Silas was a provincial newcomer who valued Boston and sought to make expressive decisions there; like Howells, Basil and Isabel are reluctant urban migrants to New York and occasionally "blink" the uncomfortable and alien realities that they confront there (Howells [1890] 1965, 48). If the "anagrammatically-named ... team of Basil and Isabel" are fictional embodiments of Howells himself (Lynn 1970, 57), as critics generally agree, then so is their anagrammatical cousin Silas.

5. Indeed *A Hazard of New Fortunes* itself involves a move in that direction (cf. Bremer 1971, 149–64).

Chapter 3: The Standard Chicago Novel

1. Addams's paired essays "The Subjective Necessity for Social Settlements" and "The Objective Value of a Social Settlement," from *Philanthropy and Social Progress* (1893), are reprinted in Addams 1965, 28–61. But Addams herself included only the first essay in her classic *Twenty Years at Hull-House* ([1910] 1961, 91–100).

2. Compare, for instance, the Fuller passage quoted below to this description by Nordenskiold (1893, 5–6): "On both sides of Mancos Cañon there extends a complicated system of lateral cañons, which in their turn send out numerous branches, the whole system thus forming a perfect labyrinth. The beds of the streams at the bottom of these lateral cañons are dry without exception.... [At] the top [of the canyon] the perpendicular cliffs of yellow sandstone rise like an insurmountable wall. The height of the mesa above the bottom of the valley is between 200 and 250 metres.... [The] caves sometimes attain a depth of 40 metres and a length of more than 100 metres.... [They] present an aspect at once singular and imposing." Rosowski and Slote's 1984 essay on Willa Cather's acquaintance with Mesa Verde directed me toward Nordenskiold's treatise as a work still known in 1916 (87).

3. These phrases refer specifically to the rapacious banker and a social-climbing woman, presented as middle-class counterparts for each other.

4. Cf. Garland's famous declaration that Chicago's cultural primacy was "a question only of time" in *Crumbling Idols* (1894); quoted in Duncan (1964, xi).

5. Recent genre criticism has joined literary naturalism intimately with "the city"; and certainly Theodore Dreiser, Frank Norris, and Upton Sinclair are key

figures for naturalism, as also for the standard Chicago novel. Treating naturalism in primarily formal terms as a thing apart, however, underestimates its continuities with other intellectual and literary works in a shared historical context. Genre criticism fails to place works like *Sister Carrie, The Pit,* and *The Jungle* properly within the larger intellectual movement to redefine American cities. The common revulsion against the economic city's mechanical dimensions, for instance, explains the curious combination of Romantic and Darwinistic strands in the naturalists' emphasis on cosmic forces; the concurrent and fearful concern of middle-class Anglo-Americans with immigrant "masses" explains its mixing of literary realism with popular journalism to document the new mass culture of American cities; and the national outsider's perspective on the urban spectacle explains the "distanced" narrative stance of the "spectator" that June Howard (1985, e.g., x, 104–41) finds so important.

In identifying the "city" with naturalism, moreover, she and Philip Fisher (1985, e.g., 10) clearly understand "city" solely in the post–Civil War industrial shape of the economic city (e.g., Howard 1985, 70–71) even though Fisher contrasts the "economic" urban world of naturalists like Dreiser to the "polis" form of settlement that he associates with historical novelists like Cooper. Without seeing both as urban forms, albeit from different historical situations, he provides a brilliant outline for the distinctions I draw between the economic city and the city-town when he argues that naturalism became "inevitable . . . once the primary plane of social life became economic rather than political, atomized rather than centered, focused on money rather than on power, and based in the lives of individuals rather than families" (16). Fisher also exemplifies the impact of definitions of "city" on aesthetic evaluation when he describes Dreiser's urban fiction as "required" (while implying that Howells and James are "merely moral and trivial") because he takes "account" of "the economic layer of life" in "the city" (21).

6. Carl S. Smith, *Chicago and the American Literary Imagination 1880–1920* (1984) provides an excellent discussion of the problem of language in Chicago novels; see esp. 2–6 on hyperbole.

7. Thus the "conceptual oppositions" that June Howard identifies as central to naturalism (1985, 36–69) *incorporate* the "sequence of deterioration" that both she (70–103) and Philip Fisher (1985, 165ff.) also identify as a defining element.

8. Generally Szuberla (1971) overemphasizes the positive side of artists' perspectives on Chicago.

9. Thus Chatfield-Taylor's *Two Women and a Fool* (1895, 154–55) makes reference to the color-coded Hull-House maps of the city's most mixed neighborhood; cf. the maps developed in fact by Hull-House researchers and printed in Kelley, ed., 1895.

10. Smith (1984, 101–20, 121–51, 152–70) also focuses on skyscrapers and railroads, along with the stockyards, as the most expressive facets of Chicago in literature, devoting a full chapter to each.

11. Cf. the building improvements that always "anticipate the city" in "After the Sky-Scrapers, What?" in Ade (1941, 105, 104–8).

12. *The Epic of the Wheat,* the title of the unfinished trilogy in which *The Pit* was to be the second volume, properly characterizes the tone established by standard Chicago novels giving mythic and detailed weight to Chicago as the epitome of American cities.

Chapter 4: Chicago's Residential Novels and their Social Roots

1. Besides Clara Burnham's *Sweet Clover* (1894), Susan Glaspell's *The Glory of the Conquered* (1909), and Alice Gerstenberg's *Unquenched Fire* (1912), Laughlin's *The Penny Philanthropist* (1912) also figures among the Chicago residential novels, all published between the world's fair and World War I. Some of Peattie's magazine short stories from that time reflect a similar perspective, as do all of Edith Wyatt's short stories in *Every One His Own Way* (1901), and a miscellany of minor plays and poems by these and other women. By way of contrast, Wyatt's ungainly family epic spanning the period from 1882 to 1921, *Invisible Gods* (1923) evidences the retrospective disillusionment that also informs Edith Wharton's *The Age of Innocence* (1920), discussed in chapter 5.

2. Gelfant privileges the perspectives of naturalism and environmental determinism toward which standard Chicago novels point. She specifies that the "active participation of the city in *shaping* character and plot" distinguishes the truly urban novel from local-color fiction merely set in a city (2–3, italics added; cf. Dale Kramer 1966, 7). Kenny Williams resolves the "confusion" about the "Chicago novel" by narrowing it even more drastically to those that focus on "the businessman as the cultural hero of the city" (1980, 443).

3. Howells's important essay explicitly celebrated the publication of *True Love.* This warm send-off was only one instance of his continued support of Wyatt, as detailed in Kirk and Kirk (n.d., 8–10).

4. Fuller's chart of this "group of individuals" combines the standard novel's emphasis on individualism with the residential emphasis on collectivity. By boxing as couples the parental generation of greedy Beldens, socially prominent Bateses, and old-family Marshalls, while aligning the separate boxes for the Marshall children no more directly with their own parents than with the Beldens and Bateses, Fuller's chart reduces collectivity to twosomes and gives equal importance to individuals. His different treatment of older and younger generations even implies a chronological shift toward the individual as "the unit of society," in keeping with the theme of *The Cliff-Dwellers.*

5. Wyatt contrasts the two homes architecturally, too (1903, 10, 47), much as Howells contrasted the Lapham and Corey homes in *The Rise of Silas Lapham;*

but Wyatt's characters move in and out of each other's homes without embarrassment or any sense of competition.

6. I think Christine Sizemore (1989, 10, 26) defines "organic" too narrowly in terms of the masculine imagery of the city as "diseased," "rigid," and with "little room for people"; these associations are results of the antinatural properties of "male images of the city." I agree with her, however, that "female novelists" see cities as "a part of nature, not a separate order from nature," and I choose "organic" as a way to convey that idea along with the idea of holistic continuity.

7. Robert Bray (1982, 98–99) agrees that, in comparison to *The Cliff-Dwellers*, *With the Procession* expresses a different "attitude" on Fuller's part toward Chicago. Bray identifies as its distinctive "subject" "the Marshall family's rediscovery—led by the oldest daughter, Jane—of their father's heritage and social worth.... [They] must learn the lessons of the past before they can resume their rightful place in the procession of the present into the future." I think, however, that *With the Procession* is more ambiguous in its presentation of history's relationship to the present and future.

8. In Garland's *Rose of Dutcher's Coolly*, the heroine has a similar experience of encountering the music of Wagner's "romantic landscape" in the Auditorium, which Bray (1982, 85) describes as an "affirmation of the continuity between country and city"; but Rose Dutcher identifies Wagner's art solely with the coolly country, paying no particular attention to the urban context of her experience. The city thus gives her means to realize a country art, not a constituent element in a cosmopolitan urban-rural vision such as Cather and Thea develop.

9. Because it marks "the turning point in her career," James Woodress (1987, 3–11) makes Cather's 1912 trip through Chicago to Arizona's Panther Canyon the prologue to her "Literary Life." Susan J. Rosowski and Bernice Slote (1984) document her continuing interest in how the Mesa Verdeans, too, were "carrying out a suggestion [from] those great natural arches of stone" in their "cliff dweller villages" and the "tempered, settled, ritualistic life" that they embodied and that she found so compatible with her own art (85).

10. Counting Addams "among my very good friends" in her unpublished autobiography (n.d., 197), Peattie publicized "Saint Jane" in a 1907 *Harper's Bazaar* short story and featured her as "little sister to the world" in a 1910 *Tribune* review of *Twenty Years at Hull-House*. In *The Precipice* she also denominates Addams a "sister of all men" (181).

11. Like Kate Barrington, Julia Lathrop went on from probation work in Chicago to become the founding head of the Children's Bureau (Bureau of Children, in Peattie's barely fictionalized form) in Washington, D.C. Like Beth Tully, but after the publication of *"Just Folks,"* Chicago probation officer Ida B. Wells-Barnett had her probationers report to her at a settlement house, the Negro Fellowship League that she had founded in 1908 as "one of four settle-

ments near black areas"; it survived until 1920 (Thompson 1979, 224, 183–89). In her extensive journalistic writing, Kate resembles Wells-Barnett, too, although Lathrop and Addams together are far more likely as Peattie's models through acquaintance. Indeed, Peattie directly opposed Wells-Barnett, also an active club woman, by arguing against admitting colored women's clubs to the General Federation of Women's Clubs because it might jeopardize the suffragist alliance of northern and southern women (Peattie n.d., 208–9). A fictionalized version of the 1902 Los Angeles convention of the General Federation of Women's Clubs, at which she made that argument, also appears in *The Precipice*.

12. So Wyatt's biographers entitle their unpublished study of her life "Edith Franklin Wyatt, Chicagoenne" (Kirk and Kirk n.d.).

13. Wyatt's and Dreiser's novels represent "pure" types, written from the perspectives most commonly associated with pre-World War I gender roles: domestic femininity and upwardly mobile masculinity. Fuller's and Cather's novels represent "mixed" types, in which a man's unexpected stasis strains against his expected attention to individual ambition, while a woman's unexpected mobility strains against her expected attention to communal ties. One could even argue that male/female and newcomer/resident variables organize a matrix in which the economic individualism expected of males either reinforces the same tendencies in the newcomer perspective or works against the social interdependency common to residents, as also the social interdependency expected of females either reinforces the same tendencies in the residential perspective or works against the economic individualism typical for newcomers.

14. A sense of home-bound Wyatt's deep longing to join the nation's "overland dream" of mobility fills her newspaper "Appreciation" of the twice-annual flights of wild geese "flying, flying, flying out of their past" (Wyatt 1914a, viii–ix). The geese also represent a natural metaphor for the mobility, discussed above, that the rural-urban continuum of her novels supported.

15. Peattie's husband, Robert (n.d., 37), credits her as editor of the *Tribune* book pages in his memoirs, although their *Tribune* colleague Burton Rascoe (1937, 324) assigns that role to Robert.

16. Duncan epitomizes this male-only view of Chicago journalism, which he considers central to Chicago's ascendency as a "literary center," while relegating the Little Theatre movement to the periphery. He also assumes that newspaper men who "had very little social life outside of the newspaper world" and "very little knowledge of family life" had "unsurpassed knowledge of the city" (1964, 114). The evidence indicates only that newspapers were established as a man's business, that most editors were men, and that women were usually assigned to the arts and society sections established late in the nineteenth century.

17. Wyatt's one-act documentary play *The Case of Francesca* ([1914–16]), about three Italian immigrants in a single tenement room, was too narrowly structured to realize the ideas that she had developed in a pamphlet on women as

home-finishing laborers (Wyatt [1907?]). One of Monroe's plays was unwelcome because it was too close to guerrilla theater in confusing performers with audience; understandably no commercial theater manager was keen to stage her *Little Davy* (1906), a drama of the Iroquois Theater fire.

18. Together these two national journals published poetry by Wyatt, Gerstenberg, and Peattie, as well as Mary Aldis, Florence Kiper Frank, Margery Currey, Monroe herself, and her chief editorial assistant, Eunice Tietjens, along with many shorter-term Chicagoans and other writers from Alaska to Paris.

19. Monroe's own breakaway from classic forms came in 1911 with a Whitmanesque catalogue of the rooms and people in New York's Waldorf Astoria; recognizing its importance, she put "The Hotel" first in her volume of poetry *You and I* (1914b).

20. Despite his published approval of Wyatt's fiction, even Howells's patronage had a personal, rather paternal tone. He gave Wyatt's first book to his brother for pleasure reading on a trip, invited her to be his table companion at a 1905 Delmonico's dinner honoring his close friend Mark Twain, and shared humorous Wyatt quotations with his family as "a constant source of joy" until his death (Mildred Howells 3 July 1920 letter, Wyatt Mss.). He paid her less attention in purely professional contexts. He did not, for instance, reinforce Wyatt's stature as his professional peer by asking her to identify members of the Chicago "army" of writers, writing instead to Fuller for a list (Fuller quoted in Duncan 1964, xiii).

21. This synthesis of social scientific scholarship on "Environmental Perception, Attitudes, and Values" notes parallel contrasts between experiential and abstracted, native and visitor, female and male perspectives—although it records no recognition of nor explanation for those parallels.

Chapter 5: New York's Megalopolitan Nightmares

1. Hughes wrote "The Ceaseless Rings of Walt Whitman" (1945) as the introduction to *Walt Whitman for Young People,* one of two anthologies of Whitman's poetry that he composed—the other entitled *Walt Whitman's Darker Brothers* (Hughes Papers). He also published an essay on Whitman's timeliness, "Walt Whitman and the Negro," in the 1955 Brooklyn College *Nocturne* (Hughes Papers).

2. Rampersad (1986; 1988, esp. 333-37) demurs from recent speculation that Hughes was homo- or bisexual, joining with acquaintances who were convinced that he was more asexual (1986, 46, 133, 196, 289; 1988, 149, 239, 351). He emphasizes Hughes's secretiveness about his private life, characterizing his sexuality as "furtive" (1986, 4). Much of Rampersad's evidence is ambiguous (e.g., 1986, 66-70, 286-88). Hughes did, however, clearly share with Crane the biographical circumstance of divorced parents, and Rampersad emphasizes his loneli-

ness and *"need"* to belong to "race" (1986, 3-4, 22). Crane's dissociated personal life was exacerbated by alcoholism, leading finally to suicide in 1932 at age thirty-three.

3. Although it includes farflung allusions to the American past and to modern popular culture—from Columbus to Woolworth Mary, from Pocahontas to a billboard's Star Dust Twins, from the ancient Mississippi to the Twentieth Century Limited train—it embodies the abstracted, ahistorical perspective that separated many post–World War I writers from old dreams of community and progress. Its opening "Proem: To Brooklyn Bridge" wilfully transforms the furious multiplicity of nature and technology, of spiraling Whitmanian seagull and "subway scuttle" alike, into its opposite, an abstracted religious essence that the bridge merely represents (3). Its eighth and closing section, "Atlantis," similarly presents the physicality of the bridge only to sever it from its moorings. Ignoring the bridge's Whitmanian potential to join commercial "mast-hemm'd Mannahatta" to the residential "hills of Brooklyn" (Whitman [1856, 1881] 1965a) and to anchor them both firmly in the land, Crane transforms it into a floating ship.

4. Lily's genteel refinement keeps undercutting her "calculations" to use the "asset" of her beauty to "profit" in "the business" of marrying wealth in the person of collector Percy Gryse or Simon Rosendale (Wharton [1905] 1964, 19, 37, 110, 14), while her love of luxury disables her from embracing the genteel "republic of the spirit" that a "poor" marriage to Lawrence Selden would mean.

5. Elizabeth Ammons (1980, 25ff.) also presents *The House of Mirth* as one of the Progressive Era's "economic novels." In my emphasis on the economic structures to which Wharton's imagery points, as in my discussion of the primacy of the city-town in Howells's *Rise of Silas Lapham,* I disagree with Annette Baxter's more simple contrast between the continuous social hierarchy in Wharton's urban imagery and the sharp socioeconomic groups in Howells's (1963).

6. Thus in book I, the figurative language of money describes her overspecialized and underfinanced equipment for the "partnership" of marriage and her failure to reckon on having to "pay up" the "interest" on any extramarital friendships (14, 153, 98). In book II, money literally defines the plot as her social standing and marital opportunities drop down to the level of her economic dependence on a hat factory job.

7. Whereas Crane was a disciple of the romantic Whitman, Dos Passos followed the "earth-feeling" Whitman (Wagner 1979, xiv–xv). Whereas Crane's fusions lack Whitman's love of sensory particularity, Dos Passos's ([1925] 1953, 3) multisensory megalopolis of newspaper headlines and jumbled traffic sounds and human bodies lacks Whitman's underlying unities.

8. The carnival atmosphere of this chapter, and indeed of the entire novel, seems much like what Dos Passos experienced on a pleasure trip with F. Scott and Zelda Fitzgerald, described in Mellow (1984, 165).

9. Following Carrie Meeber Drouet Wheeler Madenda's footsteps to the stage,

Ellen changes her first name as well as her last—Ellen, Elaine, and Ellie all on one page (54–55), and Thatcher, Oglethorpe, Herf, and Butler as she moves from one man's home to another's. She early wishes that she had a boy's privileges, while her first husband, John Oglethorpe, turns out to be homosexual and her second husband, Jimmy Herf, was called "girlboy" as a child (64, 97).

10. With the birth of the Pulitzer Prizes in the 1920s and the awarding of Nobel Prizes in literature to Americans in the 1930s, American literary artists became media celebrities. Fitzgerald's widely reported life was "so woven round with a cocoon of fiction and fantasy"—only partly of his own making—that James Mellow (1984, 207) calls his biography of Scott and Zelda Fitzgerald *Invented Lives,* complaining that "it was difficult to know where the real substance was." Anzia Yezierska's personal life betrays similar "invention" but in ways that helped to link her to the Lower East Side Jews she called "my people," as discussed in chapter 7.

11. Fitzgerald was also criticized for following Wharton too closely in his early writing, and he "made a great hit" with her when they first met in Edmund Wilson's office at Scribner's in 1923 (Mellow 1984, 180, 170).

12. His mother's family was in fact well established as wealthy and respected there, although he always thought of them as "straight potato-famine Irish" and preferred the more romantic image of his father's southern gentility and Revolutionary War ancestry (Eble 1963, 18–20).

13. Only when he announces the destruction of these two other dreams of New York in the "whoopee mammas who prance before its empty paraquets" after the crash, when he realizes that all of New York "had limits," does he allow a hint of irreverence to tinge his "lost city" of "metropolitan urbanity": "And Bunny, swinging along confidently with his cane toward his cloister in a carnival, has gone over to Communism and frets about the wrongs of southern mill workers and western farmers whose voices, fifteen years ago, would not have penetrated his study walls" (Fitzgerald [1934] 1945a, 32–33). Even then, he criticizes less "the cloister in a carnival" than the man who abused its precious sanctuary when he "went over" to politics.

14. Fitzgerald weathered the war with more public display and less real work than Wharton. The past that Jay Gatsby "can't repeat" is specifically identified with his similarly romantic wartime past of whirlwind courtship (Fitzgerald 1925, 111).

15. Cf. David Weimer's recognition (1966, 91) that Fitzgerald's west/east theme "is conceived in . . . broad geographical terms rather than being fastened to city and hinterlands."

16. Cf. Bryer and Kuehl's comment (1973, xvi) that Fitzgerald "thought class even more a psychological than an economic condition."

17. Mellow (1984, 165) tells of an evening during which Dos Passos did indeed visit a carnival with the Fitzgeralds.

18. One of Fitzgerald's several preferred titles, *Under the Red, White, and Blue,* emphasized the novel's implied commentary on the state of the nation, as Prof. Thomas E. Daniels pointed out to me; see Bruccoli (1974, 31–32).

19. He did so en route to his wealthy western friend Dan Coty's yacht *Tuolomee,* named after a wilderness meadow in Yosemite and apparently a hospitable, free-floating environment for Gatsby's dream of a new self (98–99). Although *The Great Gatsby,* unlike *The Age of Innocence,* does not require that dreams be enacted in order to last, it does suggest that they can be sustained by an appropriate, hospitable setting—one that minimizes the impact of Euro-American history on the New World.

20. Thus West's title character in *The Dream Life of Balso Snell* (1931) articulates a version of the dreams-in-dirt motif that I associate with countercultural perspectives in chapter 7. Light (1961, 16–19) discusses West's "rejection" of his Jewishness at some length. Jay Martin (1970, esp. 78–81) discusses his name change more positively as an affirmation of literary and modern values—which I see as part and parcel of megalopolitan abstraction.

21. On the numerous parallels between Fitzgerald's and West's urban settings, see Reid (1967, 97–100) and Wells (1973, 49–70, 103–21).

22. Connie Biggar, Jean-Marie Birk, Mary Strenn, and other students in my fall 1975 course "The City in American Literature and Arts" at the University of Wisconsin–Green Bay, pointed me toward the realization that *Miss Lonelyhearts* shows practically no work ever being done on the newspaper, although it opens as a publishing deadline nears. I am grateful to them for this and other insights into West's novel.

23. West deleted the name, Thomas Matlock, given his central character in an early draft (Daniel 1971, 52).

Chapter 6: The Urban Home of the Harlem Renaissance

1. Particularly for the younger set, short stays in Harlem were the norm. Biographers James R. Giles (1976, 23) and Robert Hemenway (1977, 60) miss this point by treating the long absences of McKay and Hurston as anomalies that detract from their status as members of the Harlem Renaissance. In this mobile light, even Jean Toomer belonged to the Harlem Renaissance; he associated with the Harlem crowd both uptown and in his own Greenwich Village apartment, involving many of them in the Gurdjieff movement. They claimed his work as one of their own, although he disavowed the connection when he moved to New Mexico and did not share in the patterns that characterize the others' literary work.

2. Hughes and others dated the beginning of the Harlem Renaissance from his

arrival, specifically because he was the first to be attracted by its Jazz Age image. Appropriately, when he died in 1967 at age sixty-five, many of Harlem's then long-removed political organizers, performers, and poets—representing the three leading groups of Renaissance creators—came back again to memorialize him with oratory, jazz, and poetry (*New York Post* 26 May 1967, Hughes Material).

3. So did being on the rolls of literary organizations like the Harlem Writers' Guild—again, whether or not one was physically in residence there. At Claude McKay's request (12 Aug. 1937, Johnson Papers), James Weldon Johnson was the first president of Harlem's later League of Negro Writers just before his death in 1937, although he was in residence at Fisk then.

4. One can imagine Hughes's mixed feelings when Fauset urged him to dedicate a poem in *The Weary Blues* (1925) to Du Bois, who had "made things possible for very many of us" through *The Crisis* (14 Oct. 1925 letter, Hughes Collection), just as Hughes was sending that first volume of his poetry to press. Ironically, the fame of its title poem might have been more properly credited to an *Opportunity* prize and publication and to its "discovery" by Vachel Lindsay, when Hughes waited on his table in a Washington, D.C. restaurant. Rampersad (1986, 116) notes that Fauset's request was apparently made to redress Countee Cullen's failure to include Du Bois among his dedicatees in *Color*.

5. Rampersad (1986, 156–57, 183–99 passim) notes that Hughes's agreement with Mason initially depended on no intermediary but that Locke was deeply involved in its dissolution. Hughes was as devastated by the withdrawal of her support in 1930 as by his discovery of hatred for his father in about 1920—reacting with violent psychosomatic illness in each case (Hughes 1940, 319–24).

6. In that regard, of course, writers have always seemed somewhat decadent to pragmatic Americans, since they produce no "hard" goods nor "necessary" services (Harris 1966, esp. 2–27, 218–53). But even outside of writing, service and entertainment offered Harlemites no clearly productive options.

7. The impulse to collect and record the black past—in effect, to make Harlem an archive for the race—had become self-conscious by 1920, so that, as Nathan Huggins (1971, 53, 3–4) has remarked, those who enacted Harlem Renaissance history were also responsible for labeling their movement a historical "Renaissance." Documenting and interpreting themselves as collective and individual makers of history, they often mixed general Harlem history and personal autobiography in the same volume.

8. Hughes's finest newspaper work used the comic tone and fictional frame that Chicago's Finley Peter Dunne had developed for urban social commentary and that Harlem-born cartoonist Ollie Harrington had adapted visually to black purposes, Harrington's Bootsie appealing so widely because he was "the average Negro from Lenox Avenue in Harlem or Hastings Street in Detroit to Central Avenue in Los Angeles or Rampart in New Orleans," according to Hughes (n.d., 1). Hughes dubbed his own "urban folk hero and...later day Aesop" (Clarke

1967) Jesse B. Semple and put into his mouth naively probing questions about racial justice in the nation's most famous ghetto, as well as the lyrics of a musical comedy, his 1950s Broadway hit *Simply Heavenly*.

9. Viewing the Harlem Renaissance from this collective, cultural perspective, I, too, "disagree entirely" with its consignment "to the domain of 'failure'" by those who focus on the small number of its individual achievements, the "provincialism" of its concern with race, or its disappointed faith in art (Baker 1987, xiv–xv, 9–12).

10. In this use of Biblical verse form to tell a classic Harlem story rather like Fisher's "City of Refuge," such words as "wise" and "riot," for instance, work simultaneously as sacred and slang terms. Only when Hurston slipped in a sly reference to Van Vechten and the Niggerati, did she have to resort to a parenthetic definition: "(which being interpreted means Negro literati)" (7).

11. In the end, the same command-refrain frames his spiritual life, too: "Hey, boy! / A bright bowl of brass is beautiful to the Lord. / . . . / At least I can offer that. / Com' mere, boy!" (28–29). Hughes's poetic evocations of Harlem often center on such realizations of beauty within degradation.

12. Also published in both *Spring in New Hampshire* (1920, 24) and *Harlem Shadows* (1922, 37–38), "Winter in the Country" vitiates, with its pastoral clichés, the possibility of an urban-pastoral art that its ending finally suggests. The country half, the poem's first three stanzas, strains credulity by presenting a New England winter of "soft sea-laden breeze," anthropomorphic trees that commune with "free limbs" and "bare hands," and a "sparrow's cheep" as "music that every heart could bless." Conversely, even if the details are more believable in the second half of the poem, the "city's dirty basement room," its "two crippled chairs," and "gaslight burning weird and dim" simply derive by way of contrast, rather than original observation, from the first three stanzas. Thus the potential for a transcendent artistic vision that the last stanza grants to the city—"And yet, and yet / This very wind, the winter birds, / The glory of the soft sunset, / Come *there* to me in words" (italics added)—has little compelling force.

13. "America" (1922, 6) also attributes an organic energy of hate-filled sexuality to the nation's urban power, which is both internalized and countered by an aroused rebel: "Her vigor flows like tides into my blood, / Giving me strength erect against her hate. / Her bigness sweeps my being like a flood. / Yet as a rebel fronts a king in state, / I stand within her walls." This second example of McKay's many protest sonnets offers, like "The White City," a powerful reversal of the metaphysical conceits in John Donne's poetic pleas for enforced submission to divine authority, for instance in "Batter my heart three personed God" (1610–15?).

14. McKay's revisions even increase that alienation. The "girls who pass / Eager to heed desire's insistent call" in *Spring in New Hampshire* become "girls who pass / To bend and barter at desire's call" in *Harlem Shadows*.

15. "England" is dated 1924 and "Farewell to Morocco" placed "On board

the Magollanes Jan., 1934," suggesting that he wrote the other poems at the various sites that he visited between 1922 and 1934, then collected and completed the group—probably adding the New York poems and the title poem—only after he returned to the United States in 1934. He used four of the twenty-one as touchstones in his 1937 autobiography *A Long Way from Home* (158, 224-25, 308, 326-27).

16. While recognizing the importance of McKay's discovery of nature in the city and the way he associated Harlem with Jamaica, Lenz fails to see that as a result McKay separates Harlem from greater New York. He also makes a stereotyped assumption that the other Harlem Renaissance writers belonged to a "traditional folk culture" in conflict with "the urban industrialized modern world of New York" (312-13).

17. The primary difference between Toomer's rural and urban vignettes is that city women are as divorced from the southern land as men and as likely as men to render sexual liaisons sterile.

18. Unfortunately the African cult was easily abused by the avant garde elite of white faddists who sought to sensationalize and exploit Harlem. The potential of the folk culture movement to include working-class and nonliterate blacks more centrally in the renaissance was undermined by the egotism of its major black proponents Du Bois, Hurston, and Hughes. Indeed, Hurston and Hughes became bitter enemies battling for the proprietary rights to produce a folk play, *Mulebone,* that they had written together in 1929-31 (Hemenway 1977, 136-58; Rampersad 1986, 184-85, 194-200; Hughes 1940, 331-34; correspondence in Hughes Papers and Hurston Collection and Hughes Papers-Mugar).

19. Today, too, Seventh Avenue, Lenox Avenue, Fifth Avenue, Broadway, Park Avenue, and Wall Street all belong to our culture's mental gazeteer—far outstripping our street knowledge of Chicago (Michigan Boulevard), Los Angeles (Hollywood and Rodeo Boulevards, Sunset Strip) and even Washington, D.C. (Pennsylvania Avenue).

20. According to Ann Petry, a renaissance descendant who won acclaim for her Harlem novel entitled *The Street* (1946), failure to recognize the life-giving vitality of Harlem's streets results partly from an obscuring distance in Anglo perspective—specifically, the perspective of the el itself. The "Harlem" article Petry wrote for *The Holiday Book of New York* (1949) dismisses the view from the el as equivalent to stereotypes of Harlem's gin mills in the 1920s. Petry takes a pedestrian point of view instead, focusing on "Harlem's thousand varied faces" as they appear when "groups rub shoulders" on the streets.

21. In fact, neighborhood networks somewhat strengthened what Cary Wirtz (1988, 24-25) refers to as the "weakening family ties" of Harlemites who had left extended families in the South and were increasingly housed in "male-absent families and subfamilies."

22. Only because Joanna Marshall will not then accept the form that her fame

takes on the streets—when Lenox Avenue "stared, pointed, laughed and enjoyed itself" (274)—does she depreciate the value of her African-American art and surrender her ambition.

23. The explosion there of suggestive names—J. Pennington Potter, the Dunns, Buckram and Nora Byle, Tony Nayle, Miss Agatha Cramp, Conrad White, Betty Brown, Shine, and Patmore (98–101)—presses beyond the grotesque subhumanity of *The Great Gatsby's* Long Island guest list (Fitzgerald 1925, 61–63) to display the penchant for linguistic play that Fisher shares with his characters.

24. Savage later protested the use of her Johnson death mask in *Opportunity's* February 1940 announcement of the plans for Barthé's memorial statue. It was "cruel," she wrote to Walter White on 14 April 1940 (Van Vechten Correspondence, Johnson Memorial), particularly since "the idea was originally mine."

25. The James Weldon Johnson Memorial Collection at Yale's Beinecke Library is a superb collection of African-American literary papers. It is comprehensive for the Harlem Renaissance; and it has been well supported by many black authors and even black collectors for Atlanta and Fisk University libraries.

Chapter 7: Neighborhood-City Dreams

1. Van Vechten was, after all, the author of Jazz Age works like *Peter Whiffle* (1922) as well as *Nigger Heaven,* and confidante to expatriate Gertrude Stein besides Harlem's elder statesman. Indeed, a deracinated, modernist fascination with art's formal possibilities informed his dealings with Harlem writers from the start.

2. Arguably, even white Americans shared something of the feelings of physical limitation and cultural inferiority during the pre–Civil War period of building on physical frontiers and trying to wrest an independent cultural nation from the colonized consciousness of European civilization.

3. Chametzky argues that American Jews now enjoy a "presumably secure Americanism," and other cultural critics have agreed that Jewish Americans now can largely choose the extent to which they emphasize their ethnic identity. Thus authors like Cynthia Ozick and I. B. Singer have chosen to embrace the material and perspectives of Jewish Orthodoxy and Yiddishkeit in their works and lives, while Norman Mailer has chosen to be a "non-Jewish Jew" (qtd. in Tuerk 1983, 134). Other white ethnic groups are "minorities" only in the numerical sense that makes Anglo-Americans a minority too today, since no one is likely to challenge on ethnic grounds their civic claims to home and urban power. Nonetheless, during the past hundred years and especially in our cities, ethnic group identity has been a very prominent issue for all but WASPs—the more so the larger the group and the further it stands from the light-skinned, North Atlantic, post-Reformation standard.

4. The last and most autobiographical of Yezierska's novels, *All I Could Never Be* (1932, 55), makes this point most ironically in a typical Yezierska exchange, when a rigidly rational Anglo man makes an emotionally expressive Jewish woman see her ghetto as "a city set on a high hill whose light could not be hid," implying that the Jewish community inherits the ancient WASP dream because of its exclusion from contemporary WASP culture.

5. This critical perspective involves the conflated dichotomy of spiritual and material values that has often been seen as the definitive tension in Jewish-American literature, as in Guttmann (1971).

6. Johnson had lived in New York City for a very brief time in 1901 as a Broadway composer when black minstrel shows were in fashion, thus helping to prepare the way for Harlem's cultural ascendancy.

7. Perhaps because it is racially less distanced, *The Rise of David Levinsky* sticks closest to the Ben Franklin/Horatio Alger tradition and its own internal critique of materialistic values. It details the ins and outs of business more fully than does *The Autobiography of an Ex-Coloured Man,* and its title echoes an earlier fictional counter-thrust within the tradition, *The Rise of Silas Lapham* by Cahan's long-time literary supporter William Dean Howells. Nonetheless, Cahan's book as well as Johnson's pursues a specifically ethnic challenge to the materialism of such success stories.

8. Indeed, *Sister Carrie* also uses drug imagery—even the same metaphor of the moth drawn to the flame—to express Chicago's economic attraction for Carrie and its addictive effect on her. But Carrie Meeber gives up no previous or communal dream in succumbing to Chicago's promises of individual success; indeed, these *are* her deracinated American dreams.

9. The nonnormative nature of their choices can be confirmed by the understanding of addiction as delusive and isolating, which Alcoholics Anonymous articulated in the 1930s and the American Medical Association now recognizes.

10. Such New York Jewish radicals often worked with unions and around the *Menorah Journal* (Wald 1987). New York Jewish novelists whose starting point is ethnic immigrant experience often dramatize assimilation and its costs along the lines sketched by *The Rise of David Levinsky*—as does Samuel Ornitz's *Haunch Paunch and Jowl,* subtitled *An Anonymous Autobiography* (1923; also Schneider 1935 and Frank 1946). Some trace families over generations to psychologically assimilated Jews who resemble the alienated grotesques of megalopolis—for example, at a "slightly sodden bacchanal" in Ludwig Lewisohn's *The Island Within* ([1928] 1975, 207; also Pinski 1931).

11. *The Education of H*Y*M*A*N K*A*P*L*A*N* (Rosten 1937, 51) works with similar elements but in the humorous Mr. Dooley tradition that borders on stereotypes. Its pseudonymous publication indicates its author's distance from the neighborhood textures of his material.

12. Specifically, Yezierska struggled more with opportunities to move onwards

and upwards on her own. In her autobiography, she admitted that she was occasionally "tempted to hide my Jewishness" to get a job or to fight "against the Jew in me" to gain social acceptance, feeling smothered by her embeddedness in a despised minority group (Yezierska 1950, 213).

13. Yezierska's writing repeatedly affirms her need to maintain communal ties. She dramatizes this through one of her fictional personae who opens a cut-rate fashion store on the Lower East Side after being inspired by the immigrants' love of beauty (Yezierska 1923b, 282).

14. The concluding half of Yezierska's last novel, *All I Could Never Be* (1932), gets so caught up in her own experience of literary success and Depression failure that it thoroughly loses track of its novelistic themes and settings. The "semifictional" character of her 1950 autobiography (Stinson 1982, 482; Kessler-Harris 1979, xi), called a "novel" by her daughter (Henriksen 1979, 260), also frustrates attempts to separate her fiction from her life. Most of the locating circumstances of her life—the who's, what's, where's, and when's—have been lost.

15. Only the spelling is slightly changed, from Hannah Hayye and Moses Rifkin in *The Promised Land* (1912).

16. Yezierska's autobiography (1950, 103, 118–19) presents the hunchback as a kind of double for Yezierska's sense of herself as monstrous to Anglos because of her Jewish heritage and monstrous to other immigrants because of her independent ambitions.

17. In contrast to Faulkner's Yoknapatawpha, Yezierska's Hester Street depends more on the sound of names than on the detailed logic of circumstances to hold it together. Yezierska needs no map of her literary world because its familiar names ring in her inner ear as she struggles "to say something and make myself heard through the deafening noise of a thousand clamouring voices" (1923a, 10).

18. Typically Yezierska's fictional artists find inspiration from the people and sounds on Hester Street such as "the raucous orchestra of voices" and the "rumbling Elevated" that constitute an "elemental struggle for existence" that "cried out" to be "adequately sung" (e.g., 1923a, 249). Just as typically, noise and music push and pull in Yezierska's work, as they do only slightly less insistently in Hughes's.

19. Roth explained his preference "to avoid commitment and obligation," in an interview with William Freedman (Roth 1975, 152), and Ellison said he was "by instinct (and experience) a loner," in an interview with Robert Steptoe and Michael Harper (Ellison 1977, 427).

20. Roth even declared that, "damn it, I became a Goy!" when he became an atheist early in his teens. It was only in the 1970s that he identified himself as a Jew again, when he became committed to Zionism. It was only then that he saw a "subconscious reserve" of Jewish mysticism in *Call It Sleep* (Roth 1969, 267, 269). Having previously declared, "I do not regard *Call It Sleep* as primarily a novel of Jewish life" (qtd. in Lyons 1976, 169), he now considered it "a very

Jewish book... written by someone who no longer felt Jewish." That reassessment reminded Roth's interviewer of Ellison as another who "wrote an inspired... book without orthodoxy" (Roth 1979, 22, 19).

21. Other contributors to this consensus include: Miller (1984, 18) and Tuerk (1983, 136–53) on Jewish literature; Garza and Rivera (1977, 50–51) and Rebolledo (1985, 145–46) on Chicano literature; Espada (1987, 250–58) on Puerto Rican literature; and Oyama (1987, 250–55) on Japanese-American literature. As summarized by Tafolla (1987, 223), Chicano writer Tomas Rivera points toward two preliminary phases—folk orality and sociohistorical documentation—that precede the development of ethnic literature in print, fitting well with what we know of the development of American Indian and African-American oral literatures and their scholarly documentation in ethnographic translations and records of slave narratives. Rivera then labels the three belletristic phases "rebellion," "conflict," and "invention," while Jules Chametzky (1986, 50–56) offers a superb set of examples of them. Contrasting "mother" in *The Rise of David Levinsky,* to "Mother! Momma!" in Michael Gold's *Jews without Money,* to "Mamma" in Saul Bellow's *The Adventures of Augie March,* he characterizes the first as language borrowed "second hand," the second as "two voices jostling for dominance" with "no synthesis," and the last as the voice of "authority" and "independent vision."

I also discuss these and corresponding "phases" in ethnic literary *criticism* in a forthcoming essay, "The Ins and Outs of United States Ethnic Literature," to be published by the University of Wisconsin-Milwaukee's Institute on Race and Ethnicity as volume 10 in its series on *Ethnicity and Public Policy.*

22. Generally, both have been warmly embraced more often by mainstream critics declaring them "classics" than by other African- or Jewish-American writers seeking to establish a viable ethnic tradition of their own. Even though Roth was a Communist Party member when he published *Call It Sleep, The New Masses* reviewers were the only ones to dissent from the "laudatory" reception accorded his novel in the 1930s (Lyons 1976, 16–17). African-American proponents of "black aesthetics," along with Irving Howe, have similarly castigated *Invisible Man* on political grounds, also in contrast to that novel's "largely favorable" reception and selection for the National Book Award in 1953 (Reilly 1970, 4).

23. As Jewish Americans are more and more accepted among the white ethnic groups of western civilization, their dreams of a promised land are finding a home in our cities and nation. But African Americans, more and more closely joined to Third World people of color, seem to require a new world altogether to make a home for their dreams. Loury (1986) develops this distinction as a primary force "Behind the Black-Jewish Split."

Chapter 8: Regional Perspectives and Situated Reflections

1. Whether an ideal but impractical alternative to the economic city, or a failed ideal and an illusory alternative to megalopolis, the country rightfully belongs to a different order of existence from the city in these novels. The South's pattern is closer to the city-town model in its emphasis on continuities among settings, although it figures the city as a release in the midst of it all. Nonetheless, the city is surrounded by the countryside in southern regional novels, whereas the countryside is a get-away in economic-city and megalopolitan novels.

2. This is so even in momentary resurgences of pleasure—as when the "joyous clanging" of the cable-car mixes with Trina McTeague's singing just before her husband loses his dental practice ([1899] 1967, 221) or when the instruments of an orchestra play "like parts of a well regulated machine" when Vandover briefly recoils from his debauchery ([1914] 1967, 183).

3. Martin Eden is also philosophically convinced that life is a mix of the ideal and the material, that human beings are "saints in slime," and he writes an essay to that effect entitled "God and Clod" (London [1909] 1973, 115, 212). For the most part, however, his story traces the dichotomization of social brutishness and artistic spirit rather than their fusion, the "dreams in dirt" of ethnic minority imagery of the city.

4. Specifically, Toth argues that "regional" has been used as a code word to cover up gender bias in our canon—as when, for example, critics illogically dismiss birthing in *The Awakening* by Kate Chopin as "regional" while they praise whaling in *Moby Dick* by Herman Melville as "universal."

5. This connection between regionalism and women's literature was suggested to me by Leonore Hoffmann's (1982, 2-3) description of a "regional approach" as "comprehensive" and her subsequent quotation from Stanley and Wolfe (1979).

6. Marx's essay goes much further than most critics have been willing toward "planning the actual landscape" in keeping with literature's "landscape of mind." His "pastoral design" encourages us to diversify our physical settings, to complement urban with rural renewal, and to make both settings available to all Americans. But having resisted attempts to expand the "classics" in American literature, his later paper on "The Puzzle of Anti-Urbanism in Classic American Writing" can only rehash his long-standing disagreements with Morton and Lucia White (1962) as to whether or not pastoralism accounts for the antiurban bias that he, too, sees in U.S. literature.

7. Sardello (1982) uses mythology and the perspective of Jungian psychology to articulate some directions similar to Sizemore's—and mine—toward a "feminine city" that centers in the hearth, respects the past, and promotes a balance between growth and limits.

8. The 1989 televised version of Naylor's novel missed the importance of dreams. It is through dreams within a dream that the women of Brewster Place identify themselves with the raped lesbian in their midst; the heroine dreams the possibility of tearing down the wall; and the real day of a tenant union's block party starts just like the same day in the heroine's dream.

Works Cited

Adams, Henry. [1880] 1908. *Democracy.* New York: Henry Holt.
———. [1907] 1961. *The Education of Henry Adams: An Autobiography.* Cambridge, Mass.: Riverside Press.
Addams, Jane. 1893. *Philanthropy and Social Progress.* New York: Thomas Y. Crowell.
———. 1899. "A Function of the Social Settlement." *Annals of the American Academy of Political and Social Science* 251 (16 May): 323–45.
———. [1910] 1961. *Twenty Years at Hull-House.* New York: New American Library.
———. 1965. *The Social Thought of Jane Addams.* Ed. Christopher Lasch. Indianapolis: Bobbs-Merrill.
Ade, George. 1941. *Stories of the Street and of the Town.* Chicago: Caxton Club.
Albanese, Catherine. 1988. "The Problem of Bias: Interpretive Strategies in Religious Studies." *Soundings* 71 (Spring/Fall): 279–94.
Allen, Gay Wilson. 1967. *The Solitary Singer: A Critical Biography of Walt Whitman.* New York: New York University Press.
Alter, Robert. 1973. "Jewish Dreams and Nightmares." In *Contemporary American-Jewish Literature.* Ed. Irving Malin, 58–77. Bloomington: Indiana University Press.
Ammons, Elizabeth. 1980. *Edith Wharton's Argument with America.* Athens: University of Georgia Press.
Anderson, Margaret. [1930] 1971. *My Thirty Years' War.* Westport, Conn.: Greenwood Press.
Antin, Mary. 1912. *The Promised Land.* Boston: Houghton Mifflin.
Anzaldúa, Gloria. 1987. *Borderlands/La Frontera: The New Mestiza.* San Francisco: Spinsters/Aunt Lute.

Aptheker, Bettina. 1977. "Introduction." In *Lynching and Rape: An Exchange of Views,* Jane Addams and Ida B. Wells, 1–21. Occasional Paper #25. New York: American Institute for Marxist Studies.

Armitage, Susan. 1980. "Women's Literature and the Frontier Myth." In *Women, Women Writers, and the West.* Ed. L. L. Lee and Merrill Lewis, 5–11. Troy, N.Y.: Whitston.

Arnow, Harriette S. 1954. *The Dollmaker.* New York: Macmillan.

Asch, Sholom. 1937. *The Mother.* Trans. Elias Krauch. New York: Putnam's Sons.

Atherton, Gertrude. [1898] 1968. *The Californians.* Ridgewood, N.J.: Gregg Press.

———. 1923. "Fighting Up from the Ghetto." *New York Herald,* Jan. 7. In Yezierska Papers 2:3.

Auchincloss, Louis. 1971. *Edith Wharton: A Woman in Her Time.* New York: Viking.

Badger, R. Reid. 1979. *The Great American Fair: The World's Columbian Exposition and American Culture.* Chicago: Nelson Hall.

Baker, Houston A., Jr. 1984. *Blues, Ideology, and Afro-American Literature: A Vernacular Theory.* Chicago: University of Chicago Press.

———. 1987. *Modernism and the Harlem Renaissance.* Chicago: University of Chicago Press.

Baldwin, James. 1974. *If Beale Street Could Talk.* New York: New American Library.

Baritz, Loren. 1964. *City on a Hill: A History of Ideas and Myths in America.* New York: John Wiley & Sons.

Baxter, Annette K. 1963. "Caste and Class: Howells' Boston and Wharton's New York." *The Midwest Quarterly* 4: 353–61.

Beck, Warren. 1960. "Faulkner in the Mansion." *Virginia Quarterly Review* 36 (Spring): 272–92.

Belenky, Mary Field, Blythe M. Clinchy, Nancy R. Goldberger, and Jill M. Tarule. 1986. *Women's Ways of Knowing: The Development of Self, Voice, and Mind.* New York: Basic Books.

Bender, Thomas. 1987. *New York Intellect: A History of Intellectual Life in New York City, from 1750 to the Beginnings of Our Own Time.* New York: Alfred A. Knopf.

Bercovitch, Sacvan. 1975. *The Puritan Origins of the American Self.* New Haven: Yale University Press.

Berger, Peter L., and Thomas Luckmann. 1966. *The Social Construction of Reality: A Treatise in the Sociology of Knowledge.* Garden City, N.Y.: Doubleday.

Bodenheim, Maxwell. 1930. *Naked on Roller Skates.* New York: Liveright.

Bontemps, Arna, ed. 1972. *The Harlem Renaissance Remembered.* New York: Dodd, Mead.

Borders, Florence E. 1975. *Guide to the Microfilm Edition of the Countee Cullen Papers 1921–1969.* New Orleans: Amisted Research Center.

Bourget, Paul. 1893. "A Farewell to the White City." *Cosmopolitan* 16 (Dec.): 133–40.

Bowron, Bernard R., Jr. 1974. *Henry B. Fuller of Chicago: The Ordeal of a Genteel Realist in Ungenteel America.* Westport, Conn.: Greenwood Press.

Boyesen, Hjalmar H. 1893. "A New World Fable." *Cosmopolitan* 16 (Dec.): 173–86.

Bray, Robert C. 1982. *Rediscoveries: Literature and Place in Illinois.* Urbana: University of Illinois Press.

Bremer, Sidney H. 1971. "Woman in the Works of William Dean Howells." Ph.D. diss., Stanford University.

———. 1981. "Lost Continuities: Alternative Urban Visions in Chicago Novels, 1890–1915." *Soundings* 64 (Spring): 29–51.

———. 1984. "Willa Cather's Lost Chicago Sisters." In *Women Writers and the City.* Ed. Susan Merrill Squier, 210–29. Knoxville: University of Tennessee Press.

———. 1989. "Introduction." In *The Precipice,* Elia Peattie, ix–xxvi. Urbana: University of Illinois Press.

———. 1990. "Home in Harlem, New York: Lessons from the Harlem Renaissance Writers." *PMLA* 105 (Jan.): 47–56.

Bremer, William W. 1965. *Radicalism among the Ghetto Pioneers: New York's Jewish Immigrants, 1900–1917.* M.A. thesis. University of Wisconsin–Madison.

Browne, Claude. 1965. *Manchild in the Promised Land.* New York: Macmillan.

Brownell, Blaine A. 1977. "The Urban South Comes of Age, 1900–1940." In *The City in Southern History.* Ed. Brownell and David R. Goldfield, 123–58. Port Washington, N.Y.: Kennikat Press.

———, and David R. Goldfield. 1977. "Southern Urban History." In *The City in Southern History.* Ed. Brownell and Goldfield, 5–22. Port Washington, N.Y.: Kennikat Press.

Bruccoli, Matthew J. 1974. *Apparatus for F. Scott Fitzgerald's "The Great Gatsby."* Columbia: University of South Carolina Press.

Bruce-Novoa, Juan. 1987. "Chicano Poetry: An Overview." In *A Gift of Tongues.* Ed. Marie Harris and Kathleen Aguero, 226–48. Athens: University of Georgia Press.

Bryant, William Cullen. [1825] 1935. *Representative Selections.* Ed. Tremaine McDowell. New York: American Book Company.

Bryer, Jackson R., and John Kuehl, eds. 1973. *The Basil and Josephine Stories.* New York: Charles Scribner's Sons.

Burg, David. 1976. *Chicago's White City of 1893.* Lexington: University Press of Kentucky.

Burnham, Clara. 1894. *Sweet Clover.* Boston: Houghton Mifflin.

Cady, Edwin H. 1956. *The Road to Realism.* Syracuse, N.Y.: Syracuse University Press.
———. 1957. "Introduction." In *The Rise of Silas Lapham,* William Dean Howells, v–xviii. Boston: Houghton Mifflin.
Cahan, Abraham. 1896. *Yekl.* New York: Appleton.
———. [1917] 1966. *The Rise of David Levinsky.* New York: Harper.
———. Papers. YIVO Institute for Jewish Research, New York, N.Y.
Caldwell, Erskine. 1932. *Tobacco Road.* New York: Grosset & Dunlap.
Carby, Hazel. 1987. *Reconstructing Womanhood: The Emergence of the Afro-American Woman Novelist.* New York: Oxford University Press.
Carroll, Peter N. 1969. *Puritanism and the Wilderness: The Intellectual Significance of the New England Frontier, 1629–1700.* New York: Columbia University Press.
Cather, Willa. 1915. *The Song of the Lark.* Boston: Houghton Mifflin.
———. 1936. *Not Under Forty.* New York: Alfred A. Knopf.
Cavell, Stanley. 1981. *The Senses of Walden.* San Francisco: North Point Press.
Chametzky, Jules. 1986. *Our Decentralized Literature: Cultural Mediation in Selected Jewish and Southern Writers.* Amherst: University of Massachusetts Press.
Chase, Richard. 1961. *Walt Whitman.* Minneapolis: University of Minnesota Press.
Chatfield-Taylor, Hobart C. 1895. *Two Women and a Fool.* Chicago: Stone & Kimball.
———. 1917. *Chicago.* Boston: Houghton Mifflin.
———. 1918. "Foreword." In *My Chicago,* Anna Morgan. Chicago: R. F. Seymour.
Chmaj, Betty. 1976. "The Cities of Our Minds." *Landscape* 21 (Autumn): 16–27.
Chopin, Kate. [1899] 1976. *The Awakening.* New York: W. W. Norton.
Clark, Dennis. 1975. "Philadelphia 1876." In *Philadelphia: 1776–2076.* Ed. Dennis Clark, 43–65. Port Washington, N.Y.: Kennikat Press.
Clarke, John Henrik. 1967. "Langston Hughes (1902–1967), Esop of Our Time: A Memorial Tribute to Langston Hughes." Hughes Material. Schomburg Center for Research in Black Culture. New York Public Library, New York, N.Y.
Cohen, Hyman, and Lester Cohen. 1930. *Aaron Traum.* New York: Horace Liveright.
Collins, Charles. [1942]. *Critics and Reviewers. Chicago Tribune* archives, Chicago, Ill.
Collins, Patricia Hill. 1989. "The Social Construction of Black Feminist Thought." *Signs* 14, 4: 745–73.
Condit, Carl. 1964. *The Chicago School of Architecture: A History of Commercial and Public Building in the Chicago Area, 1875–1925.* Chicago: University of Chicago Press.

Cooper, James Fenimore. [1823] 1959. *The Pioneers*. New York: Holt, Rinehart Winston.
———. [1838] n.d. *Home as Found*. Boston: Colonial Press.
Cowan, Michael. 1967. *City of the West: Emerson, America, and Urban Metaphor*. New Haven, Conn.: Yale University Press.
Crane, Hart. [1930] 1946. "The Bridge." In *The Collected Poems of Hart Crane*. Ed. Waldo Frank, 1–58. New York: Liveright.
Cronon, William. 1983. *Changes in the Land: Indians, Colonists, and the Ecology of New England*. New York: Hill and Wang.
Cullen, Countee. 1925. *Color*. New York: Harper & Bros.
———. 1932. *One Way to Heaven*. New York: Harper & Bros.
Daniel, Carter A. 1971. "West's Revisions of *Miss Lonelyhearts*." In *Nathanael West: A Collection of Critical Essays*. Ed. Jay Martin, 52–65. Englewood Cliffs, N.J.: Prentice Hall.
Davidson, Marshall. 1957. "Whither the Course of Empire?" *American Heritage* 8 (Oct.): 52–61, 104.
Davis, Angela. 1987. "Strong Beyond All Definitions..." *Women's Review of Books* 4 (July–Aug.): 1, 21.
Davis, Rebecca Harding. [1861] 1972. *Life in the Iron Mills*. Old Westbury, N.Y.: Feminist Press.
———. [1867] 1968. *Waiting for the Verdict*. Upper Saddle River, N.J.: Gregg Press.
De Forest, John W. 1875. *Honest John Vane*. New Haven, Conn.: Richmond & Patten.
Demos, John. 1970. *A Little Commonwealth: Family Life in Plymouth Colony*. London: Oxford University Press.
Didion, Joan. 1970. *Play It As It Lays*. New York: Farrar, Straus & Giroux.
Dimock, Wai-Chee. 1985. "Debasing Exchange: Edith Wharton's *The House of Mirth*." *PMLA* 100 (Oct.): 783–92.
Dos Passos, John. [1925] 1953. *Manhattan Transfer*. Boston: Houghton Mifflin.
Doubleday, Neal Frank. 1972. *Hawthorne's Early Tales*. Durham, N.C.: Duke University Press.
Dreiser, Theodore. [1900] 1959. *Sister Carrie*. Ed. Claude Simpson. Boston: Houghton Mifflin.
———. 1914. *The Titan*. New York: John Lane.
———. 1928. "Preface." In *McTeague,* Frank Norris, vii–xi. Garden City, N.Y.: Doubleday Doran.
Du Bois, W. E. Burghardt. 1903. *The Souls of Black Folk*. Chicago: A. C. McClurg.
Duffey, Bernard. 1956. *The Chicago Renaissance in American Letters*. East Lansing: Michigan State University Press.
Duncan, Hugh Dalziel. 1964. *The Rise of Chicago as a Literary Center from 1885 to 1920: A Sociological Essay in American Culture*. Totowa, N.J.: Bedminster Press.

———. 1965. *Culture and Democracy*. Totowa, N.J.: Bedminster Press.
Dunne, Finley Peter. 1962. *The World of Mr. Dooley*. Ed. Louis Filler. New York: Crowell-Collier.
DuPlessis, Rachel Blau. 1985. *Writing beyond the Ending: Narrative Strategies of Twentieth-Century Women Writers*. Bloomington: Indiana University Press.
Eble, Kenneth. 1963. *F. Scott Fitzgerald*. New York: Twayne.
Eliade, Mircea. 1959. *Cosmos and History: The Myth of the Eternal Return*. Trans. William R. Trask. New York: Harper.
Ellison, Ralph. 1952. *Invisible Man*. New York: New American Library.
———. 1963. Interview. In *Writers at Work: The Paris Review Interviews*. Ed. George Plimpton, 317–34. New York: Viking.
———. 1977. "Study and Experience: An Interview with Ralph Ellison," Robert Steptoe and Michael Harper. *Massachusetts Review* 18: 417–35.
Emerson, Ralph Waldo. [1836] 1960. "Nature." In *Selections from Ralph Waldo Emerson*. Ed. Stephen E. Whicher, 21–56. Boston: Houghton Mifflin.
———. [1841–42] 1957. "The Poet." In *Selections from Ralph Waldo Emerson*. Ed. Stephen E. Whicher, 222–41. Boston: Houghton Mifflin.
———. 1909–14. *Journals of Ralph Waldo Emerson*. Ed. E. W. Emerson and W. E. Forbes. Boston: Houghton Mifflin.
Espada, Martin. 1987. "Documentaries and Declamadores: Puerto Rican Poetry in the United States." In *A Gift of Tongues*. Ed. Marie Harris and Kathleen Aguero, 257–66. Athens: University of Georgia Press.
Farrell, James T. 1934. *Studs Lonigan: A Trilogy containing "Young Lonigan," "The Young Manhood of Studs Lonigan," "Judgment Day."* New York: Vanguard Press.
Faulkner, William. [1931] 1932. *Sanctuary*. New York: Modern Library.
———. 1932. *Light in August*. New York: Random House.
———. 1936. *Absalom, Absalom!* New York: Random House.
———. 1957. *The Town*. New York: Random House.
———. 1959. *The Mansion*. New York: Random House.
———. [1962] 1966. *The Reivers: A Reminiscence*. New York: Random House.
Fauset, Jessie Redmon. 1924. *There Is Confusion*. New York: Boni and Liveright.
———. 1929. *Plum Bun*. New York: Frederick A. Stokes.
Ferguson, William M., and Arthur H. Rohn. 1987. *Anasazi Ruins of the Southwest in Color*. Albuquerque: University of New Mexico Press.
Festa-McCormick, Diana. 1979. *The City as Catalyst*. Rutherford, N.J.: Fairleigh Dickinson University Press.
Fiedler, Leslie A. 1960. "Henry Roth's Neglected Masterpiece." *Commentary*, 102–7. Roth Papers. Mugar Library, Boston University, Boston, Mass.
———. 1968. *The Return of the Vanishing American*. New York: Stein and Day.
Fisher, Philip. 1985. *Hard Facts: Setting and Form in the American Novel*. New York: Oxford University Press.

Fisher, Rudolph. 1925. "City of Refuge." *Atlantic Monthly* 135 (Feb.) 178–87; rpt. in *The New Negro.* Ed. Alain Locke, 57–74. New York: Albert and Charles Boni, 1925.
———. 1928. *The Walls of Jericho.* New York: Alfred A. Knopf.
———. [1932] 1971. *The Conjure-Man Dies!: A Mystery Tale of Dark Harlem.* New York: Arno Press and *New York Times.*
Fitzgerald, F. Scott. [1918] 1971. City Dusk. In *In His Own Time: A Miscellany.* Ed. Matthew J. Bruccoli and Jackson R. Bryer, 66. Kent, Ohio: Kent State University Press.
———. [1920] 1951. "Bernice Bobs Her Hair." In *The Stories of F. Scott Fitzgerald.* Ed. Malcolm Cowley, 39–60. New York: Charles Scribner's.
———. 1925. *The Great Gatsby.* New York: Charles Scribner's Sons.
———. [1925] 1926. "The Rich Boy." In *All the Sad Young Men,* 1–56. New York: Charles Scribner's Sons.
———. [1934] 1945a. "My Lost City." In *The Crack-Up.* Ed. Edmund Wilson, 23–33. New York: New Directions.
———. [1936] 1945b. "The Crack-Up." In *The Crack-Up.* Ed. Edmund Wilson, 69–85. New York: New Directions.
———. 1945c. "Early Success." In *The Crack-Up.* Ed. Edmund Wilson, 85–90. New York: New Directions.
———. 1973. "First Blood." In *The Basil and Josephine Stories.* Ed. Jackson R. Bryer and John Kuehl, 186–203. New York: Charles Scribner's Sons.
Frank, Florence Kiper. 1915. "The Song of the Women." In *The Jew to Jesus and Other Poems,* 8–10. New York: Mitchell Kennerley.
Frank, Waldo. 1946. *Island in the Atlantic.* New York: Duell, Sloan, and Pearce.
Franklin, H. Bruce. 1978. *The Victim as Criminal and Artist: Literature from the American Prison.* New York: Oxford University Press.
Frederickson, George M. 1965. *The Inner Civil War.* New York: Harper & Row.
Fuller, Henry Blake. [1893] 1968. *The Cliff-Dwellers.* Ridgewood, N.J.: Gregg Press.
———. [1895] 1965. *With the Procession.* Chicago: University of Chicago Press.
———. 1897. "The Upward Movement in Chicago." *Atlantic Monthly* 80 (Oct.): 534–47.
———. 1901. "Our 'Young Lady Novelist,'" 1 June, Fuller Papers.
———. 1903. " 'Lady Rose's Daughter' Displays Mrs. Ward's Genius in Maturity." 28 Feb., Fuller Papers.
———. Papers. Newberry Library, Chicago, Ill.
Gadamer, Hans-Georg. 1975. *Truth and Method.* Trans. and ed. Garrett Barden and John Cumming. London: Sheed & Ward.
Garland, Hamlin. [1895] 1899. *Rose of Dutcher's Coolly.* New York: Macmillan.
———. 1930. *Roadside Meetings.* New York: MacMillan.
———. 1931. *Companions on the Trail.* New York: Macmillan.

Garza, Rudolpho O. de la, and Rowena Rivera. 1977. "The Socio-Political World of the Chicano: A Comparative Analysis of Social Scientific and Literary Perspectives." In *Minority Languages and Literature: Retrospective and Perspective.* Ed. Dexter Fisher. New York: Modern Language Association.

Gates, Henry Louis, Jr. 1988. *The Signifying Monkey: A Theory of Afro-American Literary Criticism.* New York: Oxford University Press.

Geertz, Clifford. 1973. *The Interpretation of Cultures.* New York: Basic Books.

Gelfant, Blanche M. 1954. *The American City Novel.* Norman: Oklahoma University Press.

Gerstenberg, Alice. 1912. *Unquenched Fire: A Novel.* Boston: Small, Maynard.

———. [1915] 1922. "Overtones." In *10 One-Act Plays.* New York: Brentano's.

———. [1962]. "Come Back with Me." Ms. Gerstenberg Papers, Chicago Historical Society, Chicago, Ill.

———. Manuscripts. Newberry Library, Chicago, Ill.

Giddings, Paula. 1985. *When and Where I Enter.* New York: Bantam.

Giles, James R. 1976. *Claude McKay.* Boston: Twayne.

Gilligan, Carol. 1982. *In a Different Voice: Psychological Theory and Women's Development.* Cambridge, Mass.: Harvard University Press.

Ginger, Ray. 1965. *Altgeld's America: The Lincoln Ideal versus Changing Realities.* Chicago: Quadrangle Books.

Glasgow, Ellen. [1932] 1979. *The Sheltered Life.* New York: Hill and Wang.

Glaspell, Susan. 1909. *The Glory of the Conquered.* New York: F. A. Stokes.

Gold, Michael. 1930. *Jews without Money.* New York: Liveright.

Goldman, Judith. 1981. "Twenty-five Years of American Prints and Printmaking, 1956-1981," *Print Review* 13: 7-13.

Green, Martin. 1967. *The Problem of Boston.* New York: W. W. Norton.

Gunn, Giles. 1982. "Literature and Religion." In *The Interrelations of Literature.* Ed. Jean-Pierre Barricelli and Joseph Gibaldi, 47-66. New York: Modern Language Association.

Guttmann, Allen. 1971. *The Jewish Writer in America.* New York: Oxford University Press.

Halprin, Lawrence. 1972. *Cities.* Cambridge, Mass.: MIT Press.

Harris, Frank. 1908. *The Bomb.* London: J. Long.

Harris, Neil. 1966. *The Artist in American Society: The Formative Years, 1790-1860.* New York: George Braziller.

Hawthorne, Nathaniel. [1832] 1965. "My Kinsman, Major Molineux." In *The Snow Image, and Uncollected Tales.* Ed. William Charvat et al. Columbus: Ohio State University Press.

———. [1852] 1965. *The Blithedale Romance.* Columbus: Ohio State University Press.

Hazo, Samuel. 1963. *Smithereened Apart: A Critique of Hart Crane.* Athens: Ohio University Press.

Hemenway, Robert E. 1977. *Zora Neale Hurston: A Literary Biography.* Urbana: University of Illinois Press.
Henriksen, Louise Levitas. 1979. "Afterword." In *The Open Cage,* Anzia Yezierska, 253-62. New York: Persea Books.
Herrick, Robert. 1898. *The Gospel of Freedom.* New York: Macmillan.
———. 1900. *The Web of Life.* New York: Grosset & Dunlap.
———. [1905] 1963. *The Memoirs of an American Citizen.* Ed. Daniel Aaron. Cambridge, Mass.: Belknap Press.
———. 1914. "The Background of the American Novel." *Yale Review* n.s. 3 (Jan.): 213-33.
Himes, Chester B. 1946. *If He Hollers Let Him Go.* Garden City, N.Y.: Doubleday, Doran.
Hoffman, Leonore. 1982. "Introduction." In *Teaching Women's Literature from a Regional Perspective.* Ed. Hoffmann and Deborah Rosenfelt. New York: Modern Language Association.
hooks, bell. 1990. *Yearning: Race, Gender, and Cultural Politics.* Boston, Mass.: South End Press.
Howard, June. 1985. *Form and History in American Literary Naturalism.* Chapel Hill: University of North Carolina Press.
Howe, Florence. 1983. Keynote address. Conference on "100 Years Teaching American Literature." University of Wisconsin-Madison.
Howe, Frederic C. 1906. *The City: The Hope of Democracy.* New York: Scribner's Sons.
Howe, Irving. 1956. "Introduction." In *The Bostonians,* Henry James, v-xxviii. New York: Random House.
———. 1976. *World of Our Fathers.* New York: Simon and Schuster.
Howells, William Dean. [1885] 1957. *The Rise of Silas Lapham.* Boston: Houghton Mifflin.
———. [1890] 1965. *A Hazard of New Fortunes.* New York: New American Library.
———. 1893. "Letters of an Altrurian Traveller." *Cosmopolitan* 16 (Dec.): 218-32.
———. 1895. Review of *With the Procession. Harper's Weekly* 39 (1 June): 508.
———. 1903. "Certain of the Chicago School of Fiction." *North American Review* 176: 734-46.
———. 1917. *Years of My Youth.* New York: Harper & Bros.
———. 1928. *Life in Letters of William Dean Howells.* Ed. Mildred Howells. Garden City, N.Y.: Doubleday Doran.
———. Papers. Houghton Library, Harvard University, Cambridge, Mass.
Huggins, Nathan Irvin. 1971. *Harlem Renaissance.* London: Oxford University Press.
Hughes, Langston. [1925] 1935. *The Weary Blues.* New York: Alfred A. Knopf.

———. 1929. *Fine Clothes to the Jew.* New York: Alfred A. Knopf.
———. 1940. *The Big Sea: An Autobiography.* New York: Alfred A. Knopf.
———. 1941. "In memory of a Man." 4 Apr., Ms. Hughes Papers.
———. [1943?] Broadcast to the West Indies. In 23 July letter to Claude McKay, McKay Papers. James Weldon Johnson Memorial Collection. Beinecke Library, Yale University, New Haven, Conn.
———. [1945]. "The Ceaseless Rings of Walt Whitman." [Aug.] typescript. Hughes Material.
———. 1945. "Introduction" to *Walt Whitman for Young People,* 27 Aug., Ms. Hughes Papers–Mss.
———. [1967] 1968. "Dream Deferred." From *The Panther and the Lamb;* rpt. in *On City Streets.* Ed. Nancy Larrick, 149. New York: Bantam.
———. n.d. "Introduction" to Harrington. Typescript. Hughes Material.
———. Material from the Vertical Files of the Schomburg Collection, 1926–67. Schomburg Center for Research in Black Culture. New York Public Library, New York, N.Y.
———. Papers. James Weldon Johnson Memorial Collection. Beinecke Library, Yale University, New Haven, Conn.
———. Papers–Manuscripts Collection. James Weldon Johnson Memorial Collection. Beinecke Library, Yale University, New Haven, Conn.
———. Papers. Mugar Memorial Library. Boston University, Boston, Mass.
Hull, Gloria T. 1987. *Color, Sex and Poetry: Three Women Writers of the Harlem Renaissance.* Bloomington: Indiana University Press.
Hurston, Zora Neale. [1925–27]. *Book of Harlem.* Hurston Collection.
———. 1934. "Race Cannot Become Great Until It Recognizes Its Talent," *Washington Tribune,* 29 Dec. Rosenwald Fund Archives. Fisk University, Nashville, Tenn.
———. [1937] 1978. *Their Eyes Were Watching God.* Urbana: University of Illinois Press.
———. Collection. James Weldon Johnson Memorial Collection. Beinecke Library, Yale University, New Haven, Conn.
Hutson, Jean. 1978. Interview by Barbara Kline. Oral History Collection. Butler Library, Columbia University, New York, N.Y.
Irving, Washington. [1812] 1984. *A History of New York.* In *Complete Works of Washington Irving,* vol. 7. Ed. Michael L. Black and Nancy B. Black. Boston: Twayne.
Jackson, John Brinckerhoff. 1972. *American Space.* New York: W. W. Norton.
Jacobs, Harriet. [1861] 1987. *Incidents in the Life of a Slave Girl.* Ed. Jean Fagan Yellin. Cambridge, Mass.: Harvard University Press.
Jacobs, Jane. 1961. *The Death and Life of Great American Cities.* New York: Random House.
James, Henry. [1886] 1956. *The Bostonians.* New York: Random House.

———. [1907] 1968. *The American Scene.* Bloomington: Indiana University Press.
Janeway, Elizabeth. 1971. *Man's World, Woman's Place: A Study in Social Mythology.* New York: Dell Publishing.
Jensen, Joan M. 1981. *With These Hands: Women Working on the Land.* Old Westbury, N.Y.: Feminist Press.
Johnson, Charles S. 1925. "The New Frontage on American Life." In *The New Negro: An Interpretation.* Ed. Alain Locke, 278–98. New York: Albert & Charles Boni.
———. 1934. *Shadow of the Plantation.* Chicago: University of Chicago Press.
Johnson, James Weldon. [1912] 1927. *The Autobiography of an Ex-Coloured Man.* New York: Alfred A. Knopf.
———. [1930] 1958. *Black Manhattan.* New York: Atheneum.
———. 1931. Speech of Resignation, NAACP. Johnson Papers.
———. 1935. *Saint Peter Relates an Incident.* New York: Viking Press.
———, and Grace Nail Johnson. Papers. James Weldon Johnson Memorial Collection. Beinecke Library, Yale University, New Haven, Conn.
Kaplan, Amy. 1988. *The Social Construction of American Realism.* Chicago: University of Chicago Press.
Kazin, Alfred. 1951. *A Walker in the City.* New York: Harcourt Brace.
Kelley, Florence. 1895. *Hull-House Maps and Papers.* New York: Crowell.
Kessler-Harris, Alice. 1979. "Introduction." In *The Open Cage,* Anzia Yezierska, v–xiii. New York: Persea Books.
Kirk, Rudolf, and Clara Kirk, eds. n.d. "Edith Franklin Wyatt, Chicagoenne (1873–1958)." In *Homage to William Dean Howells.* Wyatt Mss. Newberry Library, Chicago, Ill.
Konvitz, Joseph. 1985. *The Urban Millennium: The City-Building Process from the Early Middle Ages to the Present.* Carbondale: Southern Illinois University Press.
Kramer, Dale. 1966. *Chicago Literary Renaissance.* New York: Appleton-Century.
Langer, Susanne. 1960. *Philosophy in a New Key.* 3d ed. Cambridge, Mass.: Harvard University Press.
Langford, Gerald. 1961. *The Richard Harding Davis Years.* New York: Holt, Rinehart and Winston.
Lankevich, George J., and Howard B. Furer. 1984. *A Brief History of New York City.* Port Washington, N.Y.: Associated Faculty Press.
Larsen, Nella. [1928] 1969. *Quicksand.* New York: Negro Universities Press.
———. 1929. *Passing.* New York: Alfred A. Knopf.
Laughlin, Clara. 1910. *"Just Folks."* New York: Macmillan.
———. 1912. *The Penny Philanthropist.* New York: Fleming H. Revell.
Lauter, Estella. 1985. *Women as Mythmakers.* Bloomington: Indiana University Press.
Lauter, Paul. 1983. "Race and Gender in the Shaping of the American Lit-

erary Canon: A Case Study from the Twenties." *Feminist Studies* 9 (Fall): 435–64.
Lenz, Günter H. 1988. "Symbolic Space, Communal Rituals, and the Surreality of the Urban Ghetto: Harlem in Black Literature from the 1920s to the 1960s." *Callaloo* 11 (Spring): 309–45.
Lerner, Gerda. 1969. "The Lady and the Mill Girl: Changes in the Status of Women in the Age of Jackson." *Midcontinent American Studies Journal* 10 (Spring): 5–15.
Levin, David. 1978. *Cotton Mather*. Cambridge, Mass.: Harvard University Press.
Levin, Meyer. 1933. "Human Being." Ms. Levin Collection.
———. Collection. Mugar Memorial Library, Boston University, Boston, Mass.
Lewis, Lloyd, and Henry Justin Smith. 1929. *Chicago: The History of Its Reputation*. New York: Blue Ribbon Books.
Lewis, R. W. B. 1975. *Edith Wharton: A Biography*. New York: Harper & Row.
Lewis, Sinclair. 1922. *Babbitt*. New York: Grosset & Dunlap.
Lewisohn, Ludwig. [1928] 1975. *The Island Within*. New York: Arno Press.
Light, James F. 1961. *Nathanael West: An Interpretative Study*. Evanston, Ill.: Northwestern University Press.
Lipset, Seymour Martin. 1963. *The First New Nation: The United States in Historical and Comparative Perspective*. New York: Basic Books.
Little Room Papers. Newberry Library, Chicago, Ill.
Locke, Alain, ed. 1925. *The New Negro*. New York: Albert and Charles Boni.
London, Jack. [1909] 1973. *Martin Eden*. New York: Macmillan.
Loury, Glenn C. 1986. "Behind the Black-Jewish Split." *Commentary* 81 (Jan.): 23–27.
Lovett, Robert Morss. 1907. *A Winged Victory*. New York: Duffield.
Ludington, Townsend. 1980. *John Dos Passos: A Twentieth-Century Odyssey*. New York: Dutton.
Lynn, Kenneth S. 1970. "Howells in the Nineties." *Perspectives in American History* 4: 27–82.
———. 1971. *William Dean Howells: An American Life*. New York: Harcourt Brace Jovanovich.
Lyons, Bonnie. 1976. *Henry Roth: The Man and His Work*. New York: Cooper Square.
Machor, James L. 1987. *Pastoral Cities: Urban Ideals and the Symbolic Landscape of America*. Madison: University of Wisconsin Press.
McKay, Claude. 1920. *Spring in New Hampshire and Other Poems*. London: Grant Richards.
———. 1922. *Harlem Shadows: The Poems of Claude McKay*. New York: Harcourt, Brace.
———. [1922–34?]. "Cities." Ms. McKay Papers.
———. 1928. *Home to Harlem*. New York: Harper & Brothers.

———. 1937. *A Long Way from Home*. New York: Lee Furman.
———. 1940. *Harlem: Negro Metropolis*. New York: E. P. Dutton.
———. Papers. James Weldon Johnson Memorial Collection. Beinecke Library, Yale University, New Haven, Conn.
McKay, Nellie. 1984. *Jean Toomer, Artist: A Study of His Literary Life and Work*. Greensboro: University of North Carolina Press.
McKelvey, Blake. 1973. *American Urbanization*. Glenview, Ill.: Scott Foresman.
McWilliams, Carey. 1946. *Southern California Country*. New York: Duell, Sloan & Pearce.
Malamud, Bernard. 1961. *A New Life*. New York: Farrar Straus & Giroux.
Marin, John. 1977. *John Marin by John Marin*. Ed. Cleve Gray. New York: Holt, Rinehart and Winston.
Martin, Jay. 1970. *Nathanael West: The Art of His Life*. New York: Farrar, Straus and Giroux.
Marx, Leo. 1964. *The Machine in the Garden*. New York: Oxford University Press.
———. 1969. "Pastoral Ideals and City Troubles." *Journal of General Education* 20 (Jan.): 251–71.
———. 1981. "The Puzzle of Anti-Urbanism in Classic American Literature." In *Literature and the Urban Experience*. Ed. Michael C. Jaye and Ann C. Watts, 63–80. New Brunswick, N.J.: Rutgers University Press.
Masters, Edgar Lee. 1933. *The Tale of Chicago*. New York: Putnam's Sons.
Mather, Cotton. [1702] 1975. "Nehemias Americanus: The Life of John Winthrop." In *The Puritan Origins of the American Self*, Sacvan Bercovitch, 187–205. New Haven, Conn.: Yale University Press.
May, Miriam. 1986. "Regional Women Writers: Challenges to Traditional Concepts of Regionalism in American Fiction." Ms., University of Wisconsin–Green Bay.
Mayer, Harold M., and Richard C. Wade. 1969. *Chicago: Growth of a Metropolis*. Chicago: University of Chicago Press.
Medill, Joseph. 1871. Editorial. *Chicago Tribune*, Oct. 11.
Mellow, James R. 1984. *Invented Lives: F. Scott and Zelda Fitzgerald*. Boston: Houghton Mifflin.
Melville, Herman. [1852] 1957. *Pierre: or, the Ambiguities*. New York: Grove Press.
———. [1853] 1950. "Bartleby the Scrivener." In *Selected Tales and Poems by Herman Melville*. Ed. Richard Chase, 92–131. New York: Holt, Rinehart and Winston.
———. [1855] 1949. "The Paradise of Bachelors" and "The Tartarus of Maids." In *The Complete Stories of Herman Melville*. Ed. Jay Leyda, 185–211. New York: Random House.
Merrell, James H. 1975. "To Build a City." Honors thesis, Lawrence University, Appleton, Wis.

Miller, Nancy K. 1981. "Emphasis Added: Plots and Plausibilities in Women's Fiction." *PMLA* 96 (Jan.): 36–48.
Miller, Perry. 1967. "The Romantic Dilemma in American Nationalism and the Concept of Nature." In *Nature's Nation*, 239–53. Cambridge, Mass.: Belknap Press.
Miller, Ross. 1990. *American Apocalypse: The Great Fire and the Myth of Chicago.* Chicago: University of Chicago Press.
Miller, Wayne Charles. 1984. "Toward a New Literary History of the United States." *MELUS* 11, 1 (Spring): 18.
Minh-ha, Trinh T. 1990. "Commitment from the Mirror-Writing Box." In *Making Face, Making Soul: Haciendo Caras.* Ed. Gloria Anzaldúa, 245–55. San Francisco: Aunt Lute Foundation Books.
Monroe, Harriet. 1895. "Workman's Song." *Chicago Times-Herald,* Sept. 30. *Poetry* Papers.
———. 1906. "Little Davy." Ms. *Poetry* Papers.
———. 1912. "The Motive of the Magazine." *Poetry* 1 (Oct.): 26–28.
———. 1914a. Editorial. *Poetry* 5 (Oct.): 32.
———. 1914b. *You and I.* New York: Macmillan.
———. 1938. *A Poet's Life.* New York: Macmillan.
———. Personal Papers. Regenstein Library, University of Chicago, Chicago, Ill.
———. *Poetry* Papers. Regenstein Library, University of Chicago, Chicago, Ill.
Monroe, Lucy. 1893a. "Chicago Letter." *The Critic,* 278 (18 Mar.): 168.
———. 1893b. "Chicago Letter." *The Critic,* 602 (2 Sept.): 157–58.
Morgan, Anna. 1918. *My Chicago.* Chicago: R. F. Seymour.
———. Papers. Chicago Historical Society, Chicago, Ill.
Morrison, Toni. 1976. " 'Intimate Things in Place'—A Conversation with Toni Morrison," Robert Stepto. In *The Third Woman.* Ed. Dexter Fisher, 167–82. Boston: Houghton Mifflin.
———. 1977. *Song of Solomon.* New York: Alfred A. Knopf.
———. 1981a. *Tar Baby.* New York: Alfred A. Knopf.
———. 1981b. "City Limits, Village Values: Concepts of the Neighborhood in Black Fiction." In *Literature and the Urban Experience: Essays on the City and Literature.* Ed. Michael C. Jaye and Ann Chalmers Watts, 35–44. New Brunswick, N.J.: Rutgers University Press.
Nabokov, Vladimir. 1962. *Pale Fire: A Novel.* New York: Putnam.
Nash, Roderick. 1973. *Wilderness and the American Mind.* New Haven, Conn.: Yale University Press.
Naylor, Gloria. 1983. *The Women of Brewster Place.* Middlesex, England: Penguin Books.
Nevius, Blake. 1962. *Robert Herrick: The Development of a Novelist.* Berkeley: University of California Press.
Nordenskiold, Gustaf. 1893. *The Cliff Dwellers of the Mesa Verde, Southwestern Colorado.* Trans. D. Lloyd Morgan. Stockholm: Norstedt & Soner.

Norris, Frank. [1899] 1967. *McTeague.* In *Complete Works of Frank Norris,* vol. 8. Port Washington, N.Y.: Kennikat.
———. 1903. *The Pit.* New York: Collier and Son.
———. [1914] 1967. *Vandover and the Brute.* In *Complete Works of Frank Norris,* vol. 5. Port Washington, N.Y.: Kennikat Press.
Oates, Joyce Carol. 1972. *Marriages and Infidelities.* Greenwich, Conn.: Fawcett.
———. 1981. "Imaginary Cities: America." In *Literature and the Urban Experience: Essays on the City and Literature.* Ed. Michael C. Jaye and Ann Chalmers Watts, 11–33. New Brunswick, N.J.: Rutgers University Press.
O'Connor, Flannery. [1955] 1972. "The Artificial Nigger." In *The Complete Stories,* 249–70. New York: Farrar, Straus and Giroux.
O'Connor, Leo F. 1974. "Howells' New York." Paper presented at Modern Language Association convention, New York, N.Y.
Ogletree, Thomas W. 1985. "Hospitality to the Stranger: The Role of the 'Other' in Moral Experience." In *Hospitality to the Stranger,* 35–63. Philadelphia: Fortress Press.
Olsen, Tillie. 1972. "Biographical Interpretation." In *Life in the Iron Mills,* Rebecca Harding Davis. Old Westbury, N.Y.: Feminist Press.
Ong, Walter J., S.J. 1977. "Oral Culture and the Literature Mind." In *Minority Languages and Literature: Retrospective and Perspective.* Ed. Dexter Fisher, 142–45. New York: Modern Language Association.
Ornitz, Samuel. 1923. *Haunch Paunch and Jowl: An Anonymous Autobiography.* New York: Boni Liveright.
Osofsky, Gilbert. 1966. *Harlem: The Making of a Ghetto: Negro New York, 1890–1930.* New York: Harper and Row.
Oyama, Richard. 1987. "Ayumi: 'To Sing Our Connections.'" In *A Gift of Tongues.* Ed. Marie Harris and Kathleen Aguero, 249–56. Athens: University of Georgia Press.
Payne, Will. [1898] 1970. *The Money Captain.* Upper Saddle River, N.J.: Gregg Press.
Peattie, Elia W. 1899. "The Artistic Side of Chicago." *Atlantic* 84 (Dec.): 828.
———. 1903. *The Edge of Things.* Chicago: Revell.
———. 1907. "Cupid and the Hurdy Gurdy." *Harper's Bazaar* 38 (Oct.): 1003–8.
———. 1910. Review of *Twenty Years at Hull-House,* Jane Addams. *Chicago Tribune,* Nov. 26: 9.
———. 1910. Review of *The Creators,* May Sinclair. *Chicago Tribune,* Oct. 29: 12.
———. 1914. *The Precipice: A Novel.* Boston: Houghton Mifflin.
———. n.d. *Star Wagon.* Ms. lent by Mark R. Peattie, Arlington, Mass.
———. [Sade Iverson, pseud.]. 1914. "The Milliner." *Little Review* 1 (July): 32–37.

Peattie, Robert. n.d. *The Story of R. B. P.* Ms. lent by Mark R. Peattie, Arlington, Mass.
Petry, Ann. 1946. *The Street.* Boston: Houghton Mifflin.
Phillips, E. Barbara, and Richard T. LeGates. 1981. *City Lights: An Introduction to Urban Studies.* New York: Oxford University Press.
Pierce, Bessie L. 1957. *The Rise of a Modern City, 1871–1893.* New York: Knopf.
Piercy, Marge. 1981. "The City as Battleground: The Novelist as Combatant." In *Literature and the Urban Experience: Essays on the City and Literature.* Ed. Michael C. Jaye and Ann Chalmers Watts, 209–17. New Brunswick, N.J.: Rutgers University Press.
Pinski, David. 1931. *The Generations of Noah Edon.* New York: Macaulay.
Poe, Edgar Allan. [1840] 1956. "The Man of the Crowd." In *Selected Writings of Edgar Allan Poe.* Ed. Edward H. Davidson, 131–39. Boston: Houghton Mifflin.
Polanyi, Michael. 1958. *Personal Knowledge: Toward a Post-critical Philosophy.* Chicago: University of Chicago Press.
Porter, Katherine Anne. [1939] 1962. "Old Mortality." In *Pale Horse, Pale Rider,* 9–61. New York: New American Library.
Porter, Ruth W. 1920. "Edith Franklin Wyatt." Wyatt Mss, Newberry Library, Chicago, Ill.
Potter, David M. [1962] 1970. "American Women and the American Character." In *The Character of Americans.* Ed. Michael McGiffert, 318–34. Homewood, Ill.: Dorsey.
Quinn, Vincent. 1963. *Hart Crane.* New York: Twayne.
Rabinowitz, Howard N. 1977. "Continuity and Change: Southern Urban Development 1860–1900." In *The City in Southern History.* Ed. Blaine A. Brownell and David R. Goldfield, 92–122. Port Washington, N.Y.: Kennikat Press.
Rampersad, Arnold. 1986. *I, Too, Sing America.* New York: Oxford University Press.
———. 1988. *I Dream a World.* New York: Oxford University Press.
Rascoe, Burton. 1937. *Before I Forget.* New York: Doubleday, Doran.
Rebolledo, Diana. 1985. "The Maturing of Chicana Poetry: The Quiet Revolution of the 1980s." In *For Alma Mater: The Theory and Practice of Feminist Scholarship.* Ed. Paula Treichler, Cheris Kramarae, and Beth Stafford. Urbana: University of Illinois Press.
Reid, Randall. 1967. *The Fiction of Nathanael West: No Redeemer, No Promised Land.* Chicago: University of Chicago Press.
Reilly, John M., ed. 1970. *Twentieth-Century Interpretations of Invisible Man.* Englewood Cliffs, N.J.: Prentice Hall.
Reps, John W. 1965. *The Making of Urban America.* Princeton, N.J.: Princeton University Press.
Reynolds, Donald Martin. 1984. *The Architecture of New York City: Histories and Views of Important Structures, Sites, and Symbols.* New York: Macmillan.
Rice, Elmer. 1937. *Imperial City.* New York: Coward-McCann.

Riis, Jacob. [1890] 1970. *How the Other Half Lives.* Ed. Sam B. Warner, Jr. Cambridge, Mass.: Harvard University Press.

Rosenthal, Bernard. 1981. *City of Nature.* Newark: University of Delaware Press.

Rosowski, Susan J. and Bernice Slote. 1984. "Willa Cather's 1916 Mesa Verde Essay: The Genesis of *The Professor's House." Prairie Schooner* 58 (Winter): 81–92.

Rosten, Leo. 1959. Interview, Robert C. Franklin. In *Popular Arts Project.* Oral History Collection, Butler Library, Columbia University, New York, N.Y.

———. [Leonard Q. Ross, pseud.] 1937. *The Education of H*Y*M*A*N K*A*P*L*A*N.* New York: Harcourt, Brace.

Roth, Henry. [1934] 1960. *Call It Sleep.* New York: Avon Books.

———. 1969. "A Talk with Henry Roth," David Bronsen. *Partisan Review* 36: 265–80.

———. 1975. "A Conversation with Henry Roth," William Freedman. *Literary Review* 18: 149–57.

———. 1979. "Henry Roth in Jerusalem: An Interview," William Freedman. *Literary Review* 23: 5–23.

———. Papers. Mugar Library, Boston University, Boston, Mass.

Sandburg, Carl. 1914. "Chicago." *Poetry* 3 (Mar.): 191–92.

Santos, Bienvenido N. 1987. *What the Hell For You Left Your Heart in San Francisco.* Quezon City, Philippines: New Day.

Sardello, Robert J. 1982. "City as Metaphor, City as Mystery." *Spring* 42:95–111.

Schneider, Isidor. 1935. *From the Kingdom of Necessity.* New York: G. P. Putnam's Sons.

Schomburg, Arthur A. Papers. Schomburg Center for Research in Black Culture. New York Public Library, New York, N.Y.

Scully, Vincent. 1975. *Pueblo: Mountain, Village, Dance.* New York: Viking.

Sennett, Richard. 1970. *The Uses of Disorder: Personal Identity and City Life.* New York: Alfred A. Knopf.

Showalter, Elaine, ed. 1978. *These Modern Women: Autobiographical Essays from the Twenties.* Old Westbury, N.Y.: Feminist Press.

———. 1988. "Women Writers Between the Wars." In *Columbia Literary History of the United States.* Ed. Emory Elliott, 822–41. New York: Columbia University Press.

Silko, Leslie Marmon. 1977. *Ceremony.* New York: Viking.

Sinclair, Upton. [1906] 1960. *The Jungle.* New York: New American Library.

Singh, Amritjit. 1976. *The Novels of the Harlem Renaissance.* University Park: Pennsylvania State University Press.

Sizemore, Christine Wick. 1989. *A Female Vision of the City: London in the Novels of Five British Women.* Knoxville: University of Tennessee Press.

Smith, Carl S. 1984. *Chicago and the American Literary Imagination, 1880–1920.* Chicago: University of Chicago Press.

Smith, Seba. [1830–59] 1978. "Selection from *Jack Downing Papers."* In *America in Literature.* Ed. David Levin and Theodore L. Gross, 1: 1151–52. New York: John Wiley & Sons.

Snyder, Gary. 1974. *Turtle Island.* New York: New Directions.

Spirn, Anne Whiston. 1984. *The Granite Garden.* New York: Basic Books.

Squier, Susan Merrill, ed. 1984. *Women Writers and the City.* Knoxville: University of Tennessee Press.

Stanley, Julia, and Susan Wolfe. 1979. "Toward a Feminist Aesthetic." *Chrysalis* 6: 57–71.

Stansell, Christine. 1986. *City of Women: Sex and Class in New York, 1789–1869.* New York: Alfred A. Knopf.

Starr, Kevin. 1985. *Inventing the Dream: California through the Progressive Era.* New York: Oxford University Press.

Stegner, Wallace. 1967. *All the Little Live Things.* New York: Viking Press.

Stein, Maurice R. 1960. *The Eclipse of Community: An Interpretation of American Studies.* Princeton, N.J.: Princeton University Press.

Steiner, George. 1973. "The City under Attack." *Salmagundi* (Fall): 3–18.

Still, Bayrd. 1956. *A Mirror for Gotham: New York as Seen by Contemporaries from Dutch Days to the Present.* New York: New York University Press.

———. 1973. "Patterns of Mid-Nineteenth-Century Urbanization in the Middle West." In *American Urban History: An Interpretive Reader with Commentaries.* Ed. Alexander B. Callow, Jr., 122–35. New York: Oxford University Press.

Stinson, Peggy. 1982. "Anzia Yezierska." In *American Women Writers.* Ed. Lina Mainiero, 4: 480–82. New York: Ungar.

Stout, Janis. 1976. *Sodoms in Eden: The City in American Fiction before 1860.* Westport, Conn.: Greenwood Press.

Strong, Josiah. 1911. *The Challenge of the City.* New York: Young People's Missionary Movement.

Sullivan, Louis. [1924] 1967. *A System of Architectural Ornament according with a Philosophy of Man's Powers.* New York: Eakins Press.

Szuberla, Guy Alan. 1971. "Urban Vistas and the Pastoral Garden: Studies in the Literature and Architecture of Chicago (1893–1909)." Ph.D. diss., University of Minnesota.

Tafolla, Carmen. 1987. "Chicano Literature: Beyond Beginnings." In *A Gift of Tongues.* Ed. Marie Harris and Kathleen Aguero, 206–25. Athens: University of Georgia Press.

Tate, Allen. [1927] 1977. "The Subway." In *Collected Poems, 1919–1976,* 19. New York: Farrar Straus & Giroux.

Taylor, William R. 1979. "Psyching Out the City." In *Uprooted Americans: Essays to Honor Oscar Handlin.* Ed. Richard L. Bushman et al., 247–87. Boston: Little Brown.

Thomas, Piri. 1967. *Down These Mean Streets.* New York: Alfred A. Knopf.

Thompson, Mildred. 1979. "Ida B. Wells-Barnett: An Exploratory Study of an

American Black Woman, 1893-1930." Ph.D. diss., George Washington University.
Thoreau, Henry David. [1851] 1968. "Walking." In *Excursions and Poems,* 205-48. New York: AMS Press.
———. [1854, 1906] 1968. *Walden.* New York: AMS Press.
Thurman, Wallace. [1929] 1969. *The Blacker the Berry.* New York: Arno Press and *New York Times.*
———. n.d. "Terpsichore in Harlem." In *Aunt Hagar's Children.* Thurman Collection I-16.
———. Collection. James Weldon Johnson Memorial Collection. Beinecke Library, Yale University, New Haven, Conn.
———, and William Jourdain Rapp. 1929. *Harlem.* Thurman Collection.
Time Magazine. 1984. Presidential Campaign. 5 Nov.: 20.
Toomer, Jean. 1923. *Cane.* New York: Boni & Liveright.
Toth, Emily. 1977. "Regionalism: A Dirty Word?" Paper presented at Midwest Modern Language Association, Chicago, Ill.
Trachtenberg, Alan. 1965. *Brooklyn Bridge: Fact and Symbol.* New York: Oxford University Press.
———. 1967. "The American Scene: Versions of the City." *Massachusetts Review* 8 (Spring): 281-95.
———. 1982. *The Incorporation of America: Culture and Society in the Gilded Age.* New York: Hill and Wang.
Tuan, Ti-Fu. 1974. *Topophilia.* Englewood Cliffs, N.J.: Prentice-Hall.
Tuerk, Richard. 1983. "Jewish-American Literature." In *Ethnic Perspectives in American Literature.* Ed. Robert J. Di Pietro and Edward Ifkovic, 133-45. New York: Modern Language Association.
Tuttleton, James W. 1972. "Edith Wharton: The Archeological Motive." *Yale Review* 61 (Summer): 562-74.
Twain, Mark, and William Dean Howells. 1960. *Mark Twain-Howells Letters.* Ed. Henry Nash Smith and William Gibson. Cambridge, Mass.: Harvard University Press.
———, and Charles Dudley Warner. [1873] 1968. *The Gilded Age.* Seattle: University of Washington Press.
Twelve Southerners. 1930. *I'll Take My Stand: The South and the Agrarian Tradition.* New York: Harper & Bros.
Tyler, Royall. [1787] 1990. *The Contrast: A Comedy in Five Acts;* rpt. in *The Heath Anthology of American Literature.* Ed. Paul Lauter, et. al., 1:1091-1131. New York: Heath.
Van Doren, Carl. 1924. "The Younger Generation of Negro Writers." *Opportunity* 2 (May): 144-45.
Van Vechten, Carl. 1922. *Peter Whiffle: His Life and Work.* New York: Alfred A. Knopf.

———. 1926. *Nigger Heaven*. New York: Alfred A. Knopf.

———. 1960. "The Reminiscences of Carl Van Vechten," William T. Ingersoll. Oral History Collection, Butler Library, Columbia University, New York, N.Y.

———, and Fania Marinoff. Correspondence. James Weldon Johnson Memorial Collection, Beinecke Library, Yale University, New Haven, Conn.

Wagner, Linda W. 1979. *Dos Passos: Artist as American*. Austin: University of Texas Press.

Wald, Alan M. 1987. *The New York Intellectuals: The Rise and Fall of the Anti-Stalinist Left from the 1930s to the 1980s*. Chapel Hill: University of North Carolina Press.

Walker, Alice. 1976. "Saving the Life That Is Your Own: The Importance of Models in the Artist's Life." In *The Women's Center Reid Lectureship*. New York: Barnard College.

Warner, Sam Bass, Jr. 1962. *Streetcar Suburbs: The Process of Growth in Boston, 1870–1900*. Cambridge, Mass.: Harvard University Press.

———. 1968. *The Private City*. Philadelphia: University of Pennsylvania Press.

Warren, Robert Penn. [1946] 1968. *All the King's Men*. New York: Bantam Books.

Weber, Michael P., and Anne Lloyd. 1975. *The American City*. St. Paul, Minn.: West Publishing.

Weimer, David. 1966. *The City as Metaphor*. New York: Random House.

Wells, Walter. 1973. *Tycoons and Locusts: A Regional Look at Hollywood Fiction of the 1930s*. Carbondale, Ill.: Southern Illinois University Press.

Wells-Barnett, Ida B., ed. 1893. *The Reason Why—The Colored American Is Not in the World's Columbian Exposition*. Chicago: Ida B. Wells.

West, Nathanael. [1933] 1962. *Miss Lonelyhearts*. In *Miss Lonelyhearts and The Day of the Locust*, 169–247. New York: New Directions.

———. [1939] 1962. *The Day of the Locust*. In *Miss Lonelyhearts and the Day of the Locust*, 1–167. New York: New Directions.

Wharton, Edith. [1905] 1964. *The House of Mirth*. New York: New American Library.

———. [1920] 1962. *The Age of Innocence*. New York: New American Library.

White, Morton, and Lucia White. 1962. *The Intellectual Versus the City*. Cambridge, Mass.: Harvard University Press.

White, Walter. 1926. *Flight*. New York: Alfred A. Knopf.

Whitman, Walt. [1856, 1881] 1965a. "Crossing Brooklyn Ferry." In *Leaves of Grass*. Ed. Harold W. Blodgett and Sculley Bradley, 159–65. New York: New York University Press.

———. [1856, 1881] 1965b. "Song of the Open Road." In *Leaves of Grass*. Ed. Harold W. Blodgett and Sculley Bradley, 149–59. New York: New York University Press.

———. [1867, 1891–95] 1965c. "One's-Self I Sing." In *Leaves of Grass*. Ed. Harold W. Blodgett and Sculley Bradley, 1. New York: New York University Press.

Williams, Kenny. 1980. *Prairie Voices.* Nashville: Townsend Press.
Willis, F. Roy. 1973. *Western Civilization: An Urban Perspective,* vol. 2. Lexington, Mass.: D. C. Heath.
Wilson, Margaret G. 1979. *The American Woman in Transition.* Westport, Conn.: Greenwood Press.
Winthrop, John. [1630] 1978. *A Model of Christian Charity.* In *America in Literature.* Ed. David Levin and Theodore L. Gross, 1: 70–79. New York: John Wiley & Sons.
———. [1653] 1978. *The History of New England.* In *America in Literature.* Ed. David Levin and Theodore L. Gross, 1: 79–94. New York: John Wiley & Sons.
Wirth, Louis. 1938. "Urbanism as a Way of Life." *American Journal of Sociology* 44 (July): 1–24.
Wirtz, Cary D. 1988. *Black Culture and the Harlem Renaissance.* Houston, Tex.: Rice University Press.
Wolff, Cynthia Griffin. 1977. *A Feast of Words: The Triumph of Edith Wharton.* New York: Oxford University Press.
Woodress, James. 1987. *Willa Cather: A Literary Life.* Lincoln: University of Nebraska Press.
Wright, Richard. [1938] 1940. "Long Black Song." In *Uncle Tom's Children,* 103–28. New York: Harper & Bros.
———. [1940] 1966. *Native Son.* New York: Harper & Row.
Wyatt, Edith Franklin. 1901. *Every One His Own Way.* New York: McClure, Phillips.
———. 1903. *True Love: A Comedy of the Affections.* New York: McClure, Phillips.
———. [1907?]. "Garment Workers at Home." In *Hand-Book of the Industrial Exposition 1907.* Wyatt Mss.
———. 1914a. "An Appreciation." 13 June newspaper clipping, in Scrapbook 1914–16. Wyatt Mss.
———. 1914b. "True to Life." *Little Review* 1 (May): 13–18.
———. 1914c. Review of *Vandover and the Brute,* Aug. [8], news clipping, in Scrapbooks. Wyatt Papers.
———. [1914–16]. "The Case of Francesca." Ms. in Scrapbook 1914–16, 30–38. Wyatt Mss.
———. 1916. "City Whistles: To H. M." *Poetry* 9 (Dec.): 114–15; rpt. 1917. *The Wind in the Corn,* 109–11. New York: D. Appleton.
———. 1923. *Invisible Gods.* New York: Harper & Bros.
———. [1935] "The Poor Old Past." In Scrapbook, n.d., 5–82. Wyatt Mss.
———. Manuscripts. Newberry Library, Chicago, Ill.
———. Papers. Newberry Library, Chicago, Ill.
Yeats, William Butler. [1922] 1940. "The Second Coming." In *The Variorum Edition of the Poems of W. B. Yeats.* Ed. Peter Allt and Russell K. Alspach, 401–2. New York: Macmillan.

Yezierska, Anzia. [1920a] 1975. *Hungry Hearts.* New York: Arno Press.
———. [1920b] 1975. "My Own People." In *Hungry Hearts,* 224–49. New York: Arno Press.
———. [1920c] 1975. "The Fat of the Land." In *Hungry Hearts,* 178–223. New York: Arno Press.
———. 1923a. *Children of Loneliness.* New York: Funk & Wagnalls.
———. 1923b. *Salome of the Tenements.* New York: Boni and Liveright.
———. 1925. *The Bread Givers.* Garden City, N.Y.: Doubleday Page.
———. 1927. *Arrogant Beggar.* Garden City, N.Y.: Doubleday Page.
———. 1932. *All I Could Never Be.* New York: Brewer, Warren & Putnam.
———. 1950. *Red Ribbon on a White Horse.* New York: Charles Scribner's Sons.
———. Papers. Mugar Memorial Library, Boston University, Boston, Mass.
Zugsmith, Leane. 1936. *A Time to Remember.* New York: Random House.
Zuñi. [1929–30] 1978. "Offering." In *America in Literature.* Ed. David Levin and Theodore L. Gross, 1: 726. New York: John Wiley & Sons.

Index

Aaron Traum (H. and L. Cohen), 173
Absalom, Absalom! (Faulkner), 190
Adams, Henry, 39, 43, 45, 60, 98
Addams, Jane, 14, 40, 61, 90, 91, 94, 100, 101, 205n, 208n
Addiction: delusive, 218n
Ade, George, 207n
African-American literature: city-town model in, 13, 15; relationship to Anasazi's union of spirit and body, 9
African Americans: in Chicago (1890), 61; at Chicago fair, 66; cultural demands on, 138–39; global links of, 142; Harlem Renaissance, 132–64
After the Meeting (Beaux), 49, 50
Age of Innocence, The (Wharton), 119–20, 124, 126, 129, 204n
Albanese, Catherine, 3
Aldis, Mary, 101, 102
Alienation, 2, 170–71, 185; African-American, 146–47; in economic city, 58–59; by gender, from continuity in industrializing city-town, 32; in Harlem Renaissance literature, 199; internal and external walls, 160; of megalopolitan authors, 116; and pastoral conventions, 145, 148; in postwar New York, 115; psychological, 115; and standard Chicago novel, 80; *With the Procession*, 85
Allen, Gay Wilson, 31–32

All I Could Never Be (Yezierska), 218n
All the King's Men (Warren), 189, 190
All the Little Live Things (Stegner), 195
Alter, Robert, 182–83
American Citizen (Herrick), 77
American City, The (Weber and Lloyd), 204n
American Scene, The (James), 34
Ammons, Elizabeth, 121, 211n
Anasazi: fusion of city with nation, 89; urban organicism of, 4–5; urban pastoral art inspired by, 9
Ancestors, 2
Anderson, Margaret, 98–99, 103, 104
Anderson, Regina (Andrews), 137
Anderson, Sherwood, 147
Antin, Mary, 167, 169
Anzaldúa, Gloria, 115
Appleton, Wis., 19
Aptheker, Bettina, 100
Architect's Dream, The (Cole), 8, 9
Architecture: Chicago school of, 66–67; literature's prescriptions for, 198
Armitage, Susan, 194
Arnow, Harriette S., 115, 186
Arrogant Beggar (Yezierska), 178, 199
Arthur Mervyn (Brown), 26
"Artificial Nigger, The" (O'Connor), 189
Asch, Sholom, 172
Atherton, Gertrude, 173, 194, 195
Atlantic Monthly (magazine), 140

Auchincloss, Louis, 121
Autobiography (Franklin), 7
Autobiography of an Ex-Coloured Man, The (J. W. Johnson), 136, 142, 161, 169, 172, 183
Awakening, The (Chopin), 2, 187, 189, 191, 199

Babbit (Lewis), 186
Badger, R. Reid, 60, 64, 67
Baker, Houston A., Jr., 135, 138, 139, 156, 165, 215n
Baldwin, James, 143
Banjo (McKay), 146
Baritz, Loren, 5
Barnes, Albert, 149
Barthé, Richmond, 163
Bartleby the Scrivener (Melville), 26
Beaux, Cecilia, 49, 50
Beck, Warren, 191
Belenky, Mary Field, 84
Bellamy, Edward, 58
Bellow, Saul, 220n
Bender, Thomas, 114, 115
Bennett, A., 114
Bennett, Gwendolyn, 134, 137
Bercovitch, Sacvan, 204n
Berger, Peter L., 3, 81
Biggers, John, 176, 177
Big Money, The (Dos Passos), 129
Bishop, Isabel, 82, 83
Blacker the Berry, The (Thurman), 142, 154, 156, 158
Black Manhattan (J. W. Johnson), 134
Blithedale Romance, The (Hawthorne), 26, 31
Boas, Franz, 149
Bodenheim, Maxwell, 139
Bomb, The (Harris), 65
Bontemps, Arna, 133, 140
Borders, Florence E., 133
Boston, 46–57
Bostonians, The (James), 34–35, 39, 47, 48–49, 199
Bourget, Paul, 67
Bowron, Bernard R., Jr., 85, 98
Boyesen, Hjalmar H., 72
"Brass Spitoons" (Hughes), 142–43
Bray, Robert C., 80, 208n
Bread Givers (Yezierska), 173, 178

Bremer, William W., 167
Breton, Jules, 89
"Bridge, The" (Crane), 116, 192
"Broadcast" (Hughes), 144
Brooke, R., 114
Brooklyn Bridge (Marin), 32, 33
Brooklyn Bridge (painting; Stella), 116, 117
Brown, Charles Brockden, 26
Browne, Claude, 167
Browne, Maurice, 101
Brownell, Blaine A., 188, 191
Bruccoli, Matthew J., 213n
Bruce-Novoa, Juan, 183
Bryan, William Jennings, 99
Bryant, William Cullen, 30
Bryer, Jackson R., 212n
Burg, David, 60, 64, 65
Burnham, Clara, 65, 67, 84, 87, 97, 106, 207n
Burnham, Daniel, 62, 66, 103
Burning of Los Angeles, The (West), 131

Cable, George Washington, 188
Cady, Edwin, 52, 57, 205n
Cahan, Abraham, 168, 169, 170–72, 218n
Caldwell, Erskine, 188–89
Californians, The (Atherton), 194
Call It Sleep (Roth), 2, 16, 178–81, 198, 219n
Cane (Toomer), 147
Cap. Frye's Birthday Party, 105, 106
Carby, Hazel, 139, 147–48
"Carnival by the Sea" (Fitzgerald), 123
Carroll, Peter N., 5, 203n
"Cat and the Saxaphone (2 A.M.), The" (Hughes), 175
Cather, Willa, 9, 16, 65, 81, 82, 89, 96, 113, 147, 205n, 208n
Catherwood, Mary, 67
Cavell, Stanley, 204n
Ceremony (Silko), 5
Chaco Canyon, 19
Chametzky, Jules, 166, 183, 217n, 220n
Chase, Richard, 31–32
Chatfield-Taylor, Hobart C., 61, 74, 105, 206n
Chevrillon, A., 114
Chicago: characterization in terms of technological achievement, 62–63

Index

"Chicago" (Sandburg), 103
Chicago: The History of Its Reputation (Lewis and Smith), 64
Chicago novel, 14, 206n; standard, 60–80, 191–92
Chicago Poems (Sandburg), 103
Chicago Renaissance in American Letters (Duffey), 109
Chicago School of Fiction, 82
Chicago Whip, 139
Children of Loneliness (Yezierska), 174, 176
Chmaj, Betty, 2
Chopin, Kate, 2, 187, 189–90, 221n
"Cities" (McKay), 146
Cities of lives, 2
Cities of our minds, 2
City: representative, national, 38–39
City Beautiful planning, 63
City from Greenwich Village, The (Sloan), 55, 82
"City in the Sea" (Poe), 35
City Lights: An Introduction to Urban Studies, 204n
City of refuge: Harlem as, 150
"City of Refuge" (R. Fisher), 140
City planning, 36, 45, 200–201
"City's Love, The" (McKay), 144
City-town, 123–24; diverse representations of, 26–27; of Eastern European Jews, 167; vs. economic city, 56–57, 121; vs. European city, 27–28; joining with urban industry (Whitman), 31–32; links to economic city in Chicago, 65–66; loss of meaning, 119; model in urban organicism, 13, 16; vs. urban industrialism, 36
City upon a hill, 7, 19–20, 167–68; Boston as, 46; fusion with Romantic individualism, 32–34; Puritan dream of, 5; replacement by "Nature's Nation" concept, 30
"City Whistles" (Wyatt), 102
Civic Club, 135
Civic family, 90, 95
Clark, Dennis, 41
Clarke, John Henrik, 214–15n
Class conflict, 1, 170–72; in economic city, 53, 57; industry and finance in Chicago, 63–64; involvement of Jewish Americans, 172; *The Jungle,* 78–79; and representation at Chicago fair, 67; separation of the poor, 74; in social work, 94; *The Web of Life,* 68
Clemens, Samuel. *See* Twain, Mark
Cliff-Dwellers, The (Fuller), 9, 64–65, 68–70, 72, 76, 80, 85, 199
Cohen, Hyman, 173
Cohen, Lester, 173
Cole, Thomas, 7, 8, 10, 30, 67
Collaboration: vs. individualism and sexual freedom, 113
Collective structure, 85–87
Collectivism, 80; collaborative work in the arts, 105–6; communal ties of blacks, 142; vs. individualism, 207n; in theater and politics, 135; of urban voice, 102
Collectivity: as an urban reality, 91
Collins, Charles, 99
Collins, Patricia Hill, 166
Colossus, The (Reed), 77
"Columbian Ode" (Monroe), 67, 103
Common Lot, The (Herrick), 80
Communal values: alienation from, 70; in built environment, 76; characteristic of city-town, 28; and common vocabulary, 139–40; and divisions in community, 161; in economic city, 58; in extended urban family, 90; Harlem, 155–56; in Harlem Renaissance, 135; in harmony with nature, 69–70; and identity, 180–81; and individual ambitions, 92; and nature, 89; neighborhood dynamics in women's experience, 111; in postwar New York, 115, 121–22; in standard Chicago novel, 74–75; and unregulated growth, 77; urban aesthetic of collaborative performance, 101; voices of, 174–75
Communication: in megalopolitan nightmare, 128
Community: vs. organization, 37–38
Company town: Pullman (in Chicago), 64
Condit, Carl, 62, 63, 64
Conflict: in intellectual life, 115
Conformity: in daily life of consumers, 36–37; resulting from industrialization, 30
Congo Songs (Lindsay), 102
Conjure-Man Dies!, The (R. Fisher), 152, 158

Continuity: in Chicago residential novel, 81; of city-town, 25–26; denial in *Age of Innocence,* 120; in economic city, 58; emphasis in women's literature, 15; future with hope in city-town, 34–35; of Harlem, with other cities, 142; in participation in city events, 111; in postwar New York, 116, 119; in standard Chicago novel, 87; urban/rural, in residential novels, 89–90; in Yezierska's works, 176
Contrast, The (Tyler), 24
Cook, George Cramm, 101
Cooper, James Fenimore, 2, 13, 16, 20–21, 22, 25–26, 39, 198
Copeland, Robert Morris, 36
Cordon Club, 108
Countercultural perspectives, 213n
Counterculture: in city-town model, 16
Course of Empire, The (Cole), 7, 8, 30, 204n
Cowan, Michael, 21, 30
Crane, Frank, 173
Crane, Hart, 116, 119, 129, 192, 210–11n
Crisis, The (magazine), 133, 173
Critic, The (magazine), 68
Cronon, William, 7
"Crossing Brooklyn Ferry" (Whitman), 26, 32, 34, 116
Crumbling Idols (Garland), 205n
Crystal, Leon, 169
Cullen, Countee, 133, 135, 137, 138, 150, 158, 214n
Cultural beliefs: about urbanization and urban imagery, 2
Cultural naturalism: separatism without equality in, 30
Cultural perspective: on Harlem Renaissance, 215n
Culture: of African Americans, 139; American, 217n; expansion in Chicago, 64; families as characters, in residential novel, 85; as grids of Them-and-Us experiences, 2; Jewish-American and African-American, 168; public/private lives and artistic value, 107; and recognition of women's work, 109–10; of residential novelists, 83–84; as symbolic basis for Boston, 46–47; urban, 1, 113–14; urban diversity of, 2–3; urban literary, 3
Currey, Margery, 100
Curtis, Nancy, 5

Daniel, Carter A., 213n
Daniels, Thomas E., 213n
Davidson, Marshall, 7
Davis, Angela, 164
Davis, Rebecca Harding, 29–30, 32, 39, 40–42, 198
Day of the Locust, The (West), 127, 130, 186
Debs, Eugene, 64
Deconstructionist theory: and myth of standards set by white males, 110
De Forest, John W., 43
Democracy: vs. elitist ethics, 92
Democracy (Adams), 39, 43–44, 45, 205n
Demos, John, 5
Determinism: in development of "ultimate metropolis," 70–71; environmental, 207n; Harlem, 156; and naturalism, 30; in urban environment, 31; in urban imagery, 45
Didion, Joan, 186
Dignity of workers, 104
Dimock, Wai-Chee, 120
Diversity: in Chicago, 60–61; ethnic, 199; in Harlem Renaissance literature, 157; in New York, 114–15; regional, 195; and urban segregation, 37
Dollmaker, The (Arnow), 186
Dos Passos, John, 122, 123, 127, 129, 211n
Doubleday, Neal Frank, 205n
Douglas, Aaron, 137, 182
Douglass, Frederick, 13, 66, 166
"Dream Deferred" (Hughes), 176
Dreams: of Harlem's community, 159–60; of neighborhood-city, 165–84
Dreiser, Theodore, 61, 64, 71–72, 76, 79, 81, 92, 96, 109, 192, 198, 205n, 209n
Du Bois, W. E. Burghardt, 132, 133, 135, 138, 149, 172, 193, 214n
Duffey, Bernard, 64, 85, 109
Duncan, Hugh Dalziel, 96, 100, 205n, 209n
Dunne, Finley Peter, 74
DuPlessis, Rachel Blau, 85

Eble, Kenneth, 212n
Economic city, 14, 36–59, 206n; alternatives to materialism of, 172; and counterculural dreams, 169; European city portrayed as, 28–29; industry and finance in Chicago, 63; life-destroying capacities of, 152; *Life in the Iron Mills*, 30; loss of meaning, 119; machinery of, in literature, 192; New York as, 53; in postwar New York, 115; pre–Civil War, 23; vs. regional literature, 187; shifting base of, 51; tensions of poverty in, in standard Chicago novel, 74; women's participation in, 99
Economic forces: in postwar New York, 122–23
Economic novels, 211n
"Eldorado" (Poe), 35
Eliade, Mircea, 30
Elitism: vs. democratic ethics, 92; vs. participatory democracy, in residential novel, 86
Ellison, Ralph, 3, 16, 168, 178–80, 219n
Emerson, Ralph Waldo, 9, 21, 25
Entertainment industry: links to Harlem Renaissance, 137. *See also* Mass media
Environment, built, 7, 9; in Chicago, 76–77
Espada, Martin, 220n
Ethics of care: vs. justice, 94
Ethnic groups: racialized, 2, 74

Family: as character, in residential novel, 85–86; connections through, 90; enmeshment in, 90; and professional life, 104; in residential novel, 88; social stability in, 96; and social status, 23; values characteristic of city-town, 28
Farrell, James T., 115, 186
Fasanella, Ralph, 116, 118, 166
Faulkner, William, 176, 189, 190–91
Fauset, Arthur, 149
Fauset, Jessie Redmon, 133, 135, 136, 142, 152, 154–55, 160, 214n
Faÿ, B., 114
Feminism: as personal battle, 48–49
Ferguson, William M., 19
Festa-McCormick, Diana, 122
Fiedler, Leslie A., 182, 194
Field, Eugene, 67

Fine Clothes to the Jew (Hughes), 139, 142–43
Fire!! (magazine), 136
Fisher, Philip, 58, 206n
Fisher, Rudolph, 112, 125, 133, 136, 139–40, 140–41, 151, 153, 156, 158, 159–60, 180, 193
Fisk University, 133
Fitzgerald, F. Scott, 16, 29, 93, 123, 125, 126, 129, 130, 211n, 212n, 217n
"Flame Heart" (McKay), 144
"Fledgling Eagle, The" (Cullen), 135
Flight (White), 142
Forest Hymn, A (Bryant), 30
Fragmentation: in postwar New York, 115, 123; urban, in *Miss Lonelyhearts*, 127
Frank, Florence Kiper, 102
Frank, Waldo, 218n
Franklin, Benjamin, 7
Franklin, H. Bruce, 110
Frederickson, George M., 37
French, Alice, 107
Freudian norms: of separation, 111
Fulda, L., 114
Fuller, Henry Blake, 9, 64–65, 66, 67, 68–71, 74–75, 76, 77, 81, 82, 85, 88, 89, 95–96, 98, 105, 108, 109, 207n, 210n
Fuller, Margaret, 26
Fullerton, Morton, 120
Furer, Howard B., 114

Gadamer, Hans-Georg, 58, 87, 197
Garland, Hamlin, 46, 65, 68, 72, 73, 74, 76, 98, 107, 205n, 208n
Garvey, Marcus, 135
Garza, Rudolpho O. de la, 220n
Gates, Henry Louis, Jr., 158
Geertz, Clifford, 3, 197
Gelfant, Blanche M., 14, 17, 82, 207n
Gelpi, Albert, 204n
Gender: of authors establishing literary versions of cities, 46–47; basis for separate and connected knowing, 84; and class distinctions, 41–42, 95–96; and collective activities in Chicago (1890), 61–62; expressions of care vs. justice, 94; and greater urban family, 90–91; and leadership in professional associations, 105–6; and patterns of professional development,

Gender (*continued*)
 98–99; and professional recognition, 108–9; split between production and consumption, 74–75; and urban experience, 14–15; women's business in residential novels, 93–94
George, W. L., 114
Gerstenberg, Alice, 65, 92, 93, 97, 98, 101–2, 104, 108, 111, 174, 190, 207n
Giddings, Paula, 137
Gilded Age, 64, 75
Gilded Age, The (Twain), 43, 205n
Giles, James R., 213n
Gilligan, Carol, 84, 111; conflict between self and other, 92; ethic of care, 94
Ginger, Ray, 61
Glasgow, Ellen, 189, 191
Glaspell, Susan, 65, 84, 88, 92, 93, 101, 207n
Glory of the Conquered, The (Glaspell), 65, 88, 92, 101
Gold, Michael, 115, 179, 220n
Goldfield, David R., 188
Goldman, Emma, 99
Goldman, Judith, 197
Gospel of Freedom, The (Herrick), 75, 76, 77
Granite Garden (Spirn), 200
Great Depression, 126–27
Great Gatsby, The (Fitzgerald), 124, 127
Green, Martin, 46
Group identity, 191–92
Gunn, Giles, 3
Guttmann, Allen, 218n

Hale, Edward Everett, 57
Halprin, Lawrence, 200
Hamilton, M. A., 114
Hard Facts (P. Fisher), 58
Harlem (Thurman and Rapp), 139, 150
Harlem: Negro Metropolis (McKay), 134
"Harlem Dancer" (McKay), 145
"Harlem Night Club" (Hughes), 155
Harlem Renaissance, 123, 124–25, 132–64; in postwar New York, 115
Harlem Shadows (McKay), 132, 144, 145, 215n
Harlem Writers' Guild, 135
Harper's Weekly, 68
Harris, Frank, 65

Harris, Joel Chandler, 188
Harris, Neil, 214n
Harrison, Carter, 64
Hawthorne, Nathaniel, 13, 23, 26, 27, 28–29, 31
Hazard of New Fortunes, A (Howells), 14, 39–40, 47, 51, 53–57, 64, 69, 122, 205n
Hazo, Samuel, 116
Hemenway, Robert E., 213n, 216n
Henriksen, Louise Levitas, 219n
"Heritage" (Cullen), 150
Herrick, Robert, 65, 67–68, 72, 73, 74, 76, 77, 78, 80, 90, 91, 95–96
Himes, Chester B., 115
Historic context: contribution to literary reality, 3
Historic continuity: of Boston, 48; of pre–Civil War city-town, 29
History of New York, A (Irving), 21
Hoffman, Leonore, 196, 221n
Home as Found (Cooper), 20, 26–27, 39
Homelessness, 80; in economic city, 57; of New York, 56
Home to Harlem (McKay), 134, 144, 145, 146, 151, 158
Homeward (Bishop), 82, 83
Honest John Vine (De Forest), 43
hooks, bell, 132
House of Mirth, The (Wharton), 119–20
Howard, June, 72, 206n
Howe, Florence, 110
Howe, Frederic C., 38
Howe, Irving, 47, 48, 167, 168, 195–96, 220n
Howells, William Dean, 13, 39, 47, 51–54, 56–58, 67, 80, 81, 87, 152, 205n, 210n, 211n, 218n
How the Other Half Lives (Riis), 37, 54
Hudson River school, 30
Huggins, Nathan Irvin, 136, 214n
Hughes, Langston, 2, 16, 32, 116, 132, 133, 135, 136, 138, 139, 140–41, 142–44, 151, 154, 155, 173, 175–76, 198, 210n, 214n, 215n, 216n
Hull, Gloria T., 137
Hull-House, 61–62, 92–93, 100
Huneker, J., 114
Hungry Hearts (Yezierska), 2, 173, 176
Hurston, Zora Neale, 133, 140, 149, 157, 158, 189, 216n

Hutchinson, Anne, 20
Hutson, Jean, 164

If Beale Street Could Talk (Baldwin), 142
"If We Must Die" (McKay), 138
I'll Take My Stand (Twelve Southerners), 192
Illusion: in literature and mass media, 130–31
Imagery: alternative to mechanized, skyscraper symbols, 12; black/white, for Chicago dream, 67; cities as grids of Them-and-Us experiences, 151; economic city as machine, 78–79; of economic city (Howells), 58; of ethnic wilderness, in standard Chicago novel, 74; Harlem as home, 132–34; innovation vs. continuities, 9; Jazz Age, 135; of nature, in residential novel, 88; organic, in Harlem life, 149; public/private spheres, 47; of science for consolidation of city, 71; of skyscrapers and machines, 78; urban, 2, 54; urban, and historic stage of development, 12–13; of urban artificiality, 125; of urban power, 145. *See also* Metaphor; Mythology
"Immigrant among the Editors, An" (Yezierska), 174
Immigrants: absent from standard Chicago novel, 73; alienation of, 79; in Boston and New York, and historic continuity, 46; in Chicago (1890), 61; at Chicago fair, 66; devaluation of (James), 34–35; segregation in industrial cities, 37; women's roles in teaching, 101
Incidents in the Life of a Slave Girl (Jacobs), 23
Incorporation of America, The (Trachtenberg), 38
Individualism: abuse of, and unregulated growth, 77–78; vs. collectivity, 207n; critique of, in standard Chicago novel, 73; economic, 209n; vs. economic city as machine, 78–79; inadequacy of, 78; and minority status, 179; in postwar New York, 115; psychic dissociation as cost of extreme, 75; and skyscraper image, 75–76; and social bonds, 91–92
Individuality: vs. mechanical ties of industrialization, 29–30; vs. privatism, 41–42; and separation, 32–34; vs. urban growth, 38
Individuals: connectedness of, 85; definition of, in terms of culture and continuity, 87; in social order of pre–Civil War city, 22–23
Infants of Spring (Thurman), 140
Insull, Samuel, 63, 78
Intellectual versus the City, The (White and White), 28
Interdependence: and improvement of city life, 95
Invention: in writers' lives, 211–12n
Invisible Man, The (Ellison), 16, 178–81, 183, 198, 200
Irving, Washington, 21, 25

Jack Downing Papers (Smith), 23
Jackson, John Brinckerhoff, 36
Jacobs, Harriet, 13, 23–24, 25, 26, 166
Jacobs, Jane, 199, 200
James, Henry, 34, 39, 47–48, 48–49, 51, 57, 198
James, William, 97
Janeway, Elizabeth, 97–98, 128
Jazz Age, 132–33
Jefferson, Thomas, 7
Jensen, Joan M., 5
Jewish-American literature: city-town model in, 15; relationship to Anasazi's union of spirit and body, 9
Jewish Americans: in Chicago (1890), 61; ethnic identity of, 217n; Nathanael West, 126–27; sense of place and race, 164; urban experience in literature of, 166–84
Jewish Daily Forward, 169
Johnson, Charles S., 132, 133, 134
Johnson, Edward, 7
Johnson, Grace Nail, 162
Johnson, Helene, 133
Johnson, James Weldon, 133, 134, 135, 136, 137, 138, 142, 151, 161–63, 168, 169, 170–71, 214n, 218n
Jordan, Kate, 104
Journalism: women's participation in, 99–100
Jungle, The (Sinclair), 14, 44, 64, 72, 73, 77, 78–79, 109, 189

Just Folks (Laughlin), 2, 65, 82, 85, 90, 92, 95, 108, 109, 124

Kaplan, Amy, 37, 53–54, 79, 96, 114
Kazin, Alfred, 166
Kessler-Harris, Alice, 219n
Kirk, Clara, 99, 207n
Kirk, Rudolf, 99, 207n
Konvitz, Joseph, 204n
Kramer, Dale, 109, 207n
Kuehl, John, 212n

Landscape (painting; anonymous), 9, 11, 32
Langer, Susanne, 196
Langford, Gerald, 30, 40, 42
Language: in Chicago novels, 206n
Lankevich, George J., 114
Larsen, Nella, 133, 136, 142, 147–49, 151, 156, 158
Last Tycoon, The (West), 127
Lathrop, Julia, 93, 208n
Laughlin, Clara, 2, 14, 61, 65, 82, 84, 90, 93, 94, 97, 99, 101, 106, 108, 124, 178, 207n
Lauter, Estella, 200
Lauter, Paul, 110
League of Negro Writers, 134
Leaves of Grass (Whitman), 32
LeGates, Richard T., 12, 204n
Legislation: inspired by *The Jungle*, 79
L'Enfant, Pierre, 45
"Lenox Avenue: Midnight" (Hughes), 155
Lenz, Günter, 146, 147, 216n
Lerner, Gerda, 24
Levin, David, 7
Levin, Meyer, 164
Lewis, Lloyd, 64
Lewis, R. W. B., 120
Lewis, Sinclair, 147, 186
Lewisohn, Ludwig, 218n
Life in the Iron Mills (E. H. Davis), 29–30, 41
Light, James F., 213n
Lindsay, Vachel, 102, 214n
Lipset, Seymour Martin, 30
Literary constructions: limitation to dominant culture, 109–10
Little Review, The, 103, 104, 108
Little Room, 104–8

Little Theater movement, 101; women's contributions to, 108
Lloyd, Anne, 12, 62, 204n
Locke, Alain, 133, 136, 149, 214n
London, Jack, 194, 221n
"Long Black Song" (Wright), 190
Looking Backward (Bellamy), 58
Lost continuities: reconstructing in counterculture literature, 17
Lost Generation writers, 119
Loury, Glenn C., 220n
Lovett, Robert Morss, 74
Lowell, Amy, 97
Lower East Side: parallels with Harlem, 166–67
Luckmann, Thomas, 3, 81
Ludington, Townsend, 122
Lynn, Kenneth, 52, 205n
Lyons, Bonnie, 219n, 220n

McCutcheon, George Barr, 106
Machine: city as, 44; identification of city with, 2–3, 203n; imagery in *Vandover and the Brute,* 193; social, of urban culture, 43–44. *See also* Mechanical forces
Machor, James L., 1–2, 7
McKay, Claude, 132, 133, 134, 138, 144–47, 151–52, 158–59, 161, 171, 214n, 215–16n
McKay, Nellie, 147
McKelvey, Blake, 22, 38
McTeague: A Story of San Francisco (Dreiser), 192
McWilliams, Carey, 130
Making of Urban America (Reps), 22
Malamud, Bernard, 186
Manchild in a Promised Land (Browne), 167–68
Manhattan Transfer (Dos Passos), 122–23, 129
"Man of the Crowd" (Poe), 27
Mansion, The (Faulkner), 189, 190
Marble Faun, The (Hawthorne), 27–28
Marin, John, 32, 33, 116
Marriages and Infidelities (Oates), 186
Martin, Jay, 127, 130, 213n
Martin Eden (London), 194
Marx, Leo, 2, 189, 197, 203n, 221n
Masculine hegemony: in economic city, 109

Mason, Caroline, 136
Mass culture: conformity in postwar New York, 115; stereotypes of, 15
Masses, The, 115
Mass media: and megalopolitan nightmares, 127, 128–29; national entertainment industry, 129–30
Masters, Edgar Lee, 64
Materialistic consumption: in postwar New York, 126
Mather, Cotton, 7
Mayer, Harold M., 62
Mechanical forces: in postwar New York, 115; as source of human control, 103; in tune with natural, human forces, 103; vs. vitality of streets in Harlem, 153–54
Mechanistic images: alternation with organic images, 193
Medill, Joseph, 63
Megalopolis, 15, 192; ascendancy of, 165; emptiness of, 115; vs. regional literature, 187
Megalopolitan alienation: dream vs. nightmare in, 16
"Meistersinger" (Whitman), 116
Mellow, James R., 123, 130, 211n, 212n
Melville, Herman, 25, 26, 27, 28, 31, 93, 124, 221n
Memoirs of an American Citizen (Herrick), 14, 64, 68, 78
Mencken, H. L., 114
Merrell, James H., 19
Mesa Verde, 5, 6, 19; comparison with Chicago, 69–70; impact on Cather, 208n
Metaphors: of battle, in describing economic divisions in Chicago, 74–75; for boundaries, 89–90; in built environment, 76; city as home, 97; city as machine, 44; city as superhuman, 71–72; for conditions of city life, 56; drug imagery in *Sister Carrie,* 218n; of el for city, 54; of family for society, 52–53; of family house for city, 98; of family vault for postwar New York, 121; of hieroglyphic social forms, 121; isolation of the individual, 31; for mobility, 209n; in named characters (Fitzgerald), 125; of "Nature's Nation," 204n; of newspaper for one-dimensional meaning, 127; for regional military rivalry, 48; in standard Chicago novel, 72; for mechanical life, 31; swarming crowds of industrial city, 41; urban "swarming," 54; of walled cities for segregation and disfranchisement, 122; of walled city, 160. *See also* Imagery; Mythology

Miller, Nancy K., 110
Miller, Perry, 7, 9, 30
Miller, Ross, 66, 84, 204n
Miller, Wayne Charles, 220n
Mills, Florence, 135
Minh-ha, Trinh T., 2
"Minister's Black Veil, The" (Hawthorne), 31
Miss Lonelyhearts (West), 126, 180, 189
Mobility: in Chicago and New York, 92; connections through, 90
"Model of Christian Charity, A" (Winthrop), 5
Money Captain, The (Payne), 78
Monroe, Harriet, 14, 67, 68, 97, 100, 101, 102–3, 105, 106, 109, 113, 209n
Monroe, Lucy, 68, 104, 106
Moral choices: in city-town, 24–25; conflict between self and other (Gilligan), 92; different voice of women, 94
Morgan, Anna, 101, 105, 106
Morrison, Toni, 2, 111, 163, 185, 186, 191, 198
Moses, Robert, 163
Mother, The (Asch), 172
"Mother to Son" (Hughes), 154, 198
Murphy, Gerald, 130
My Chicago (Morgan), 101
"My City" (J. W. Johnson), 162
"My Kinsman, Major Molineux" (Hawthorne), 12, 23, 28
"My Lost City" (Fitzgerald), 123
"My Own People" (Yezierska), 174–75, 178
Mythology: of arrival home, 140; of arrival in Harlem, 180; bases for "Nature's Nation," 7; of Chicago arising from ashes, 66; of Chicago fair, 72; of city-town in postwar New York, 124; effect of mass media on, 127; of Harlem arrival, 141; of industrial city, 40–41; of powerful tycoon, 78; in standard Chicago novel, 110; of urban culture (James), 43–44

NAACP, 100, 133, 135
Nabokov, Vladimir, 161
Narrative of the Life of Frederick Douglass, The, 2, 24, 26
Nash, Roderick, 7, 203n
Native Americans: spirit stories of, 4
Native Son (Wright), 186
Naturalism: central conceptual oppositions, 206n; in genre criticism, 205–6n
Nature: in city, 88; fusion with city in residential novel, 89; preservation in cities, 62–63; recognizing city as part of, 200; within urban society, 148–49
"Nature's Nation," 9, 65
Naylor, Gloria, 200, 222n
Negro Fellowship League, 93
"Negro Speaks of Rivers, The" (Hughes), 140
Neighborhood literature: feminine nurturing associated with, 200–201
Nevius, Blake, 82
New Jerusalem: early American dream, 7
New Life, A (Malamud), 186
New Masses, The, 115, 180
New Negro, The (magazine), 135, 140
New Orleans, 188, 190
Newsboy, The (E. O. Smith), 26
New World Symphony (Dvorak), 89
New York, 113–31; comparison with Boston, 46–57; privacy in, 49
"Niggerati," 133, 157, 215n
Nigger Heaven (Van Vechten), 139, 156, 157
Nordenskiold, Gustaf, 69, 205n
Norris, Frank, 64, 72, 74, 75, 76, 78, 84, 97, 192, 193, 194, 195, 199, 205n
Novel, Chicago. *See* Chicago novel; Residential novels

Oates, Joyce Carol, 2, 186
Objectifying language, 69–70, 146; in Crane, 116
"O Black and Unknown Bards" (J. W. Johnson), 163
O'Connor, Flannery, 189
O'Connor, Leo F., 57
Ogletree, Thomas W., 199
"Old Mortality" (Porter), 189
Old New York (Wharton), 129
Olsen, Tillie, 30

One Way to Heaven (Cullen), 158
Ong, Walter, 176
"Open Road" (Whitman), 198
Opportunity (magazine), 132, 135, 137
Oppression: expression in white women and African Americans, 166
Organic community, 5, 9, 16–17
Organic continuity: comparison of American and European cities, 27; definition of, 208n
Organic images: and prescriptive models for planning, 197–98
Organization, technological: deadening effects of, 56
Organizational gatekeepers: in black community, 135–36; constrictions imposed by, 150
Organized privacy, 49
Ornitz, Samuel, 177, 218n
Osgood, James R., 57
Osofsky, Gilbert, 133
Overtones (Gerstenberg), 101–2
Oyama, Richard, 220n

Pale Fire (Nabokov), 161
Palmer, Bertha Honoré, 14, 66
Parade on Seventh Avenue (Van Der Zee), 152, 153
"Paradise of Bachelors, The" (Melville), 28, 124
Parsons, Lucy E., 100
Passing (Larsen), 142
Pastoral conventions: used by writers of Harlem Renaissance, 147
Pastoral design, 189, 221n
Payne, Will, 73, 76, 78, 106
Peattie, Elia W., 2, 14, 65, 74, 82, 84, 88, 89, 90–91, 92–93, 96, 97, 99, 100, 101, 104, 105, 109, 111–12, 160, 207n, 208n, 209n
Peattie, Robert, 96, 209n
Penn, William, 13, 40
Penny Philanthropist (Laughlin), 94
Perspective, urban, 38–39
Petry, Ann, 166, 216n
Phelps, William Lyon, 174
Philadelphia, 40–42
"Philadelphia Story, The," 42
Phillips, E. Barbara, 12, 204n
Pierce, Bessie L., 63

Piercy, Marge, 2, 151
Pierre (Melville), 25–26, 31
Pinski, David, 218n
Pioneers, The (Cooper), 2, 13, 20, 21–22, 26
Pit, The (Norris), 14, 64, 72, 74, 75, 78, 84, 192, 193
Play It as It Lays (Didion), 186
Plum Bun (Fauset), 142, 152
Poe, Edgar Allan, 27, 28, 35
Poetry (magazine), 97, 102–3, 108
Polanyi, Michael, 110
Political criticism: of literary works, 220n
Population: in Chicago, 60–61; and urban growth, 38
Porter, Katherine Anne, 189
Porter, Ruth W., 99
Post, Alice Thacher, 88
Potter, David M., 110
Pound, Ezra, 99
Precipice, The (E. Peattie), 2, 65, 81–82, 85, 88, 89–90, 90–91, 108, 111–12, 160
Privacy: symbolic of various cities, 48–49
Problem of Boston, The (Green), 46
Professional associations: compared with intellectual life of ethnic neighborhoods, 115–16
Professionalism, 114
Promised Land, The (Antin), 167–68
Psychological alienation, 1, 115. *See also* Alienation
Public/private conflict: between city and individuals, 56; commitment to domestic and civic goals, 91; Howells's views of, 49; military metaphor for, 48; personal honesty and social communication, 136
Public/private images, 47, 161; and artistic value, 107; city as subject of novel, 53–54; of family, 92; integration of, 49; in *Overtones*, 101–2; pre-Romantic, 13
Publishing business: in Chicago, 67; New York as center of, 46–47
Pullman, George, 63, 64
Pullman Strike, 68

Quicksand (Larsen), 142, 148–49, 150, 156, 158
Quinn, Vincent, 116

Rabinowitz, Howard N., 191
Race: in economic city of Chicago, 66; sense of, 164
Railroads: contribution to standardization, 37–38; focus on, 206n; metaphors using, 76
Rampersad, Arnold, 210n, 214n, 216n
Rapp, William Jourdain, 139
Rascoe, Burton, 109, 209n
Ray, Ethel (Nance), 137
Read, Opie, 67, 77
Reagan, Ronald, 19
Reality: fusion with dreams, 182; vs. illusion in megalopolitan nightmares, 130; as limitation on progress, 29
Reason Why, The (Wells-Barnett), 66
Rebolledo, Diana, 220n
Redburn (Melville), 27–28
Regional perspectives, 185–201; and feminism, 221n; reality of, 25; status of Boston in, 45–46
Reid, Randall, 213n
Reification: of Brooklyn Bridge, 116, 119; of Chicago, 15; of city (Emerson), 9
Reilly, John M., 180, 220n
Reivers, The (Faulkner), 189
Religion: organic community and God's will, 5; spiritual values and natural forms, 7, 9
Reps, John W., 20, 22, 28, 40, 45
Residential novels, 65; Chicago, 81–112
Reynolds, Donald Martin, 114
"Rich Boy, The" (Fitzgerald), 123
Rigidity, social: in post–Civil War city, 41–42
Riis, Jacob, 37, 54, 167
Rise of David Levinsky, The (Cahan), 169, 172, 183
Rise of Silas Lapham, The (Howells), 39, 47, 51–53, 205n
Rivera, Rowena, 220n
Rivera, Tomas, 220n
Rohn, Arthur H., 19
Romanticism: emphasis on isolation of individuals, 31; and nature, idealized, 7
Rosenthal, Bernard, 204n
Rose of Dutcher's Coolly (Garland), 65, 72, 73, 74
Rosowski, Susan J., 205n, 208n
Rosten, Leo, 130, 218n

Roth, Henry, 2, 16, 178–79, 198, 219n, 220n
Rothschild, P. de, 114
Rural/urban interactions, 24–25; Emerson on, 9; nineteenth-century idealization of, 7. *See also* Urban/rural dichotomies

Sanctuary (Faulkner), 189, 191
Sandburg, Carl, 103, 116
San Francisco, 47, 192
Santos, Bienvenido N., 195
Sardello, Robert J., 200, 221n
Savage, Augusta, 162
Schneider, Isidor, 218n
Schomburg, Arthur A., 133, 134, 164
Scully, Vincent, 5
Segregation: communal ties in, 142–44
Sennett, Richard, 199
Sense of place, 163, 185; and participation in city events, 111
Separatism: in professional organizations, 107–8
Sexual politics: of Harlem Renaissance, 151
Sheltered Life (Glasgow), 189
Shotguns (Biggers), 176, 177
Showalter, Elaine, 110
Shuffle Along (Mills), 135
Silko, Leslie Marmon, 5
Sinclair, Upton, 44, 64, 72, 73, 76, 77, 79, 97, 205n
Singh, Amritjit, 153
Sister Carrie (Dreiser), 14, 61, 64, 71–72, 109, 198
Sisterhood, cities of, 2
Sizemore, Christine Wick, 90, 197, 207n
Skyscraper image, 1, 2, 206n; in Chicago, 66–67; *The Cliff Dwellers,* 69–70; contrast with traditional cultural models, 9; economic city in, 14; in historic context, 17; powerlessness engendered by, 75–76; projected onto ethnic neighborhoods, 186; as surrogate for alienation, 2. *See also* Mechanical forces; Mechanistic images
Sloan, John, 55, 82
Slote, Bernice, 205n, 208n
Smith, Carl S., 206n
Smith, Elizabeth Oakes, 26
Smith, Henry Justin, 64

Smith, Seba, 23
Snider, Denton J., 66
Snyder, Gary, 5
Social action: regional base of, in Chicago residential novel, 81
Social construction, 81; of reality, 3
Social democracy: in tension with elitism, 86–87; women's roles in supporting, 101
Social ethics, 86; of care (Gilligan), 94; and collectivity, 91
Social justice: and aesthetic concerns, 2
Social Lion, The (M. Potter), 77
Social welfare organizations: women's participation in, 100
Society of Midland Authors, 108
Sodoms in Eden (Stout), 24, 27–28
Song of Solomon (Morrison), 191
Song of the Lark, The (Cather), 9, 65, 81, 82, 84, 89
Song of the Lark, The (painting; Breton), 89
"Song of the Open Road" (Whitman), 35
"Song of the Women, The" (Frank), 102
Souls of Black Folks, The (Du Bois), 149
Southern literature, 187–92
South, the: privacy in, 49
Spiritual city: critique of, 71; split from material city, 66
Spiritual values: hunger for, 130; in megalopolitan nightmare, 128
Spirn, Anne Whiston, 200
Spring in New Hampshire (McKay), 144, 145, 215n
Squier, Susan Merrill, 2
Stanley, Julia, 196
Stansell, Christine, 94, 172
Starr, Kevin, 130
Steffens, Lincoln, 38
Stegner, Wallace, 195
Steiner, George, 19
Stella, Joseph, 116, 117
Stereotypes: of African-American culture, 139; ethnic, in residential novels, 93; limitations imposed by, 137; of newspapers, 128; overcoming prejudices of, 94; racist, 149; rural southerner lost in city, 141–42; vs. self-dramatization in Harlem Renaissance, 158
Still, Bayard, 61, 114
Stinson, Peggy, 219n

Stout, Janis, 24, 25, 27–28, 31
Street, The (Petry), 166
Strong, Josiah, 38
"Subway, The" (Tate), 192
Suffrage: and the club movement, 113
Suffragist campaign, 15
Sullivan, Louis, 63, 66
Summer on the Lakes in 1843 (M. Fuller), 26
Sunday Afternoon (Fasanella), 116, 118, 166
Survey Graphic, 135
Sweet Clover (Burnham), 65, 67, 84, 87
Symbolic construction: and determinism, 58
System of Architectural Ornament (Sullivan), 63
Szuberla, Guy Alan, 73, 206n

Tafolla, Carmen, 220n
Taft, Lorado, 108
Tale of Chicago (Masters), 64
Tar Baby (Morrison), 186
"Tartarus of Maids, The" (Melville), 28, 29
Tate, Allen, 192, 199
Taylor, William R., 1
Technology: domination by, 141; and exclusion, 144
Tensions: between nature and technology, 147; truth and pretense in art, 158; in views of Chicago as national city, 73
"Terpsichore in Harlem," 154
Their Eyes Were Watching God (Hurston), 189, 191
There Is Confusion (Fauset), 135, 142, 154–55
Thomas, Piri, 166
Thompson, Mildred, 66, 209n
Thoreau, Henry David, 9, 29
"Threnody" (Cullen), 137
Thurman, Wallace, 133, 137, 139, 140, 142, 150, 154, 156–57, 158
Tietjens, Eunice, 100
Titan, The (Dreiser), 64; unregulated growth and tyranny, 77
"To a Little Lover-Lass Dead" (Hughes), 155
Tobacco Road (Caldwell), 188
Toomer, Jean, 147, 213n, 216n
Toth, Emily, 196, 221n

Town, The (Faulkner), 190
Trachtenberg, Alan, 3, 36–37, 38, 119
Transit symbolism: the el and technological organization, 56; and missed connections, 122. *See also* Railroads
"Tropics in New York, The" (McKay), 145
True Love: A Comedy of the Affections (Wyatt), 65, 82, 86–87, 88, 108, 109, 198, 207n
Truth: and illustrative power in art, 170
Tuan, Ti-Fu, 111, 197
Tuerk, Richard, 217n, 220n
Turner, Frederick Jackson, 14, 65
Turtle Island (Snyder), 5
Tuttleton, James W., 121
Twain, Mark (Samuel Clemens), 43, 57, 204n
Twenty Years at Hull-House (Addams), 205n
Two Women and a Fool (Chatfield-Taylor), 206n
Tyler, Royall, 24

Unions: Jewish-led, 168
Universal Negro Improvement Association, 135
Unquenched Fire (Gerstenberg), 65, 91–92
Urban League, 135
Urban pastoralism, 1–2
Urban/rural dichotomies, 215–16n; as Gesellschaft/Gemeinschaft dichotomies, 111; in McKay's work, 144–45; in residential novel, 88; source of image of, 191–92. *See also* Rural/urban interactions

Van Der Zee, James, 152, 153
Van Doren, Carl, 135
Vandover and the Brute (Norris), 84, 192, 193, 194
Van Vechten, Carl, 136, 137, 139, 141, 156, 157, 161–64, 165, 172, 217n
Vinde, V., 114

Wade, Richard C., 62
Wagner, Linda W., 122, 211n
Waiting for the Verdict (R. H. Davis), 39, 198; Philadelphia as representative city, 40–41
Wald, Alan M., 218n

Walker, Alice, 196
Walker in the City, A (Kazin), 166
"Walking" (Thoreau), 9
Walking city, 204n
Walls: as disruptions in human relations, 89–90; limitations as, 112; New York as a "Walled City," 75
Walls of Jericho, The (Fisher), 112, 136, 140, 153, 156, 158, 160, 193, 200
Walrond, Eric, 134
Warner, Charles Dudley, 43
Warner, Sam Bass, Jr., 42, 62
Warren, Robert Penn, 189, 190
Washington, D.C., 43–45
Weary Blues, The (Hughes), 2, 136, 138, 154, 155, 175
Weber, Michael P., 12, 62, 204n
Web of Life, The (Herrick), 68, 72, 74, 76–77, 79, 80
Weimer, David, 212n
Wells, Walter, 130, 186, 213n
Wells-Barnett, Ida B., 66, 93, 100, 208–9n
West, Dorothy, 133
West, Nathanael, 119, 126–29, 130, 182, 186, 190, 213n
Wharton, Edith, 114, 119, 124, 126, 129, 204n, 207n, 211n, 212n
What the Hell for You Left Your Heart in San Francisco, 195
"When Dawn Comes to the City" (McKay), 144
"When Sue Wears Red" (Hughes), 175
White, Lucia, 2, 3, 28, 187, 203n, 221n
White, Morton, 2, 3, 28, 187, 203n, 221n
White, Walter, 133, 136, 142, 160–61, 163, 217n
"White City, The" (McKay), 145, 171
Whitman, Walt, 26, 31, 34–35, 103, 116, 198, 211n
Wilderness: the city as, 44–45; urban, 54
Williams, Kenny, 82, 207n
Williams, Roger, 20

Willis, F. Roy, 36
Wilson, Edmund, 29, 124, 212n
Wilson, Margaret G., 104
Winthrop, John, 5, 19, 22, 46, 47
Wirth, Louis, 15, 111, 191
Wirtz, Cary D., 134, 216n
With the Procession (Fuller), 65, 68, 69, 85, 87, 88
Wolfe, Susan, 196
Wolff, Cynthia Griffin, 120, 121
Woman's Club (Chicago), 100
Woman's work: in Harlem Renaissance, 137; and patterns of professional development, 99; public service roles, 104
Women of Brewster Place (Naylor), 200
Women's literature: and regional literature, 196
Women's voices: public, 102; and urban experiences, 96
Wonder-Working Providence (Johnson), 7
Woodress, James, 208n
"Workman's Song" (Monroe), 103
World of Our Fathers (Howe), 195–96
World's Columbian Exposition, 14; public contradictions in, 64–68
Wright, Richard, 179, 186, 190
Writers Guild, 108
Wyatt, Edith Franklin, 14, 46–47, 65, 74, 82, 84, 85, 86–87, 88, 89–90, 93, 97, 99, 101, 102, 103, 106, 109, 111, 192, 198, 207n, 209n
Wynne, Madeline Yale, 104–5

Yekl (Cahan), 169
Yerkes, Charles, 63, 77
Yezierska, Anzia, 2, 16, 167, 173–75, 178, 183, 199, 212n, 218–19n
You and I (Monroe), 210n

Zuñi, 5, 25

A Note on the Author

SIDNEY H. BREMER, professor of humanistic studies at the University of Wisconsin–Green Bay, has taught courses in literature, women's studies, urban studies, and American studies. She is the author of numerous articles as well as the introduction to a new edition of Elia Peattie's *The Precipice*.